OSWEGO:
Its People and Events

cover by
frank kroth

Also by Anthony Slosek

Oswego: Hamlet Days 1796-1828

Stories of Old Oswego

Oswego County to 1796

OSWEGO:
Its People and Events

by
Anthony M. Slosek

Oswego County Historian

Anthony M. Slosek

Heart of the Lakes Publishing
Interlaken, New York
1985

Library of Congress Cataloging in Publication Data

Slosek, Anthony M.
    Oswego : its people and events.

    Bibliography: p.
    1. Oswego (N.Y.)--History.   2. Oswego County
(N.Y.)--History.   I. Title.
F129.07S59   1985   974.7'67   85-959
ISBN 0-932334-23-7
ISBN 0-932334-71-7 (pbk.)

ISBN: 0-932334-23-7 (Cloth)
ISBN: 0-932334-71-7 (Paper)
Manufactured in the United States of America

A *quality* publication of
Heart of the Lakes Publishing
Interlaken, New York 14847

This book is dedicated to my wife:

Margaret Even Slosek

Contents

Preface

The Technical Leaflet 21, issued by The American Association for State and Local History, on Methods of Research by Richard W. Hale, Jr., states: "Never do work that somebody has already done. It is amazing how much repetitive research is done. It is even amazing how many shortcuts for researchers are overlooked." With that admonition in mind, this writer has supplemented his research with that of others in the field. The reader will find some stories of other writers included in this book which were done with a view to avoid repetition and, without doubt, well researched.

This writer was aware and adhered to a certain extent to what Daniel Boorstin (who in 1975 became the 12th Librarian of Congress) expressed in his thoughts on history. "My kind of history tries to deal with the total human experience" he said, "not just political history." My aim of this book is to show how history could be made more interesting, and even gripping, by tracing the lives of real people rather than merely recounting dry facts. It is hoped that the continuity of human nature in history has surfaced again.

My obligations to others for assistance is very great. This book is dedicated to my wife for her patience and devotion over many years to the cause of local history. I am indebted to many people for their aid: to Richard Palmer, of the Syracuse Newspapers, Mara Crowell, Curator of Oswego County Historical Society, Nicholas Todaro, President of Oswego Town Historical Society, Richard N. Wright, President of the Onondaga Historical Association, Oswego City Library Staff, and others specifically noted in the list of sources.

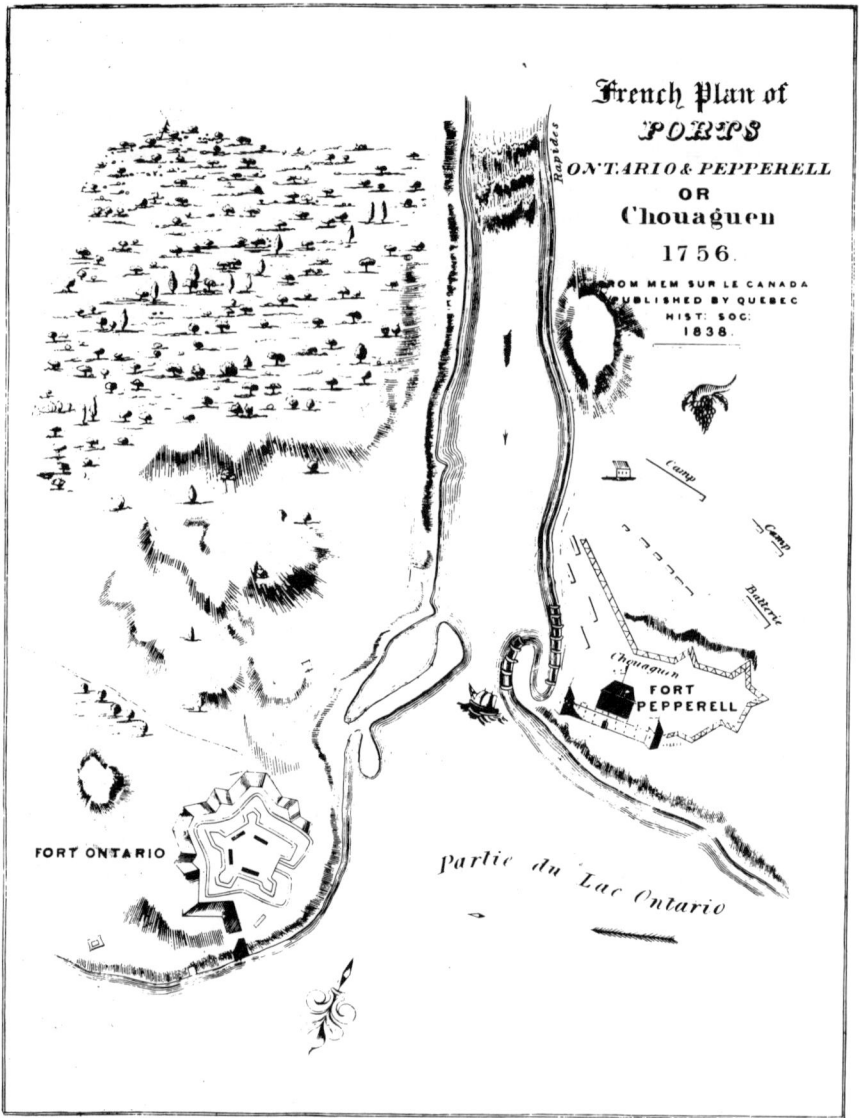

French Plan of *Ports* ONTARIO & PEPPERELL OR Chouaguen 1756.

FROM MEM SUR LE CANADA PUBLISHED BY QUEBEC HIST: SOC: 1838.

FORT ONTARIO

Chouaguen FORT PEPPERELL

Partie du Lac Ontario

Documentary History of New York

French and Indian Wars

Background

The campaign plans of both English and the French for the year 1756 bore a striking similarity; the control of Lake Ontario, the valley of the Hudson River and the valley of the Ohio River. General William Shirley's council of war had arrranged to seize Fort Frontenac (Kingston), Fort Niagara and Toronto; capture Crown Point and Ticonderoga and finish the work William Johnson failed in the year before; reduce Fort Duquesne (Pittsburg) with a devastating incursion down the Chaudiere River upon Quebec. The high-minded and accomplished Marquis de Montcalm was determined to redeem Lake George, to capture Oswego and retain Fort Duquesne.

With the approach of Spring the English were active providing for the campaign on Lake Ontario. Besides providing soldiers and men to navigate several thousands of batteaux, 300 sailors were sent from New York to Oswego to navigate the four armed ships on the lake. There were two more ships under construction, with plans for more. Smiths, carpenters, and other artificers had already arrived.

The French were also busy preparing for the campaign against the English. A fortified camp was established on Niaoure Bay, now called Henderson Bay, in Jefferson County. The camp was intended as a base for scouting parties toward Oswego and the Mohawk River valley. Captain Louis Coulon, Sieur de Villiers, one of the most partisan leaders of Canada, was sent with 800 Canadians and Indians to establish the camp. He was the only man who ever fully Conquered Major George Washington (at Fort Necessity two years before). De Villiers was soon busy sending out scalping parties of Indians or Indians and French combined.

The Episode

On May 12th one of de Villiers detachments attacked a party of ship carpenters at work only 300 yards from Fort Oswego. (There is a marker at the foot of West First Street designating its location). A description of the attack was reported in the New York Mercury, May 31, 1756. "On my arrival I [Colonel John Bradstreet?] heard, that a few days ago, a Party of Indians came to some ship Carpenters cutting timber not 300 yards from the Town [referring to Oswego]; & before a Party could be turned out, Killed and carried off Twelve: They were pursued by the Party, but could not get sight of them: Our People found one Killed, which they Scalped, & threw his Body in the [Oswego] River."

About the same time two parties of Indians left Fort Niagara on May 7th for Oswego and returned on the 15th (a distance of 140 miles one way) with 12 scalps and three English prisoners - carpenters and sawyers who were working upon vessels near the fort.

An episode is an incident or action occurring in the regular course of events. This one parallels other incidents of Indian depredation and capture. On July 5, 1757, there came into Fort Herkimer, two men who made their escape from the French; one of them was a Virginian, and said he was an Ensign when taken; the other young man, a carpenter taken at Oswego. They unfolded the following story:

Two young men, one named Peter Luney, belonging to Virginia, and the other William Phalps, an apprentice to Jones Wright, of a Boston shipwright. The latter was taken at Oswego, the 11th of May, 1756, in company with Charles Carter, of Philadelphia, and James Flanagan, and Lewis Dunning of New Jersey, cutting timber for vessels then being built on Lake Ontario. Lewis Dunning being wounded by a shot from the Indians and unable to keep pace with them in their march, they, therefore, killed and scalped him. The party arrived at Niagara in four days. Carter and Flanagan were soon sent to Montreal, but one of the Indians adopted William Phalps for a son. William was obliged to go with him to their country, where he remained all summer, and was used extremely well by them. They often entreated him to forget his own country, and be contented to live with them, but he always testified his unwillingness to remain in that situation, they delivered him up to the commander of Fort Niagara the 28th of September 1756, where he remained till the 19th of June 1757. At that time he and Peter Luney (who came to Niagara with a few Indians from the westward trade) contrived means to facilitate their escape. Accordingly they set out with

12

only one gun, 30 charges of powder and ball, and no food. They were obliged to subsist for six days on two rotten fish. In order to prevent being tracked by the Indians, they walked several miles in the water;sleeping all day in the woods and traveling at night. Eventually they arrived at Oswego where they saw nothing but the ruins of that place. It will be recalled that Marquis de Montcalm laid waste to the three forts at Oswego on August 14, 1756, and sent 1600 prisoners of war to France. The two escapees then made their way to Fort Herkimer.

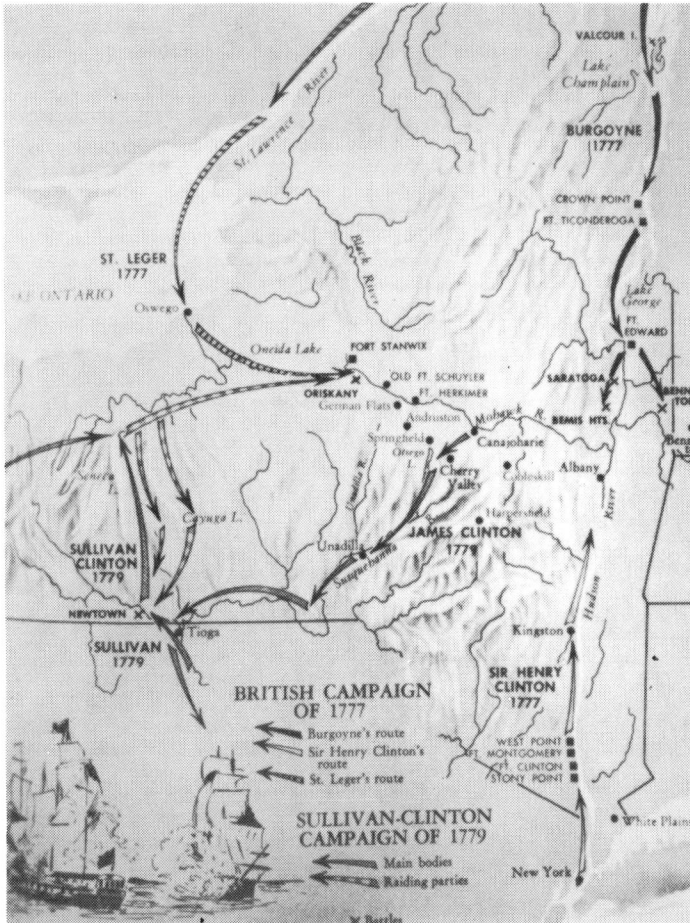

Silas Town — An American Spy

The battles fought in New York during 1777 were most important; indeed, the New York campaign ultimately proved to be the most decisive of the war for independence. Basically, the plan was to divide the American colonies in two parts, by siezing the interior waterways of New York. General John Burgoyne was to advance along the Great Warpath (the Lake Champlain-Lake George Route) toward Albany; an auxiliary column of British under Lieutenant Colonel Barry St. Leger was to meet Burgoyne at the mouth of the Mohawk River, near Albany by way of Lake Ontario and the Oswego route; General William Howe was to proceed up the Hudson to Albany. The failure of the plan was in its execution. Howe received his orders on August 17, which he should have received in April or May. He received the news of Burgoyne's surrender at Philadelphia. Colonel St. Leger, with his 1,300 - 1,400 men ("fifth clumn") brought Oswego County to the attention of historians.

Lieutenant Colonel Barry St. Leger was the nephew of the 4th Viscount Doneraile and of Hugenot descent. At this time about forty years of age (born about 1737), he had behind him a rather extended military career. He entered the British service as an ensign in the 28th Regiment of Foot in 1755 and the following year accompanied the regiment to America, where it served under General Abercrombie. In 1758 he was promoted to captain in the 48th Regiment, then also serving in this country, and in the same year participated in the seige of Louisburg. He accompanied Wolfe to Quebec in 1759, participated in the battle in the Plain of Abraham. In July the following year he was appointed brigadier major and in 1762 he became major of the 95th Foot. In 1772 he became lieutenant colonel in the army; lieutenant colonel of the 34th Foot, May 1775; and the next spring his regiment formed a part of the reinforcement sent over to Sir Guy Carleton. He assumed command under Burgoyne on June 2, 1777. It was Lord Germain's order of March 26, addressed to Sir Guy Carleton, that it was "the King's pleasure that you put under the command of Lieutenant Colonel St. Leger (certain specified troops), together with a sufficient number of Canadians and Indians, ... you are to give him orders to proceed forthwith to and down the Mohawk

River to Albany, and put himself under the command of Sir William Howe."

St. Leger's force left Lachine on June 21, 1777, for the capture of Fort Stanwix (modern Rome). Omitting the details of his movement from Canada, Colonel St. Leger stopped at the mouth of Salmon Creek, now called Mexico Point.

Colonel Daniel Claus, in his official report, gave a description of the situation there:

The 24th of July, I received an express from Brigadier St. Leger, at Salmon Creek, about twenty miles from Oswego, to repair thither with what arms and vermillion I had, and that he wished I would come prepared to march through the woods. As to arms and vermillion I had none, but prepared myself to go upon the march, and was ready to set off when Joseph (Brant) came into my tent and told me that as no person was on the spot to take care of the number of Indians with him, he apprehended in case I should leave them they would become disgusted and disperse, which might prevent the rest of the Six Nations to assemble, and be hurtful to the expedition, and begged I would first represent the circumstances to the Brigadier by letter. Brigadier St. Leger mentioned, indeed, my going was chiefly intended to quiet the Indians with him, who were very drunk and riotous, and Captain Tice, who was his messenger, informed me that the brigadier ordered the Indians a quart of rum apiece, which made them beastly drunk, and in which case it is not in the power of man to quiet them. Accordingly, I mentioned to the brigadier, by letter, the consequences that might affect his Majesty's Indian interests in case I was to leave so large a number of Indians that were come already and still expected. Upon which representation and finding the Indians disproved of the plan, and were unwilling to proceed, the brigadier came away from Salmon Creek, and arrived the next day at Oswego with the companies of the 8th and 34th Regiments and about 250 Indians.

Of all the veterans of the American Revolution buried in the Town of Mexico, Silas Town, who lies in the soil of Spy Island at the mouth of the Salmon Creek, is the only one who performed a part of his war services within the present town, at that time a wilderness uninhabited by white men. It was he who, concealed on that island, listened to the plans of St. Leger for his advance on Fort

Stanwix in the summer of 1777 and carried his information by a short cut through the woods to the commandant of the fort (Colonel Peter Gansevoort), while St. Leger sailed for Oswego.

The sixth child of Silas (a Deacon) and Susannah Town was born August 5, 1755, at Oxford, Massachusetts. His contemporaries described him as a man of more than ordinary ability, tact, shrewdness, and penetration of mind—"very smart with an eye like an eagle's". He was sent on a mission to Canada where he was arrested. After spending two years there on parole, he managed to escape. Upon his return to the American Colonies, he went again into the service of the United States. He was ordered to shadow St. Leger, get as much information as possible and report to the commanders at Fort Stanwix, Colonel Peter Gansevoort and Lieutenant Colonel Marinus Willett.

Fortunately, an account of his exploit is preserved:

Town made the journey from Fort Edward to Lake Ontario. He was fortunate in reaching the lake before St. Leger came along the shore. He secreted himself on an island at the mouth of Salmon Creek and was concealed there when the British reached th Point. St. Leger at this place came to a halt with a view of leaving the lake and going across country to Fort Stanwix. Some delay and considerable talk were used to persuade the Indians; but no, they would go only by way of Oswego and Oswego River. As soon as the command moved on, Town made haste to return and report at Fort Stanwix what he had seen.

Silas Town returned to Mexico in 1799. He made his home just before his death with Esquire Hamilton who then lived on the shore of Lake Ontario on the east bank of Salmon Creek near the mouth of the stream. The Mexico Independent, quoting Mr. Goodwin, wrote: "To Mr. Hamilton Silas Town gave the charge to bury him in a spot which he selected in advance and pointed out where he should like to have his body repose." That spot was the little island where he had listened to St. Leger's plan nearly thirty years before. He died in the Hamilton home in 1806, aged 51 years.

In 1871 a monument in memory of Silas Town was erected on the island over his grave. The monument is of limestone, consisting of base about 4 by 5 feet and 8 inches in thickness. From this rise a shaft of 2 feet by 15 inches at the base, tapering 12 inches square at the top, and about 12 or 13 feet long surmounted by a tasteful capstone. Facing the lake is a polished surface bearing the description "Erected July 4, 1871 to the memory of Silas Town, an officer under Washington. Died 1806." The island has been called Monument Island, Grave Island, Town Island, Deadman's Island, but now popularly and legally known as Spy Island.

MEXICO POINT, — SILAS TOWN MONUMENT.

Courtesy of Euloda Fetcha

Colonel Willett's Expedition Against Oswego

BEAUTIFUL SNOW! when a delicate thaw
Makes the air chilly and damp and raw!
Beautiful snow! they may sing when it suits—
I object to the stuff, 'cause it soaks through my boots.

The Revolutionary War to all intents was over in every field when General Charles Cornwallis surrendered at Yorktown in October 1781. At long last General Frederick Haldimand, Governor-General of Canada, realized the risks he had run by neglecting Oswego. On February 18, 1782, he directed Major John Ross, commanding at Carleton Island, to proceed to Oswego as soon as the ice broke in the spring, because a post was to be established there with all speed. Oswego would be of prime importance should a drive by the Americans be directed at Quebec. The risk must be prevented by "a more Early Exertion, and as the first object to be considered is to secure yourself from insults, you will pay your whole attention to it, taking advantage of what remains of the old Bastions and afterwards proceed to Buildings."

Construction plans were outlined in detail. Captain Turis of the Engineers would communicate to Ross his plans for the works and the Adjutant General would advise regarding ordinance, size of garrison and other details. Ross pushed the rebuilding at Oswego though the works were in bad shape and tools available at Carleton were few. Transport vessels, including the scow "Haldimand", would be ready to sail from Carleton in April and the troops should know nothing of their destination until they were embarked. Ross requested as many as possible of the Eight Regiment of British Foot stationed at Fort Niagara.

It is doubtful if the fortification changed from that of 1759. In the case of an earth and timber fortification the first decay usually became evident within five years of its construction and the average life of such a fort was only forty years. The repairs made in 1782 were principally the buildings that were burned in 1778 rather than to ramparts, traverses, timberwork and palisades. Fortunately a description of the fort at that time exists. Colonel Marinus Willett, in command of all levies, militia, and state troops, writing to General Washington, December 7, 1782, gave the following description:

19

MARINUS WILLETT.

I have thought it might not be amiss to give your Excellency some description of the fort which according to the accounts I have received is a regular built Fortification on the north (sic east) side of the river, consisting of five angles, with a bastion to each angle. The angles, are all nearly of a length supposed about one hundred yards each. The fassse (moat) is about twenty feet wide and nine feet deep. From the bottom of the fasse to the top of the parapet is about thirty feet, except the angle where the sally port is placed at which port it is represented to be not more than twenty feet. And the fasse is not wide as in other ports. It is said the fort is surrounded with glassis (earth embankment) but which does not appear to be protected with any kinid of frieze work. There is a row of Pickett's perpendicularly fixed in the center of the fasse, and another row of horizontal ones placed along the wall seven or eight feet above the beam. The gateway is secured by a drawbridge. At the entrance of the gate on one side is the guard house and on the other side a house for the

20

commandant. Within one of the bastions is placed the magazine. The other four bastions and curtains are filled with barracks. All the buildings are made of logs and are said to be Bumproof. Three of the angles of the fort front the lake and the river, and in some parts lay very near to those waters.

Residents of New York State, and particularly those residing in the Mohawk and Champlain Valleys, were much worried during 1782, by the re-establishment of Fort Ontario by the British and the concentration there of many of the British forces maintained to the north and west of New York State. A further concentration took place almost simultaneously in Lake Champlain at Isle Aux Noix.

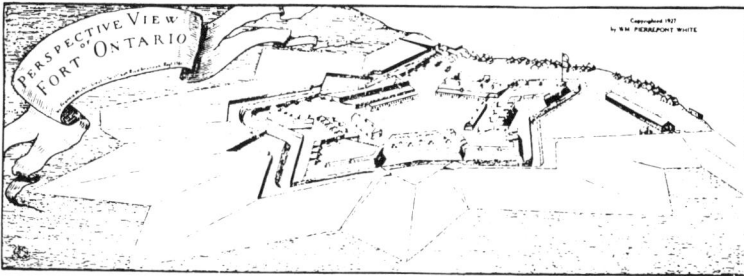

Permission for use from the son of W. P. White

Perspective view of Fort Ontario by Francis Pfister, Lieutenant in the 1st Battalion Royal American Regiment 1761.

At the end of November 1782 Colonel Willett set out for Albany. He then went to Fishkill for his wife, intending to take her to his quarters with him during the winter. As the headquarters of General Washington were at Newburgh, directly opposite Fishkill Landing, Colonel Willett went to pay his respects to him, and remained to dinner. As soon as dinner was over, he rose to take his leave. The General rose also, and following him out asked him to go to his office. He then inquired as to his success in recruiting, the strength and situation of the regiment; said the clothier-general should have particular orders respectiong clothing; and mentioned that it would be proper to place no reliance on a speedy peace, but be as well prepared as possible for another campaign. He then inquired of Colonel Willett if he was acquainted with the situation of the enemy's garrison at Oswego, and if he thought it might be surprised by an expedition in the winter. The conversation finished

21

by the General desiring him to think of the project and write him his opinion.

In accordance to General Washington's request, Colonel Willett, about a week later, wrote in favor of the enterprise. A correspondence ensued between General Washington and Colonel Willett beginning on December 7, 1782, and terminating on March 5, 1783.

In the dead of winter of 1783, the last military expedition of the Revolutionary War was directed against Fort Ontario. It was commanded by Lieutenant Colonel Marinus Willett in command of New York and Rhode Island troops. The expedition had been personally planned by General Washington, who wrote out full and detailed instructions for Willett's guidance. Washington gave strict orders that if from any circumstance, the enemy learned of the presence of the Americans, Willett was not to attack at all but lead his men away. In the words of Washinton (Washinton to Willett, February 2, 1783), "it is to be remembered, and I wish to impress it upon you, that, if you do not succeed by surprise the attempt will be unwarrantable." It took six days to travel the 190 miles to Oswego.

The troops, 470 men, assembled at Fort Herkimer on the Mohawk Rver on February 8; crossed the ice of Oneida Lake, in some 120 sleighs till they reached Fort Brewerton. Here they left their sleighs under a guard. About 2 P. M. they arrived at Oswego Falls, Fulton today. At this place they went into the woods and made eight ladders. Their prospects were as promising as they could wish. All the necessary preparations for entering the enemy's works were completed; and every officer was made acquainted with the particular part he was to perform.

It was scarcely 10 o'clock (February 12) at night when the troops reached a point of land about three or four miles from the fort (Minetto). Here, on account of the weakness of the ice, they were obliged to take to the land; and in doing this they had to ascend an eminence which caused some difficulty in getting up the ladders.

Colonel Willett had procured a young Oneida Indian, called Captain John, and two other Indians, as guides. Not a thought entered his mind of the least danger of losing their way, as they were then four miles from the fort and there were still four long hours to elapse before moon set, which was the time fixed upon entering the

22

fort. Colonel Willett's attention was constantly engaged in encouraging the men whose business it was to carry the ladders; a labor, which from the inclemency of the season, the depth of the snow, and the difficulties of the woods, was a very arduous one. His attention thus occupied, and not having the least apprehension that his guides would lose their way, two hours passed without discovering an opening in the woods which he had been in some time expecting. This circumstance led him to hasten to the front of the line of march where he was informed that the Indian pilot had not been seen for some time, though they were pursuing his tracks as fast as they could. Colonel Willett immediately set out to follow his tracks himself, with a quick a step as possible and in about half an hour overtook him. He found him standing there still apparently lost and frightened. They had by this time got into a swamp and some of the men had their feet frozen in sunken holes. In this deplorable situation, ignorant where they were, the hope of taking the fort vanished. The orders of General Washington were peremptory; that, if they failed in surprising the fort, the attempt would be unwarrantable. All then was left for the troops to do was to retrace their steps.

At daybreak the attackers found themselves on a hill overlooking the fort. It seems they assembled on the crest of Oak Hill. While the offficers were conferring on a course of action, five British carrying axes presumably to gather firewood, were seen approaching in the direction of the hill. A sudden rush captured two British soldiers but three escaped to the fort to give warning. Soon the Americans heard drums beating a call to arms and saw soldiers shoveling away from the guns of the fort.

Leaving their scaling ladders near the hill, the troops made an about face and trudged back to the sleighs at Brewerrton and on to Fort Herkimer. Many of them suffered much from the cold; three were frozen to death, 130 frostbitten and some so badly as to require constant assistance to get them along. Two men, Henry Blackmer and Joseph Perrigo, who afterward both settled on the west side of Oswego above the falls, were badly frozen on this expedition. Such was the gloomy end of an enterprise, which, at ten o'clock at night presented so far a prospect of success.

General Washington with great magnanimity consoled the dejected Willett in a letter, March 5, 1783, which terminated their correspondence on the subject. Among other things he said:

I cannot omit expressing to you the high Sense I entertained of your perservering Exertions and Zeal on your Expedition; and begging you to accept my warm Thanks on the occasion; and that you will be pleased to communicate my Gratitude to the Officers and men under you command for their share they have taken in the service.

As to the probable success of storming Fort Ontartio, another opinion differs from the Willett version. Two of Willett's men, badly frozen, entered the fort in the morning, surrendering themselves prisoners, from whom the garrison learned the object of the enterprise. A party of British soldiers went and brought in ladders left by Willett. An American prisoner (there since the spring of 1782), Moses Nelson (and two other lads) said that the longest ladder reached only about two-thirds of the way to the top of the pickets. It was the opinion of Nelson that the accident which misled the troops was most providential tending to save Colonel Willett from defeat and most of his men certain death since the post was strongly garrisoned.

Colonel Willett's expedition gave Fort Ontario the distinction as the last hostile movement of American troops against British in the Revolution. During his march to Oswego, Congress received news of the signing of the provisional articles of peace. Shortly after Colonel Willett's return to Fort Rensselaer, he went to Albany (in April) where he heard the peace proclaimed by the town clerk at the city hall to the rejoicing inhabitants. He dispatched messengers to Major Andrew Fink, commander in Willett's absence, who in turn sent Captain Alexander under a flag of truce to Major John Ross at Oswego.

It would be of interest to note that besides Henry Blackmer and Joseph Perrigo, Captain Edward O'Connor (1753—7/2/1831) came to Oswego in 1796. The Captain, an Irishman of good education and pleasing manner was in charge of a company in Willett's expedition. He built a log house on Lot No. 46, 174 West First Street, the site of the Palladium building, but removed the first winter to Salt Point, now Syracuse, being fearful of the terrible winters which prevailed here. He returned to Oswego in 1802. He and his wife, Christina, (4/21/1756—1/27/1829), had three daughters: Cecilia, unmarried; Mary (1795—10/27/1870), Married Alvin Bronson in 1815; Catherine (d.3/4/1870) married John H. Lord, Jr., in 1819, who founded the oldest newspaper in Oswego

County, the Palladium. The Lords built a wooden dwelling on the east portion of Lot No. 46, (facing West First Street in 1817 and ten years later, built another wooden dwelling on the west portion of the lot, facing West Second Street.

Captain O'Connor taught school in a log cabin, probably being the first man to do so in the community. He also held a position in the Customs House under the first collector, Joel Burt. He had the reputation of being a scholar, a gentleman, and was a respected, prominent citizen.

By the UNITED STATES of AMERICA in Congrefs affembled.

A PROCLAMATION,

Declaring the Ceffation of Arms, as well by Sea as by Land, agreed upon between the United States of America and His Britannic Majefty ; and enjoining the Obfervance thereof.

WHEREAS Provifional Articles were figned at Paris on the Thirtieth Day of *November* laft, between the Minifters Plenipotentiary of the United States of America for treating of Peace, and the Minifter Plenipotentiary of His Britannic Majefty, to be inferted in and to conftitute a Treaty of Peace propofed to be concluded between the United States of America and His Britannic Majefty, when Terms of Peace fhould be agreed upon between their Moft Chriftian and Britannic Majefties : And Whereas Preliminaries for reftoring Peace between their Moft Chriftian and Britannic Majefties were figned at Verfailles, on the Twentieth Day of *January* laft, by the Minifters of their Moft Chriftian and Britannic Majefties : And Whereas Preliminaries for reftoring Peace between the faid King of Great Britain and the King of Spain were alfo figned at Verfailles, on the fame Twentieth Day of *January* laft.

By which faid Preliminary Articles it hath been agreed, That as foon as the fame were ratified, Hoftilities between the faid Kings, their Kingdoms, States and Subjects, fhould ceafe in all Parts of the World ; and it was farther agreed, That all Veffels and Effects that might be taken in the Channel and in the North Seas, after the Space of Twelve Days from the Ratification of the faid Preliminary Articles, fhould be reftored ; that the Term fhould be One Month from the Channel and North Seas as far as the Canary Iflands inclufively, whether in the Ocean or the Mediterranean ; Two Months from the faid Canary Iflands as far as the Equinoctial Line or Equator ; and laftly, Five Months in all other Parts of the World, without any Exception or more particular Defcription of Time or Place : And Whereas it was Declared by the Minifter Plenipotentiary of the King of Great-Britain, in the Name and by the exprefs Order of the King his Mafter, on the faid Twentieth day of *January* laft, that the faid United States of America, their Subjects and their Poffeffions fhall be comprifed in the above-mentioned Sufpenfion of Arms, at the fame Epochs, and in the fame Manner, as the three Crowns above-mentioned, their Subjects and Poffeffions refpectively ; upon Condition that on the Part and in the Name of the United States of America, a fimilar Declaration fhall be delivered, exprefsly declaring their Affent to the faid Sufpenfion of Arms, and containing an Affurance of the moft perfect Reciprocity on their Part   And Whereas the Minifters Plenipotentiary of thefe United States, did, on the fame Twentieth Day of *January* in the Name and by the Authority of the faid United States, accept the faid Declaration, and declare, that the faid States fhould ceafe all Hoftilities with his Britannic Majefty, his Subjects and his Poffeffions, at the Terms and Epochs agreed upon between His faid Majefty the King of Great-Britain, His Majefty the King of France, and His Majefty the King of Spain, fo, and in the fame Manner, as had been agreed upon between thofe Three Crowns, and to produce the fame Effects : And Whereas the Ratifications of the faid Preliminary Articles between their Moft Chriftian and Britannic Majefties were exchanged by their Minifters on the Third Day of *February* laft, and between His Britannic Majefty and the King of Spain on the Ninth Day of *February* laft :— And Whereas it is Our Will and Pleafure that the Ceffation of Hoftilities between the United States of America and His Britannic Majefty, fhould be conformable to the Epochs fixed between their Moft Chriftian and Britannic Majefties.

WE have thought fit to make known the fame to the Citizens of thefe States, and we hereby ftrictly Charge and Command all our Officers, both by Sea and Land, and others, Subjects of thefe United States, to forbear all Acts of Hoftility, either by Sea or by Land, againft His Britannic Majefty or his Subjects, from and after the refpective Times agreed upon between their Moft Chriftian and Britannic Majefties as aforefaid.

And We do further require all Governors and others, the Executive Powers of thefe United States refpectively, to caufe this our Proclamation to be made Public, to the end that the fame be duly obferved within their feveral Jurifdictions.

DONE in Congrefs, at Philadelphia, this Eleventh Day of April, in the Year of our Lord One Thoufand Seven Hundred and Eighty-Three, and of our Sovereignty and Independence the Seventh.

ELIAS BOUDINOT, Prefident.

Atteft,   Charles Thomfon, Sec'ry.

STATE OF NEW-HAMPSHIRE. } In Committee of Safety, Exeter, April 24th, 1783.

ORDERED, That the foregoing Proclamation be immediately printed and difperfed throughout this State, to the end that the fame may be duly obferved.

M. Weare, *Prefident.*

BY ORDER OF THE COMMITTEE.

J. Pearson Deputy Secretary.

Printed at Exeter.

25

OLD SWAGO

A few stanzas of a ballad — sung to music —
based on Willett's Expedition

Come all you valiant heroes,
Unto my song attend!
And unto you I will relate
The lines that I have penned.

Concerning of a sad distress
Which late we did receive,
A marching to Old Swago,
Our country to relieve.

The drums did beat so merrily,
The fifes did play so free
Commanded by John Holden,
Old Swago for to see.

And then spoke our Colonel,
And unto us did say:
"I'll place in front, boys,
All for the bloody fray."

Then up spoke our officers,
With courage stout and bold:
Be of good cheer, my brave boys,
We're not born to be controlled.

Then set out their works to storm,
And boldly marching on,
Were guided by an Indian
Some called him Captain John.

O'er hills and dales we marched
Until the break of day;
But little did we think or know
That we were led astray.

Then our provisions being out,
Then back we did return;
It was enough to make even
A Pharoah's heart to mourn.

For the terrible sufferings
Which to our band befell;
No pen can e'er describe them
No tongue can ever tell.

Some of our men were frozen,
And left upon the snow;
And others they were starving,
As onward we did go.

For in the piercing cold,
Our feet and hands did freeze
While endeavoring to make a fire,
From branches of the trees.

As to that treacherous Indian,
The cause of all our woe;
We put a bullet through his head
And left him on the snow.

But now we are returning,
Unto our own abode;
Here's health unto Old Swago,
That dark and dismal road.

Now to conclude my ditty,
The lines which I have penned;
Huzza! Huzza! America!
The war is at an end.

A Soldier's Experiences in the War of 1812

In the War of 1812 the frontiers of New York were continually open to attack. General Henry Dearborn was sent to command the northern army and General Jacob Brown was stationed at Ogdensburg with a body of New York militia. To secure the mastery of Lake Ontario, General Dearborn and Commodore Isaac Chauncey decided to attack York (Toronto since 1834). Chauncey's fleet, with 1700 soldiers, left Sackets Harbor in April 1813, and in five days afffected a landing about three miles from York. General Pike headed the attack. Let us digress for a moment.

Zebulon Montgomery Pike, of New Jersey, was a regular and thorough bred soldier, nearly all his life spent in the little army of the United States. He entered the army as a youth when it consisted of only a few hundred men, under Washington's presidency. After serving in frontier garrisons through Washington's, John Adams', Jefferson's, and Madison's administrations, attained the rank of Major. In the War of 1812 Major Pike became a brigadier general, and regarded as one of our best commanders.

General Pike led the assault with such vigor that the enemy fled in precipitation. But before quitting their ground they blew up their magazine, killing and wounding about 200 of the American attacking force. The town capitulated on April 27. General Pike, unfortunately, was among those gravely wounded by the explosion. He was carried to the American flag-ship, the *Madison,* and there the hero of York battle died, his head pillowed by the flag to which he gave his heart's devotion. General Pike is buried in the cemetery at Sackets Harbor.

Following this initial success the small American fleet proceeded in the direction of Fort George at the mouth of the Niagara River. There Colonel Winfield Scott landed the troops and, attacking the British outside the fort, defeated them. The garrison, following the tactics of the garrison at York, fired their magazines and fled. Thus, on May 27, one more signal victory was chalked up to American credit. So much for the background of the scenes of action. Now for the experiences in the life of the soldier as told by him in a letter to his brother.

This letter was written by A. W. Barns to his brother Ephraim Barns in New Haven, Oswego County, and came into the possession of George L. Barnes of West Second Street, Oswego, New York, a descendent. This is his sketch of the part of his life dealing with his war experiences:

I went to old Fladley to live with a man by the name of Hooker. I lived with him about two years. My chance for an education with him was very limited and my usage was bad. I concluded to leave him, but where to go I knew not, as our Father's situation was such that I knew he had no use for me at home. So I concluded to run away and go to Barnum in the Town of Fairfield, Herkimer County, State of New York. Here I knocked around about two years. Here my chance of education was limited and here I became a very rude boy having no home or master. I tried to get a blacksmith trade, but did not succeed, so I concluded to go and enter the army. Accordingly I left Fairfield in March, 1813, for Utica and arrived there same day and enlisted in the 13th Regiment United States Infantry. Putman Farrington commanded the 13th Regiment of New York Militia in the War of 1812, first as Lieutenant Colonel and then as General. Here you know was a poor place for creature, but it proved a good schooling to me for they brought me to it fast.

I was marched soon to Sacket's Harbor. After remaining there a few days we were put on board the fleet and sailed across the lake to Little York, now called Toronto. There we met a very warm reception. Together with the explosion of their magazine we succeeded in capturing the Fort with the loss of our brave General Pike and many brave men and officers. We soon left here and sailed to Fort Niagara. From here in the month of May, we crossed again into Canada and here we met another warm reception, but we succeeded in taking Fort George. The next day our brigade was ordered to pursue the enemy.

We overtook the enemy at Stoney Creek about forty miles distant. Here we had a bloody fight in the night and made a kind of a draw game of it, though we got many prisoners. We returned to Fort George and remained there during the summer of 1813. Here we had a great deal of fighting but nothing serious. In the fall of 1813 we left Fort George and went down the lake for the purpose of taking Montreal and taking up our quarters there for the winter, but, I suppose through some treachery, we never reached there. On our way down the River St. Lawrence, at what was Cristler's Fields, we had a fight with the enemy, which lasted two hours and a half. The British got the best of the fight, owing to bad mismanagement of our General Wilkinson. (General Dearborn was removed from his command and General James Wilkinson became his successor). This day I had five of my mess mates shot down by my side and I, the only one left of my mess. Here we lost many good officers and men. From here we proceeded down the River St. Lawrence to the French mills. Arrived here I think, late in October, 1813, and had to lay in tents till after New Years before we could get barracks built and lived half rations and badly clothed and had to endure extreme cold weather, in this half clothed situation. Soon after getting fixed in barracks, we had to leave and march to Plattsburgh. Many suffered severly on this march in the month of March, 1814. We marched into Canada to the Cole Mills down towards Montreal. Here we had a fight with the British at the Mills. We gained nothing, except many wounded and killed. From here we returned to Plattsburgh, and soon after that splendid victory, our brigade was ordered into Upper Canada to join General Brown at Fort Erie. Here we had hard fighting the balance of the campaign. In this sketch I have to leave out many particulars that came under my notice.

I will take room to mention in 1813, when we lay at Fort George, there was a post on one of the picket guards which was so situated as to render it very dangerous in the night on account of the British and Indians. It fell to my lot to stand that post one night. I being a boy, the officer of the Guard, put another young man on post with me as we had to stand post (with) all night, for the relief did not dare to come to relieve us in the night. The British and the Indians crept upon close before we discovered them. I fired my gun at the body of them and run. They fired a platoon (about 12 men) at the flash of my gun, but none hit me, though shaved me close. The other man they caught before he had time to fire and run. He got away from them when Captain Chapens and his men retook them on the lake shortly after. My man's name was John McSigler. He belonged to the town of Canadagua, State of New York.

31

At the end of this campaign we returned in the fall of 1814, to Sacket's Harbor into winter quarters, the spring of 1815 after frees and the desiring wars men got their discharge, we the five years men of the 13th, 211 Regiment called the Fifth Regiment. We were then ordered to Detroit, Michigan Territory. We were there at the Great Treaty made with the Western Indians in 1815. I remained there at Detroit until my five years expired, in the spring of 1818. I always had good luck to have the confidence of my officers. On the day that my commanding officer gave me my discharge, he said to me, "Now go and be as good a citizen as you have been a soldier and not re-enlist.

A. W. Barns remained in the West, settling at Canton, Illinois.

Selleck's Shore Store brochure

Evacuation of Fort Ontario *by Charles Henry Grant*

"I do not wonder this was the last place left by the British; Oswego is so beautiful I wonder that they every went away."

General Horace Porter

The Cable

The British attacked, captured and destroyed Fort Ontario on May 6, 1814. A description of the affair is written in detail in the writer's publication, Oswego: Hamlet Days 1796–1828. The first part of this story, under the heading, Battle of Sandy Creek, is taken from the above work.

Lieutenant Colonel George E. Mitchell retreated to Oswego Falls (Fulton) accompanied by Captain Melancthon Taylor Woolsey. It was planned to transport the naval stores to the mouth of Stony Creek and portage them overland to Sackets Harbor. The stores including twenty-two long 32-pounders, ten 24 pounders, three 42 carranades and twelve large cables were loaded on nineteen boats. The main cable for the *Superior*, a warship nearing completion at Sackets Harbor, measured twenty-two inches in circumference, and weighed 9,000 pounds.

On the night of May 28, Captain Woolsey, with Major David Appling's 130 riflemen, slipped out of Oswego with the flotilla. In spite of the dismal rain, the rowers reached the mouth of the Salmon River, with one boat missing. Here Woolsey was joined by 150 Oneida Indians. The warriors, stripped and painted for battle, each arrayed only in breachcloth and a crest of feathers, and armed with rifle, tomahawk and scalping knife, strode proudly along the sandy shore abreast the flotilla.

Captain Woolsey surmised that the missing boat was intercepted by the Britsh, which indeed it was. He spied a schooner coming toward his boats which hastily disapperared. At noon the flotilla entered at Sandy Creek and proceeded a mile upstream. He dispatched runners for reinforcements.

Major Appling's description of the action that followed is brief and to the point:

Our commander, apprehending an attack, placed the riflemen and Indians in the woods on each side of the creek, and sent a few raw militia with a show of opposing the enemy's landing. The plan succeeded. The militia retreated on the first fire, pursued by the enemy, but as soon as they passed the Indians and riflemen who were in ambush, these last attacked them in the rear, while a battery of four field pieces opened up on them in front. Thus cut off in their retreat, after a smart

South East View of Sacketts's Harbour c.1815

action of twenty minutes in which they had 20 killed, 40 or 50 wounded, the whole force of the enemy, 137 in number, surrendered with their gun-boats, five in number. One of these gun-boats carried a 98 pound carronnade, one two long twelves and two brass field pieces, one of which they threw overboard. Not a man escaped to carry the news to Sir James Yeo.

Perhaps it would be of interest to the reader to obtain a description of the skirmish at Sandy Creek from a boatman's view point.

Matthew McNair, who was 85 years old, paid a visit to the office of the Oswego Commercial Times. In its March 15, 1859, edition, Mr. McNair, in the course of their conversation, stated that the *Traveler* was a vessel of 53 tons burthen, begun at Liverpool, on Onondaga Lake, in 1813. She was run down to the mouth of the river at Braddock's Reef (Lower Dam), and kept till after the war, when she was purchased by Mr. McNair and was on the lake in 1818.

Captain Israel Adams, in his Narrative, gave a boatman's view of an incident of the War of 1812.

At this time a man by the name of J. W. Smith, of Liverpool, who was engaged in building four boats and two schooners on his own account, employed me in making the sail for the whole of them, which occcupied me through the winter. In the spring of 1813, (sic) another fleet of boats were taken down the river to Oswego, and I was again employed to pilot them, which I did to the satisfaction of all concerned. These boats were employed to transport guns and rigging to fit out three new vessels for service, then building at Sacketts Harbor, and as the enemy then had command of the Lake, it was unsafe for us to be seen in the day time. We therefore sailed out of Oswego in the evening, expecting to reach Sandy Creek before daybreak, the distance being thirty miles, but the wind not being so strong as we expected, it was 9 o'clock before we reached Sandy Creek. We here learned that the enemy were in possession of the coast between this and Sacketts Harbor. We then concluded to ascend the creek as far as possible, which we accordingly did, shoving our boats around a bend of the creek, which there was a small copse of woods which sheltered them in part from the sight of the enemy, a few of our masts only could be seen. We formed a determination to defend our boats as long as possible; and early in the morning the enemy made their appearance, coming up the creek and firing at us with 68 (sic) pound shot, and some smaller calibre from their gun boats. We had a small party of riflemen, thirty in number, commanded by Capt. Applin, to whom we gave the command of the defence. We armed ourselves as well as we could, but could only arm 100 men, including riflemen. About a mile from the mouth of the creek, at a bend in the stream, was a copse of woods, below which, on either side of the creek, were meadows—at the mouth of the creek, on each side, were high banks. Here the enemy landed a part of their forces, but finding they could not proceed by land, they again embarked on board the boats and proceeded up the creek until they reached the meadows, when a party landed on each side of the creek, and kept along with the boats. They commenced firing from the boats immediately on entering the creek, from their largest piece. There were boats, carrying 14 guns in all, and the number of the enemy was four hundred, well armed.

Captain Applin drew up his party in the copse of the woods. Behind the woods, in the bend of the creek, lay our boats, the masts of which the enemy had discovered. The enemy were now advancing, keeping up a continual fire, which did no other damage than to cut the limbs of the trees. Each of us were ordered to keep behind the stumps of the trees until Captain Applin fired, which was the signal for all to fire—then we were to load and fire as fast as we could, and not to waste ammunition. The enemy were now within six rods of us. They had loaded their big guns with a bag of musket balls, and as the gunner was taking aim at us, Captain Applin fired, and the rest of us at the same instant—there were seven balls through the gunners body. Every man loaded and fired as fast as he could. The battle was general on both sides—it lasted not more than twenty minutes before the enemy surrendered prisoners of war, they having 40 killed and 87 wounded. We had none killed, and but one wounded, who died of his wound the third day after the battle.

How the supplies were carried from that point to Sackets Harbor is well described by the story of a participant. This article is found in the *Watertown Daily Times*, February 9, 1880, under the heading, "A Patriotic Job In 1814—Eighty-Four Men Carry Five Tons of Ship Cable On Their Shoulders From Sandy Creek to Sackets Harbor"

During the War of 1812, Sackets Harbor was a naval station, and in the winter of 1813–14 many war vessels were built at that place.

In (Dr. Franklin B.) Hough's, History Of Jefferson County, it is related that in the spring of 1814 the frigate *Superior* (66 guns) was launched and the *Mohawk* and *Jones* were launched on the stocks. The rigging and armament for these vessels were transported via the Mohawk River and Wood Creek and so on to Oswego, at which point they were loaded in boats to proceed to Sackets Harbor. But a British fleet having stationed itself at the Galoup Islands, the boats were prevented from passing around Six Town Point. Accordingly, an attempt was made to reach the mouth of Stony Creek, from which point to Henderson Harbor a land carriage of only three miles intervened. But the boats were chased into Sandy Creek where the guns, rigging, etc., were loaded on to wagons for transportation to Sackets Harbor a distance of twenty miles.

There remained, however, one large cable which could not be loaded on any vehicle. It was then suggested to bear it upon the shoulders of men:

> The proposal was cheerfully adopted by the citizens who had assembled, and they, being accordingly a arranged in the order of their stature, shouldered the ponderous cable and took up their line of march for Sackets Harbor, being as near together as they could walk. This travel procession passed by way of Ellis Village and Smithville, and on the second day reached Sackets Harbor. As they approached the town, the sailors came out to meet them and with loud cheers relieved them of their burden and marched triumphantly into the village.

The subjoined letter from Silas Lyman who was an actor in the scenes described above, and who assisted in bearing the cable, will be found a valuable contribution to local history, and will be read with interest. The venerable writer of the letter is now in his 86th year, but his handwriting is distinct and business like, and as will be seen, his mind is clear and vigorous.

I have been requested by many to give some account of the cable that was taken up and carried on men's shoulders from the mouth of Sandy Creek to Sackets Harbor, a distance of about twenty miles. The cable weighed nearly five tons, and eighty-four men took it up and carried it from McKes's Landing to Ellis Village, where we got a few recruits and went to Belleville, and thence to place called Four Corners, finding ourselves then pretty well drilled out. The people at the Corners most liberally furnished us with supper and barn lodging and breakfast, all freely given and thankfully received. Then the rope was taken up and on through Smithville and to the Harbor. Some of our men tired out, but others volunteered in their places. One man left his team with his boys, saying we should not do the job alone. He was a stout fellow, and put his shoulder to the work. As we advanced, men kept falling in, and the people along the route cheered us lustily. And as we advanced toward the end of our rope job, there was loud cheering the whole length of the cable, which was about thirty-six rods (594 feet) long and the size of a seven-inch stove pipe.

As we went into the town, there were as many men as could walk under it, and with good music the big cable was landed in the ship yard in care of the sailors. A stout man stood on the cable and held a flag, and a boy stood on the man's shoulders and played the drum. The boy may be living to tell for himself, but looking around I can find no man living that took part in carrying the cable—not one.

The men who first took up the cable were Ellisburg and Lorraine men principally, about 120 lbs each man.

This was the last of the property driven into Sandy Creek by the British fleet, consisting of guns, and rigging for the old ship now on the stocks.

Of the old ship I will just say, I was at work on a big oak tree about a mile south of the Harbor, when the word came, 'no more ship timber.' Peace was declared.

I resided in Lorraine sixty years, and had quite extended acquaintances in the south part of Jefferson County with many choice friends and good neighbors who are gone the way of earth. To such as remain, I say farewell—meet me in Heaven. I am in my eighty-sixth year.

Silas Lyman

Battle Ship *New Orleans* Built 1812.

Keel 187 ft—Beam 56 ft—Depth of Hold 30 ft Measurment.

3200 Tons—120 Guns—Portrait Taken Aug 1881—Sackets Harbor, N. Y.

The New Orleans

On December 18, 1814, Commodore Isaac Chauncey ordered New York shipbuilders Adam and Noah Brown and Henry Eckford to "make selection of such spots as in your opinion may be the most eligible for building with dispatch two ships of the Line and one Frigate. Your selection will not extend beyond Storr's Harbor."

What is remarkable about the rapidity of shipbuilding at Sackets Harbor is the number of men employed in construction. By mid January, 1815, more than 600 ship carpenters were on the scene. A newspaper correspondent noted that the men were "busily engaged in getting timber ready to build two seventy-fours and a Frigate of the first class. Although surrounded by spies, our government have reason to congratulate themselves on this very essential point—that the whole of the materials for the increased naval force to be established on this lake has been contracted for, and ready for delivery in six weeks." The article was written on January 11, 1815.

On February 1, Chauncey advised B. W. Crowninshield, Secretary of Navy, that work on the ships was progressing rapidly and the frames had been raised. "The builders," said Chauncey, "assure me that they shall both be launched in April—the Frigate is not yet commenced but the materials will be prepared for her so that she can be built in a short time."

Also employed in the shipbuilding frenzy at Sackets Harbor were 60 shipjoiners, 75 blacksmiths, 25 block and pump-makers, 10 boat builders, 10 spar-makers, 18 gun-carriage makers, 16 sail masters, 10 armorers and five tin men, for a total of 829.

Governor D. D. Tompkins was advised by Chauncey on February 16th that caulking could commence in two days and would be ready to launch by the last of March "unless peace prove true and stops us where we are." The Treaty of Ghent ending the War of 1812 was signed on December 24, 1814, but the news did not reach Sackets Harbor until late in February, 1815.

In a letter to Crowninshield on February 25, Chauncey wrote:
I have suspended all contracts and stopped the transportation of all stores except those between this place and Utica which must come here for safe keeping. I have directed Messrs. Eckford & Brown to discontinue all building—these gentlemen however state to me it is impossible for them to

stop so suddenly because they have upwards of 800 men employed which must be paid work or play until they arrive in New York—consequently it costs no more to keep them at work than suffer them to remain idle—they reduce their gangs thirty to forty men per day which is as many as they can find transport for.

Chauncey continued to write: "If left on the stocks they must be housed or they will decay in a few years."

Chauncey subsequently had the naval fleet on Lake Ontario dismantled. Most of the vessels built at Sackets Harbor were laid up in ordinary and the merchant vessels resold back to their original owners. Upon Chauncey's advice shiphouses were erected over the *New Orleans* and *Chippewa* in August 1815, at a cost of $25,000. The *Chippewa* was broken up and burned on the ways for her old iron in 1834.

An eulogy on the old ship published in the *Jefferson County Journal*, Adams, New York, March 31, 1880 (first published at Sackets Harbor, September 10, 1872) is presented:

THE NEW ORLEANS

Old and rotten, and worthless now,
No waters shall ever feel her prow
To cleave away her laughing sides
As over the foaming crest she rides.

They've kept her here like a corpse in state,
For curious gaze and idle prate,
To gather no halo around her name,
And lie unchristened, unknown to fame.

The tooth of time is ever at work;
The mould and worm in her vitals lerk
The hulk that our fathers had builded stout,
Has sat on her haunches and rusted out.

She has stood aloof from the water's soak,
And out-lived the age of her heart of oak;
In the ponderous clutches of iron mail,
Her wooden walls are as eggshell frail.

And yet to go like the *Cumberland* down,
Unscrewed by the *Merrimac's* ugly frown,
Her last gun fired from under the wave,
And her proud flag flying above her grave—

Eluding the cumbersome "Southron's" grip,
To hold forever the good old ship,
Would leave her record of moral worth,
As everlasting as God's green earth.

Then why should her unused life be sold,
For the common sin of growing old?
Her keel was laid by the nation's brave,
To drive the foe from Ontario's wave.

Their hammers are still. The dip of their oars,
Has fled from Ontario's shelving shores,
And their old gray heads are pillowed too low,
To heed Ontario's ebb or flow.

Their staunch old craft has stood on her "ways,"
The treasured relic of troublous days
Till they have finished their ground-work here,
And gone to build in a brighter sphere.

Then let her abide as the nation's guest,
Till she rots to Ontario's heaving breast,
When the winds and waves in frolic, and gust,
Will bear to their secret caves her dust!

> O. D. K., in the Brookfield Courier

The Navy finally decided to dispose of the *New Orleans* and held a public auction. On September 24, 1883, Syracuse business man Alfred Wilkinson found himself the proud possessor of an authentic War of 1812 ship of the line (unfinished) for $427.50. The editor of the Jefferson County Journal reported on January 13, 1884:

The old ship is a thing of the past; she is a mass of ruins which once was of such massive proportions and gazed at with so many curious eyes. She was erected in 1812 (sic 1815) in 29 days from standing timber. She had been covered over with

43

a house but from delay and want of repair, it fell about two years since, and last year the old ship was sold at auction by the government. Thus passes away an old landmark, regretted by all that its last days should be marked by such a scene of horror.

The "Patriot War"

The Caroline Affair and Its Effect on Oswego

The causes and details of the uprising of dissidents against the government of Upper Canada is not in the purview of this survey, only so far as it relates to Oswego. Willliam Lyon Mackenzie, publisher of a weekly newspaper in Canada, supported the liberal viewpoint of the period. The Reform Party fought for responsible government for the province. Mackenzie engaged in constant warfare with the political clique known as "The Family Compact".

Eventually the Reformers undertook an armed rebellion against the govermnent of Upper Canada. In an effort to capture Toronto, there was a skirmish on December 7, 1837, in which the insurgents were routed and dispersed. The leaders and others escaped to the United States.

Mackenzie arrived at Buffalo on December 11. There he began to recruit a "Patriot army" with the purpose of invading Canada and winning its independence from Great Britain. The volunteers moved across the Niagara River by boat to Navy Island, a small Canadian island three miles above Niagara Falls near the mainland. On the island a Provisional Government for Upper Canada was set up. Announcement was made to the world as to the objectives of the ambitious young "government" which included perpetual peace founded on a government of equal rights for all, a written constitution guaranteeing civil and religious liberty, the abolition of hereditary honors and laws of primogeniture and entail, a republican form of government chosen by popular election, freedom of the press, trial by jury, free trade and the opening of the St. Lawrence to world trade. It also promised 300 acres of "fair and fertile" lands to those who enlisted in the "army" being set up on the island for the purpose of invading Canada.

The influx of volunteers was so great at Navy Island a few days after Mackenzie had established his provisional government with its fair promises there, that the supplying of food and other supplies for the "army" became an acute problem. To meet the situation, Mackenzie arranged for an American-owned steamer "Caroline" of 40 tons to be cut free from the ice which had frozen her in at her

Schlosser Landing   Sketch by Cap. Van Cleve

CAROLINE

Captain James Van Cleve records that the *Caroline* had been built by Cornelius Vanderbilt "about 1825 at a cost of $6,000 for service along the Atlantic coast. About 1834 the *Caroline* came through the canal to Oswego and went thence into service as a ferry boat between Ogdensburg and Prescott. Later she went through the Welland Canal to Lake Erie and ran between Buffalo and Schlosser. During the Canadian attack upon her two or three were wounded December 29, 1837. Her bowsprit was picked up at Fort Niagara by Col. E. Jewett. Her figure head is now in the Buffalo Historical Society."

---

dock, and placed in immediate service. It began transporting supplies for the men on the island, bringing in fresh recruits daily and transporting visitors who came to see the "troops" who were engaged in setting up defense works there. It was reported that there was an arrival of "28 young men from Oswego in a single party" who entered the service of the "Patriot" army.

It came to the attention of Colonel Allan McNab, commanding the Canadian forces at Chippewa, opposite Navy Island, that the *Caroline* had begun making trips between the United States mainland and Navy Island. He dispatched Captain Andrew Drew, an officer of the Royal Navy and Alexander McCleod, deputy sheriff of the Niagara District to reconnoitre the island. With this infor-

46

mation Col. McNab and Capt. Drew hit upon a plan to render useless the *Caroline*. Capt. Drew was asigned the execution of the plan. The 50 or 60 volunteers on the night of December 29, were instructed to: "Take and destroy the *Caroline* wherever you shall find her."

Instead of being tied up on the eastern side of the river, the *Caroline* lay alongside a wharf on the American side. The Canadians succeeded in seizing the boat. There were 33 persons in all on board, 10 of whom were her crew and the others were persons asleep on board because there was not room for them in the Schlosser hotel (located two miles above the American Falls) which stood nearby. In the melee one American, Amos Durfee, was killed outright.

The *Caroline* was cut from her mooring, set on fire, towed to the center of the river, and allowed to drift down stream. Soon her woodwork above the water line was pretty much destroyed. Her engine went to the bottom, her copper bottom having given away first. Contrary to popular belief, the ship did not go over Niagara Falls.

The chain of events which followed in the wake of its destruction very narrowly avoided bringing the United States in a state of war with Canada and Great Britain. In the United States the slogan "Remember the *Caroline*" soon became prevalent along the border.

Restoration of Fort Ontario

A public meeting was held at Market Hall on January 20, 1838, to take action bringing to the attention of the United States authorities to the need which the citizens of the community felt as the result of incidents along the border for the rehabilitation and garrisoning of Fort Ontario.

On motion of William Lewis, Jr., Col. Theophilus S. Morgan was made chairman; on motion of Moses P. Hatch, William Lewis, Jr., was made secretary of the meeting.

The following resolutions were adopted:

Whereas, it is deemed the policy of the national government to place the northern frontier in a condition by which it may be better secured against foreign aggression, and whereas, it is the duty of our government to be prepared for any emergencies that may grow out of relations with neighboring powers, and that to prepare for war in time of peace is the dictate of reason and the surest guarantee of public tranquility.

Resolved, That the importance of Oswego as a place of business and its commanding position as a frontier post require that it should be placed in a state of defense by the national government.

Resolved, That for the purpose of carrying into effect this object, the president of this village be requested to correspond with General Scott, directing his attention to this point, and obtain his views as to the expediency of repairing Fort Ontario and establishing a military post at this place.

Resolved, That chairman of this meeting designate a committee to prepare a memorial to Congress for the promotion of this object.

Pursuant to the last resolution Chairman Morgan appointed the following committee to memorialize Congress: David P. Brewster, Llewellyn Jones, Milton Harmon.

The full text of the memorial to Congress as prepared by this committee was published in the Palladium of Januray 31, 1838. It was a strong document, and undoubtedly was helpful in bringing about the appropriation Congress made a short time later for reconstructing Fort Ontario after arrangements had been made for the transfer of the land the fort occupied from the State to the United States government so long as it should be used for military purposes.

General Scott in replying to the letter sent him by the Village President Brewster at the request of the mass meeting, said according to the *Commercial Herald* of February 1:

Headquarters—Eastern Division, Buffalo,
Jan. 29, 1838

Dear Sir:

I had the honor to receive your letter of the 23rd instant, and also have a copy of the memorial addressed to Congress, respecting the establishment of a military post at Oswego.

I am well acquainted with the topography of your place and its importance in a commercial and military point of view.

In a recent report on the frontier of my division, I had occasion to speak of Oswego as a military station, and

48

Barber & Howe, 1841.

An 1841 drawing showing Fort Ontario. At the far right are Oswego's first lighthouse and lightkeeper's hous built in 1821, still standing. At left is Oswego's second lighthouse built in 1837 and made higher in the late 1860s.

---

recommended, in a certain contingency, that a large force should be alotted to it. I am also of the opinion that it would be wise to erect a fort at that place, to cover the force and protect the harbor.

I trust that the memorial may produce the desired result.
With great respect
I remain, sir, your ob't serv't,
Winfield Scott

Public confidence was somewhat assured when General Winfield S. Scott, on July 12, sent a detachment of U. S. regulars to Oswego under the command of Lieut. R. E. Temple for the better protection of the place. As Fort Ontario was not at this time habitable, the soldiers were quarterd at the United States Hotel which stood on West Seneca Street.

Oswego Guards Organized

Two Oswego County militia regiments had their headquarters in Oswego at this time, the 172d Regiment of Infantry, commanded by Col. Charles G. Rumrill, in a private capacity he was also the jailer of Oswego jail then located in the basement of the Market House. The 28th Regiment of Riflemen was commanded by Col. L.

49

Parkhurst. No very great reliance was placed in the militia, however, by the local folk or apparently by the State government either. Both the state and federal officials encouraged the formation at this time of new, military companies in the cities along the border for their greater security. Here the "Oswego Guards" were organized in the summer of 1838 largely as a result of desire on the part of local citizens for greater protection to be accorded Oswego, and because of the tardiness of Congress in acting upon General Scott's recommendations for a larger army and more troops for the important border posts with which General Scott classed Oswego.

The organization meeting of the "guards" was held July 19, 1838, with a young lawyer, William F. Allen, later to become one of the most distinguished member of the state bench ever produced in Oswego County, acting as chairman of the meeting. C. L. Cole was secretary; Sidney S. Hurlbut, captain; James Ransom, lieutenant; and Zadoc Strong, ensign.

Drilling was started immediately in the "great hall" on the third floor of the Market House which from this time forward was used by the "Guards" as a drill hall for many years. At the time of its organization, the company included in its ranks many young men who were destined to be numbered among the leading citizens of the village. One of the early acts of the "guards" was to make an offer to the War Department to take over the garrisoning of Fort Ontario until a regular garrison could be provided. The "Guards" saw no active service, however, in connection with the "Patriot War". Later they were reorganized as the 48th Separate Company of the New York State Guard, and became the forerunner of Oswego's National Guard companies of the modern period.

Two incidents occurred that had an effect on Oswego; one was burning of the steamboat *Sir Robert Peel*, and the other the firing upon the American owned *Telegraph*. The *Sir Robert Peel* was boarded and burned, at Well's Island, near Clayton, while she stopped to take on wood (while enroute to Oswego). Four days after the burning of *Sir Robert Peel*, Saturday morning, June 2, 1838, the steamer *Telegraph*, American owned, plying her regular schedule between Kingston and Lewiston via Oswego, was first boarded and searched, and then fired upon. Apparently as an act of retaliation, this happened while lying at her dock in Brockville by a company of about fifty Canadian militiamen. In commenting on this incident the *Oswego Commercial Herald*, said: "Everyone who has any regard for the preservation of peace between the two countries, will look upon the burning of the *Sir Robert Peel,* and also the outrage of the *Telegraph,* as acts of piracy, calculated to impair those amicable and friendly relations which should be strictly observed by the citizens of both governments.''

For some days following the development of the *Peel* and *Telegraph* incidents, all communications between Port of Oswego and Canadian ports was cut off. The daily steamers between Oswego and Toronto ceased running. Upon arriving in Oswego the steamer *United States* was advised not to visit Kingston. Commerce between the two countries as it normally moved through Oswego came to a stop. Some American skippers said that they would not sail for Canadian ports until they have been provided with an armed guard. As matters quieted down again, the strain became less intense and gradually commerce was resumed once more.

Steamboat *United States*

Before relating the episode about the steamer *United States,* it is necessary to say something about the ''Hunters''. The ''Hunters'', organized in 1838, was destined to become the largest and by far the most important of all the ''patriot'' secret societies. It soon became the boast that it had a lodge in every considerable village and town of the north. The ''Hunters''' headquarters in Oswego were in rooms above the West First Street store of Millis & Leverich where at this period a dozen or more shoemakers were employed in the establishment. The lodge rooms could only be reached from the interior of the store. J. Clark Cooley of Oswego was a local leader of the movement. John Grant, Jr., was referred to as the grand treasurer of the ''Hunters'' by George H. McWhorter, the Custom Collector. Grant was a second Judge of the Court of Common Pleas of Oswego County in 1820; served as postmaster for Oswego for two terms following 1825; appointed collector of the Port of Oswego in 1826; served as President of the village in 1833 and 1834; and was a merchant and manufacturer. He died in Oswego May 26, 1850. According to Col. E. J. Worth, commander of the United States forces along the Ontario and St. Lawrence frontiers from Sodus to Ogdensburg in 1838, said: ''Many [public officers] are notoriously active partisans. There are, however, some honorable exceptions—a

LAKE ONTARIO--1839.

THE STEAM-BOAT

United States.

sad state of things this when private persons usurp the functions of the authorities and violations of the law, no matter how criminal the manner, is hailed as the highest indication of partriotism."

High winds whipped up giant waves in Lake Ontario through the greater part of the week which opened Sunday, November 4. So strong were the waves that pretty much of all the shipping in the Port of Oswego, sail or steam, was for safety held there. The pasengrer steamer *United States*, largely Oswego-owned and the last word in luxury travel on the lake for that period, was among these. Her captain was James Van Cleve, one of the ablest and most farseeing lake captains of his day, and a man who would rise to a considerable degree of fame in the lake region. Two other ships held in Oswego harbor during the storm were the schooners *Charlotte of Oswego* and *Charlotte of Toronto*. The first named lay at a wharf near the Market House just north of the Lower Bridge.

The storm receded on Saturday and the *Charlotte of Oswego* slipped out of port that night of November 10. Somewhere down the lake after a few hours she was joined by another schooner, the *Charlotte of Toronto*, and the two proceeded towards the St. Lawrence keeping always each other's sail in view. (Both had heavy human cargoes aboard as well as freight).

The regularly scheduled time of the departure of the *United States* on this trip would have been 5 P. M. Thursday, November 8, but left Sunday morning, November 11. On board were at least 60 Oswego County residents. Among them were Neils S. Von Schoultz [Polish] "general" in command of the expedition against Canada. Also on board were two of the owners of the steamer, Col. Theophilus S. Morgan and Lucius B. Crocker, both of Oswego, whose partnership in the ownership of the steamer were principally Ogdensburg residents.

Captain Van Cleve seems to have entertained some doubts as to the purposes of the motley crowd of the deck passengers who boarded the *United States* at Oswego that morning. He hesitated about putting out with them for fear his passengers might get the boat in trouble. Finally Van Cleve was assured by Messrs. Morgan and Crocker that his doubts were probably groundless and that they would assume any risk involved. Reassured, Captain Van Cleve steamed away from the dock at 9 o'clock in the morning. A stop was made at Sackets Harbor and 20 or 30 men were taken on, and at Cape Vincent 10 or 11 more came aboard.

A little below Millen's Bay, near the entrance to the St. Lawrence River, the *United States* overtook the two schooners which had left Oswego on the night of November 10, while the steamer was still in port—the *Charlotte of Oswego* and the *Charlotte of Toronto*. An arrangement had been made by an unidentified passenger on board ship soon after Cape Vincent had been left behind for the *United States* to pick-up and tow the two schooners to Ogdensburg where the man who posed as a merchant said he desired to have the goods on the ships in port the next morning. Captain Van Cleve stopped his steamer, arranged his tows, one on either side of his ship, and proceeded on his way. What happened next is best described by a person who was present at the scene.

An unidentified gentleman, accompanying as a guest of Col. T. S. Morgan and L. B. Crocker, became an eye-witness of the events of the voyage to Ogdensburg. In a letter to the *Albany Argus*, written on board the *United States*, penned one of the best and most comprehensive accounts of these events. The letter was reprinted in the Oswego *Commercial Herald* under the date of November 28. In part the text of this letter follows:

53

Correspondent of the Argus
Steamboat *United States*
Wednesday, Nov. 14, 1838

Editor Albany Argus

Sir: Having had an opportunity to acquire some information relating to the recent hostile movement near Prescott, I have thought it might not be uninteresting to you if I should employ the leisure which this mode of traveling affords me to send to you a brief account of what I have witnessed within the last three or four days.

I came to Oswego last week, with a view to transact some business there, and then to proceed by steamboat to Ogdensburgh where, I had also some business. According to the advertisement the steamboat United States, Capt. Van Cleve should have left Oswego last Thursday evening for Ogdensburgh, but owing to a storm upon the lake which prevailed all last week she was not able to get out until Sunday morning. I went on board after breakfast and found among others, Col. Morgan and Mr. Crocker of Oswego, part proprietors of the boat who were going to Ogdensburgh to meet the other proprietors, to make arrangements for closing up the season's business.

Soon after I came aboard a body of men came on to the boat and took deck passage to the number of seventy or eighty. The circumstance did not surprise me at the time, as I knew that emigrants were constantly passing in considerable numbers; and being myself in the cabin while they were on deck, I took but little notice of them. At Sacket's Harbor, 20 or 30 more came on board, and at Cape Vincent and French Creek, 15 or 20 more.

Soon after we left the latter place my attention was most particularly directed to the character of the passengers. A large proportion of them appeared to be American citizens, with a sprinkling of Canadians, French and English; but they were very quiet—said little, drank nothing that I observed, and apparently were without arms. I was satisfied that they were not ordinary passengers, but concluded that they were making their way to Lower Canada to take part in the operation against the government in that province.

When we were a little below Cape Vincent, Capt. Van Cleve was applied to by a passenger of respectable appearance to take in tow two schooners which he said were lying in the river below, loaded with merchandise for Ogdensburgh, which he was desirous of getting into port the next morning; and upon inquiry by the captain, he asssured him that the vessels had no connection with the passengers, who by this time were understood to be patriots (as they were called). The captain unfortunately yielded to the request of this individual, and the vessels when reached were taken in tow—one being lashed on each side of the steamboat. They had boxes and barrels on deck, and just men enough in sight to navigate them.

The facts relating to these vessels thus far I derived from Captain Van Cleve. I knew nothing of them until some time after they had been fastened to the boat. The weather was very cold, and I had kept below until after the event. The captain added that it was a common occurrence to take vessels in tow on the river, that having become somewhat suspicious of the character of his passengers, he thought the presence of the crews of the vessels would be of some protection to his boat.

Immediately after I became acquainted with the presence of the schooners, I observed men climbing from them into the steamboat and it was soon obvious that their holds were filled with men similar character with those already on the boat, and that they in all probability contemplated a descent upon some of the Canadian towns upon the river. They were then more open in their conduct. I remarked a sword under the cloak of one, and pistol in the hands of another.

One of the schooners was under the command of "Bill" Johnston, commander of the "Patriot Navy" and Von Schoultz is said to have assumed direction of the other. They climbed on board of the *United States* to join "General" John W. Birge, their commander-in-chief. A Council of War then took place on the steamer.

The account continued to say:

At this time I was desired by Col. Morgan to confer with Mr. Crocker and the captain, as to the course of conduct to be pursued in this emergency. We had an interview on the upper deck—the patriots all crowded into the cabin. It was evident that we were entirely in the power of an armed force of about 200 men and we could have no doubt that any attempt to

55

thwart them would be resisted. We dared not, therefore, cast off the vessels, as they would then doubtless have ordered the steamboat to be taken to the place they designed to attack. The course finally determined upon and adopted was to lay by at Morristown, 10 miles above Ogdensburgh—to communicate the facts to a magistrate and to send an express on to Ogdensburgh—remaining ourselves at Morristown until the express should have time to communicate the facts to the marshal of the Northern District who, we were informed, was at Ogdensburgh.

As we were going into the harbor at Morristown, the Patriots voluntarily unfastened their vessels, after having transferred to them about 100 men, perhaps an equal number yet on board the steamboat. We remained about three hours at Morristown—causing information to be given to a magistrate, started the express immediately on our arrival with directions to inform a magistrate of the facts which had transpired, in case the marshal have luck. We then got under and at about 3 o'clock in the morning reached Ogdensburgh.

Col. Morgan and myself immediately communicated the facts in our possession to several individuals in Ogdensburgh. Captain Van Cleve informs me that subsequently he went to his boat and found that the passengers had left her, and that she was then made fast to the dock and thought secure from any other intrusion.

While I was dressing the same morning I heard cheering at the wharf a few rods from the hotel, and on going there, found that the steamboat was in the possession of the patriots and filled with armed men—a hundred of them having rushed on board and taking possession by force. One of the schooners with which we parted company at Morristown, was aground on the shoals in the river, near opposite Prescott, and the other at anchor near her—the decks of both were covered with men. I have since learned that on leaving the steamboat they had laid their course for Prescott but owing to some mismanagement they did not come up to the wharf at the point, but became entangled with each other and in an attempt to draw off towards the American side, one of them ran upon the bar. The design was to have taken Prescott by surprise in the night, which was prevented by the mistake in coming to the wharf.

56

Soon after daylight the schooner which had not grounded sailed down the river and landed her men 1-1/2 miles below Prescott at a place known as Wind Mill Point, on the British side, to the number, as near as I can learn, of about 150. She remained off that point several hours and then came up and lay near the American shore, opposite the lower part of the Village of Ogdensburgh.

The *United States* after being seized by the patriots first stood out towards the vessel on the bar, but finding it impractical owing to the shallowness of the water to come near enough to get her off, came back to the wharf at Ogdensburgh for rope with which to effect that object and proceed again towards the schooner. The account of this second trip is derived from the individual who acted as pilot but who was forced, as he declares to me, to go on board and assume conduct of her by threats of his life should he refuse. [Captain William Schuyler Malcolm of Oswego, in Ogdensburgh as a deputy United States Marshal on secret duty, He was a grandson of Gen. Philip Schuyler of American Revolutionary War fame.] The incidents of this trip are fully corroborated by my observation from the shore. He went towards the schooner, but found that he could not get near enough to get her off with rope which had been procured.

He then went around the schooner, between her and the British shore, and as soon as he got her in the channel, which at this place is near the British shore the steamboat *Experiment* [used as a gun boat against the 'Patriots'] now in the British service, came out from Prescott and fired upon the *United States* with her cannon. Neither of the two shots which were fired at this time took effect; the *States* then ran down towards Wind Mill Point to the other schooner [the *Charlotte of Toronto*] which had not then come up, the *Experiment* following her down. The lower steamer [the *Paul Pry*] then got underway and came up towards the grounded schooner [the *Charlotte of Oswego*] with a view to take off her men, and was convoyed by the *United States* to protect her from the *Experiment* and during this time, the *Experiment* fired some five or six shots at her also without effect. This lower schooner then ran over to Ogdensburgh side and anchored under the shore as before mentioned. The *United States* again ran down

57

to Wind Mill Point and by means of small boats landed 110 of her men. The notorious 'Bill' Johnston at that point of time went over from the American shore in a small boat and assisted in landing the men from the steamboat.

In the meantime the *Paul Pry*, a small American steamboat which ordinarily plied as a ferry-boat between Ogdensburg and Prescott, was manned by the "Patriots". It pulled the stranded vessel and rescued her, bringing her to the American side. All this time the *Experiment* running up and down firing on both vessels. Under the circumstances, this fete of the *Paul Pry* was among the most courageous acts of the day. To continue:

After landing her men at the Point the *United States* was to return to [Ogdensburgh] and in doing so as the channel is very near the British shore, she had again to encounter the hostility of the *Experiment* and the musketry from the shore. Accordingly as she came opposite Prescott a shower of bullets came from the shore, most of them hitting, breaking lights of glass but doing no other damage. The men, about 25 in number, who had remained after the disembarkation all stood upon the promenade deck and cheered the discharge as they came. At the same time the 'Experiment' commenced her cannonade, she discharged her pieces repeatedly without effect until at length just as the *United States* was coming around the bar, one of the shots passed through the wheel house and killed the helmsman, Solomon Foster. It hit his head which was nearly shot away. My informant [Captain William Schuyler Malcolm] then took the wheel and after sustaing one more discharge from the cannon, the boat was worked into the harbor at Ogdensburgh.

On the return of the steamboat, she was given up by the 'Patriots' and taken possession of by her owners, and immediately received by the authorities of the United States. At the request of Messers. Morgan and Crocker, I accompanied them on board. Col. Worth of the United States Army and two companies of U. S. troops arrived at Ogdensburgh on Monday evening, accompanied by Mr. Garrow, the marshal. The colonel immediately took into custody all the crafts which had been employed by the 'Patriots', including this steamboat, the two schooners and the *Paul Pry*. I had a brief interview with Col. Worth and it is owing to his indulgence that I am permitted to return on this boat. She is towing the two schooners to Sackett's Harbor where they are to await appropriate legal proceedings.

After a few months the *United States* was returned to her Oswego owners when the court became convinced that the owners of the ship and her captain had no part in carrying out the plans of the "Patriots". Her owners returned her to passenger service on the lake in May 1839, under Captain Joseph Whitney.

The 450 tons *United States* had been built at Ogdensburg by William Capes, a New York City shipbuilder. She was launched in November and made her first trip July 4, 1832, under the command of Captain Elias Trowbridge of Oswego, a former resident of New Haven, Conn., where he had been engaged in the West Indian trade. A clerk on the steamer in her first year of navigation was James Van Cleve who was to become her captain from 1835 to 1838.

Among the original subscribers for shares in the steamer were Gerrit Smith and Henry Fitzhugh, his brother-in-law, of Oswego who subscribed $1,000 each; George H. McWhorter and D. W. Cole of Oswego who had subscribed $500 each; John T. Trowbridge & Co. of Oswego who had subscribed $6,500. In all $9,500 of the ship's stock had been subscribed in Oswego and $15,000 had been taken at Ogdensburg. The Trowbridge shares were later redistributed to D. P. Brewster, Bronson & Crocker, T. S. Morgan and Frederick Carrington of Oswego. Eventually, and after her participation in the "patriot war", the steamer passed under the exclusive control and ownershop of her Oswego share-owners. According to Van Cleve a Dutchman named Bunkle became her principal stockholder.

In 1840 the *United States* and the *Great Britain* met in a collision off Genesee River. [The latter steamer was owned by Sir John Hamilton, built at Kingston, and at one time commanded by Captain Joseph Whitney.] The *United States* nearly sank before she could be gotten into port. In the fall of 1841 on her way down the lake at night soon after passing the Genesee River, Capt. W. S. Malcolm of Oswego who was mate with Captain Whitney on board the *United States* took the watch and by some strange fatality was run on shore at Lyons Point 7 or 8 miles below the river. The hull of the wrecked steamboat was sold to John Cockran of Oswego in 1843 and the ship was broken up. One of her engines was replaced in the steamer *Rochester*. Incidentally Captain Whitney died

October 11, 1841, from a fever brought on by the excitement and fatigue incident to the accident and Malcolm finished out the season as commander.

Steamer *Great Britain*

The deluxe passenger steamer *Great Britain* was the rival of the Oswego-owned steamer *United States* for speed laurels and passenger trade. The two vessels, built about the same time, and making approximately the same stops on the run from Lewiston to Ogdensburg and vice versa, competed for popular favor. The *Great Britain* made Oswego a regular port of call upon her up and down trips over the lake. In 1840 two attempts were made to cause an explosion aboard her as she was tied up at her west side wharf near the foot of West Cayuga Street with the object of setting her on fire in view of the strained relations yet existing following the border disturbances incident to the "Patriot War". Benjamin Lett, native born Canadian, who had blown up the monument of Sir Isaac Brock of 1812 fame committed other acts of crime and violence, was arrested in Oswego a few hours after the second attempt to blow up the *Great Britain* had been successful up to a point of having caused a small fire aboard ship following an explosion and causing injury to one passenger. An accomplice of Lett in causing

60

the explosion, who was also arrested, turned states' evidence at the trial with the result that Lett was convicted and sentenced to Auburn prison. He escaped from a deputy sheriff while being transported from Oswego to Auburn, and was at large many months with a reward offered by the Governor for his arrest. Soon after the amount of the reward was doubled, Lett was arrested on board in Buffalo harbor and transferred thereafter immediately to Auburn prison to start serving out the term under the sentence imposed upon him at Oswego. He was pardoned, however, in 1845, when he developed tuberculosis in prison and physicians certified that his only chance for life would be for him to be set free.

Wind Mill Point

It is not in our purview to discuss the five days fighting that took place at Wind Mill Point. Let it be said that fighting ceased on Friday when the "Patriots" surrendered. In the entire battle the British losses were: 2 officers, 14 men killed and 60 wounded. The "Patriots" lost at least 20 killed and possibly 40 wounded. The surrendering "patriots," numbering in all 160, including 18 wounded, were lined up by the British between two files of regulars and marched to Prescott where they were held over night at Fort Wellington. Next day they were marched to Fort Henry at Kingston where those among them who were British subjects were charged with treason and those who were American citizens where charged with "brigandage". Within a few weeks their trial would open, each facing separately a court martial, and the guilt or innocence of each being determined by a separate vote of the court.

The court martial was held at Kingston on November 26. Gallows were erected on the glacis of Fort Henry at Kingston. Executions went on until all 17 of the "invaders" had paid for their errors of judgment with their lives. Among them were Neils S. Von Schoultz, first in command and "Col." Dorephus Abbey, second in command of the "patriots".

Dorephus Abbey had been the first printer in Oswego County in 1817 when he came to Oswego to establish a job printing shop later publishing the first newspaper in the county, the *Oswego Palladium*. Abbey and his brother Seth A. had been operating a commercial printing office in Albany until the spring of 1817 when they bought the *Watertown Advocate*. With the Abbey brothers came John Haines Lord, Jr., the first editor of the *Oswego Palladium* in 1819. Dorephus Abbey remained in Oswego for some time, and then returned to Jeffferson County to become once more associated with his brother there in the publishing and printing business. After, however, removing a few years later to New Jersey he had returned about 1830 to engage in farming, near Watertown. He some how became associated with the "Hunters".

Many of the men over 20 years of age were sentenced to spend the remainder of their lives in Von Dieman's Land [Tasmania] where there was a penal colony. Among those from Oswego County who were sent to Sandy Bay, Hobart Town, Von Dieman's Land were Jehiel H. Martin, John Berry and Samuel Washburn of Oswego; John Bartlett, David Allen, Enos Fellows of Volney; Joseph Lee and Alanson Owens of Palermo; and Thomas H. Baker of Hannibal.

A change in policy by the Canadian authorities caused most of prisoners to be unconditionally pardoned. The release of the prisoners started in March. Others were set free in May, July, and August. In all 90 were pardoned and released who had been subject to execution having been found guilty upon trial. Following the rapid improvement of relations between the United States and Great Britain after the ratification of the Webster—Asburton Treaty, the Brisish government granted free pardons to all of the 78 men who had been transported to Van Dieman's Land for life. With only one or two exceptions the men had returned to their homes in the States or in Canada by 1845.

Of those prisoners who came before the court martial, but six were acquitted because of the lack of evidence and 10 were discharged for turning "state's evidence". Two of the wounded died before release.

In retrospect, it might be said that many of those from the "States" who entered the "patriot" ranks doubtless did so believing and hoping that a Canadian revolution would result in the over-throw of the British power in Canada and result eventually in the annexation of Canada to the United States at the desire of the Canadians, were doomed to utter disappointment. Many of the youths and some of the relatively few men of mature years from south of the border who participated in the expedition against Pres-cott were truly "patriotic" in their motives, if misguided, and made

62

the tools of others. They were sympathetic towards a people they believed to be down-trodden, anxious to be freed from their oppressors and eagerly awaiting the aid of their American cousins to help them accomplish their purposes.

The Vandalia

The *Vandalia* was the first scew-propelled vessel on the Great Lakes. John Ericsson, the Swedish inventor of the Ericsson screw propeller, was induced to come to the United States in 1839 by his friend Francis B. Ogden, United States Consul at Liverpool, for the primary purpose of introducing his propeller to American waters. Two years previously he applied for and received a United States Patent.

Captain James Van Cleve, a "lake captain", on Lake Ontario was responsible for the introduction of the screw propeller on the lakes. Perhaps the best description of Captain Van Cleve's early connection with Ericsson and introduction of the invention to the Great Lakes is contained in Captain Van Cleve's book which he presented to the City of Oswego in 1877. Captain Van Cleve's account is as follows:

While on a vist in the City of New York in the month of December 1840, I was called upon by Josiah J. Marshall, formerly one of the firm of Bronson, Marshall, & Company, of Oswego, who informed me that - our friend Sanderson of Brockville, Canada, who had boats on the Rideau Canal had requested him to examine Ericsson's propeller and give him his opinion as to its application to the propelling of boats on the canal. Mr. Marshall stated that as he had no practical experience in steam machinery. He wished me to go with him to the engine works of Messrs. Hogg and Delanader and examine the propeller hung there upon a shaft for the examination of all parties interested and give him my opinion which he would transmit to our friend Sanderson.

After examining the propeller with great care I stated to Mr. Marshall that it was my opinion it would produce a revolution in the propelling of vessels and must result in the complete change in the steam marine of the Lakes.

He then requested me to go with him and he would introduce me to Captain John Ericsson, the patentee, who had rooms at the Astor House. After a conversation of about two hours with Capain E., respecting the commerce of the Lakes he got up from his chair, walked two or three times across the room, then made the following proposition:

"Capt. Van Cleve, if you will put a vessel in operation with my propeller on the Lakes within one year, I will assign to you one-half interest in my patent for all the North American Lakes."

I accepted his proposition, the papers were drawn accordingly and I left for Oswego. After exhibiting a model of the propeller and plans a short time, I had partly arranged with a party to introduce the propeller in a vessel already built when an arrangement was concluded with Sylvester Doolittle, who had a shipyard in Oswego, to build the vessel.

The parties interested in the vessel were Sylvester Doolittle, one-quarter, Bronson and Crocker, one-quarter, Captain James, one-quarter, Captain Rufus Hawkins, one-quarter. I then went to Auburn and concluded a contract with C. C. Dennis to build the engine for the vessel with which when launched was named *Vandalia*. She was a sloop rigged and made her first trip in November 1841 to the head of Lake Ontario, experiencing good and bad weather and proved a success, thus carrying out my contract with Capt. Ericsson in eleven months. In the Spring of 1842 the *Vandalia* passed through the Welland Canal and visited Buffalo where she was examined by all classes with much interest.

Having in my possession the papers, drawings, of the *Vandalia* engine sent for C. Dennis builder contract of the engine, and relating my arrangement or agreement with Capt. Ericsson for the introduction of the propeller, upon the Lakes, I have considered it proper I should make this record that the public and various historical societies may have facts relating to so interesting a subject.

James Van Cleve

Captain Van Cleve also stated that his quarter interest in the *Vandalia* was taken over by Sylvester Doolittle before the *Vandalia* was launched. The Doolittle shipyard where the *Vandalia* was built was located on Water Street near the foot of Cayuga Street.

When Captain Van Cleve returned to Oswego from New York City, he made arrangements, as noted above, to build a screw propelled vessel. He also let it be known that he had the agency for the building of similar vessels. This advertisement appeared in the Oswego County *Whig*, March 17, 1841:

TO OWNERS OF VESSELS ON THE NORTH AMERICAN LAKES—the subscriber, having the agency, and being a joint proprietor in the right [on the waters] of 'Ericsson's Propellers', a recent important invention, by which vessels can be propelled, in the absence of favorable winds, at the rate of seven miles an hour, at a trifling expense - thus enabling vessels to make about double the trips made with canvass only. The weight of machinery necessary for a vessel of one hundred fifty tons, including water in boiler, five and half tons. In point of speed, certainty of economy, this improvement cannot but be received most favorably by all interested, and is confidently recommended for their consideration. For further partriculars inquire of—J. Van Cleve.

The keel of the *Vandalia* was laid as soon as weather permitted possibly early in April 1841 as it was necessary to have her in service before December 1841 to meet the terms of Captain Van Cleve's agreement with John Ericsson. The *Vandalia* was so named for the then Capital of the State of Illinois. She was a sloop rigged vessel, 91 feet long on deck; her beam was 20 feet 2 inches, with a depth of hold of 8 feet 3 inches. Her displacement was 138.19—95 tons.

Captain Van Cleve's sketch of the vessel as she appeared when she first came out showed a trim looking ship with deckhouse amidships and a smaller deckhouse or cabin aft. The small smoke stack from her boiler is shown projecting up through the top of the rear deckhouse.

Space was provided at the stern for a small deck and a life boat or dinghy suspended over the stern of the vessel, and her bow appears to have been fitted with an ornamental carving. The *Vandalia* was fitted with cabins for passengers as well as for her crew. The propulsion equipment consisted of twin propellers about 5 feet in diameter, one being located on either side of the rudder. Contrary to popular belief that twin screws are of fairly recent origin, it would seem that practically all of the early vessels had twin screws or propellers.

Ericsson's description of the propeller depicted it as—"A rotary propeller consisting of a series of segments of a screw attached to a thin broad hoop supported by arms so twisted as also to form part of the screw."

The steam engine was a vertical two-cylinder engine, with cylinders 14 inches in diameter and a stroke of 22 inches. Each cylinder was connected independently to the two propeller shafts through double connecting rods and the valves for admission and exhaust of steam were driven through a train of gears from the propeller shafts.

Ericsson's original drawing showing an end view of the patented engine is in Captian Van Cleve's book and a facsimile of an original drawing by Ericsson showing a side view of the engine is found in the book *Inland Seas* by James C. Mills. There seems to be a dearth of information about the boiler used for generating steam, but judging from the description of the boilers used at that time, the pressure carried was probably between five and ten pounds and forced draft was obtained with a blowing engine, of Ericsson design.

C. C. Dennis of Auburn, New York, was given the contract for building the engine and presumably the propellers and the boilers. The St. Catherine [Ontario] Journal in the fall of 1841 stated that "the Ericsson propellers were built at Auburn State Prison under the supervision of Messrs. Dennis & Wood, who carry on an extensive business in that line near the prison." The firm of Dennis and Wood apparently operated as the Continental Iron Shop. Their plant was located on State Street and in turn by the Osborne Hotel. It was estimated that complete propulsion equipment for a vessel of the size of the *Vandalia* cost about $2,000 and that the cost of fuel for a trip between Oswego and Cleveland, Ohio, would be about $25. The vessel was completed in the Fall of 1841 and late in November made her maiden voyage to the head of Lake Ontario with a cargo of 130 tons of merchandise for Niagara and Hamilton.

The first trip of the *Vandalia* was made under a special permit issued by the Oswego Custom officials. Her regualar papers were not taken out until the Spring of 1842. Apparently with the intention of determining how the vessel would operate in the Welland Canal, she proceeded through the canal as far as St. Catherine's, Ontario. The success of the trip through the canal is attested in the following quotation from the *St. Catherine's Journal*:

She steers as helmsmen term delightfully—the movement of the screws assisting rather than retarding the operation of the rudder. This point was satisfactorily ascertained, in the circuitous route of the canal, from Port Dalhousieto St. Catherine's, where we had a full opportunity of testing the merits of this ingenious and novel invention. She glided along without any perceptible motion of the water; so that not the least injury to the banks of the canal need be apprehended from the swell of the water which arises from the paddles of an ordinary steamer.

After passing one of the smallest locks on the canal at this place at ease, and staying an hour or two for the inspection of the inhabitants generally, she returned to Port Dalhousie on her route to Oswego.

The *Vandalia* returned to Oswego in the last week of November, making the run between Niagara and Oswego in 18-1/2 hours, partly under sail and partly under the propulsion of the new equipment. During the experimental trip she experienced rough weather which demonstrated her seaworthiness and the ship was pronounced a complete success. On her first trip to the head of the Lake the *Vandalia* was in command of Captain Rufus Hawkins, one of the owners. A Mr. Taylor was the engineer, and it is known that Sylvester Doolittle, the shipbuilder, was a passenger.

Captain Van Cleve had stated that Captian Daniel H. Davis was the first captain of the *Vandalia*, the assumption being that he was placed in command of the vessel in the Spring of 1842. He also stated that the *Vandalia* was later enlarged to a vessel of 320 tons and her name was changed to *The Milwaukee*. The *Vandalia* was sunk off the head of Lake Erie in a collision with the schooner *Fashion*, October 27, 1851.

Although the screw propeller was planned primarily for use in canal service, in the case of the *Vandalia*, one of the primary advantages of the screw propeller was in its ability to successfully navigate the Welland Canal. The advantages of the propeller on larger bodies of water was soon realized and accounts for the rapid spread of this form of propulsion.

The experimental run of the *Vandalia* fulfilled the terms of Captain Van Cleve's agreement with John Ericsson, to place a vessel in operation on the Great Lakes within the year's time. It seems that Captain Van Cleve pushed the sale of screw propellers on the Lakes, and therefore the number of vessels propelled by the screw increased very rapidly. Before we go into the description of the new vessels constructed at Oswego, it would be well to show the need for such vessels.

Let us consider the conditions prevailing at this particular time

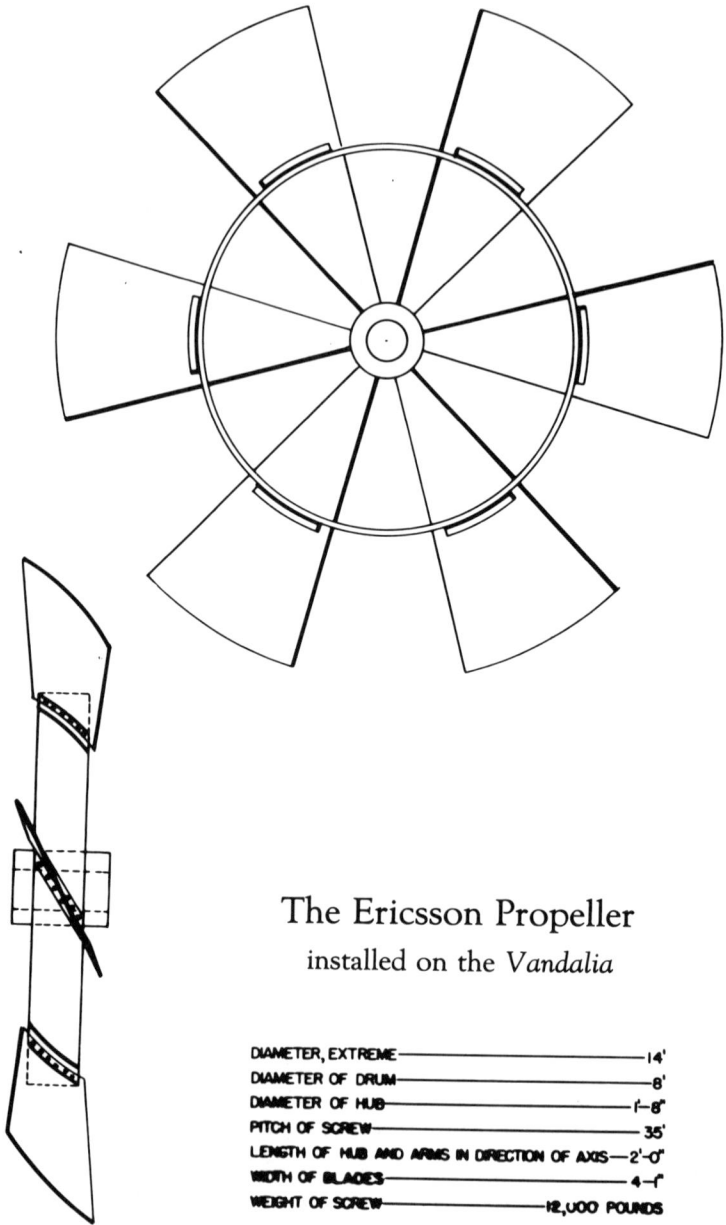

The Ericsson Propeller

installed on the *Vandalia*

DIAMETER, EXTREME	14'
DIAMETER OF DRUM	8'
DIAMETER OF HUB	1'-8"
PITCH OF SCREW	35'
LENGTH OF HUB AND ARMS IN DIRECTION OF AXIS	2'-0"
WIDTH OF BLADES	4'-1"
WEIGHT OF SCREW	12,000 POUNDS

and the advantages that the shippers of the Port of Buffalo enjoyed over their Oswego rival. The following account from the Oswego Palladium of March 24, 1841, sums up the situation as viewed by the Oswegonians:

THE ERICSSON PROPELLER

The progress of the experiments for the application of steam power in aid of sails of ships, schooners, and other sailing craft, has been observed at this place with great solicitude.

There is probably no place in the Union which will derive such immediate and extensive advantages from the invention of Mr. Ericsson as Oswego. It is affirmed by one of our first forwarding merchants that, with the aid of this propeller, goods from New York by the Oswego route can be delivered at Cleveland, Ohio, at less cost than the actual charges which must be advanced upon freights in their transportation from New York to Buffalo.

In the cheapness of transportation for the Western trade, the Oswego or Ontario route always had a very great advantage over the inland or Buffalo route. A very clear admission was made of this by the general combination of forwarders last year in stating the charges by the Oswego route to be four dollars per ton less than by the inland route. The latter route, however, had always had a great advantage over the Oswego in speed, and certainty in reference to time. The freight vessels from Oswego bound to the Upper Lakes were all schooners. From Buffalo, a large propotion were steamers.

The prevalent winds upon the Lakes are westerly. Perhaps in the season of navigation they are from that quarter more than two-thirds of the time. While, therefore, the descending passage from the Upper Lakes to Oswego was usually as quick as was desirable, the ascending trip was often tedious and dilatory. This was a serious objection to Western Merchants desirous of receiving their goods at early dates. They were desirous of despatch and certainty, and to obtain them submitted to heavy charges beyond those demanded on the Oswego route. But the Ericsson propeller applied to our Lake Vessels the Welland Canal becomes navigable for steam vessels, and freights from New York by the Oswego route can be delivered at Cleveland as soon or sooner than they can be delivered at Buffalo.

Thus, while the Oswego route will continue to enjoy all the advantages of its superior cheapness, it will equal the inland route and surpass it in speed.

Here is the matter for consideration with the advocates of the enlargement of the Erie Canal. The grand object to be gained is the Western trade; and yet it is certain that should the state realize the full results of the Seward and Ruggles policy in extending our debt to 40 millions, yet the channel it will have provided will not equal that which nature furnished, and through it the bulk of the Western trade will refuse to pass.

We learn with pleasure that two vessels at this port are about being fitted out with Ericsson propellers, and the necessary machinery. One of them is a new vessel, the keel of which is about being laid at S. Dolittle's shipyard. The other, one of our present craft. So that ere long Lake Erie will be visited by steam vessels from Lake Ontario.

A spirited controversy in print took place between the editors of the Oswego and Buffalo newspapers all during that period that the was being constructed. The editorials were vitriolic and rich in sarcasm, the *Buffalo Journal* branding the *Vandalia* as another "Oswego Humbug". The following quotation from the *Oswego Palladium* under the date of April 21, 1841, is a typical example of the exchange of words between the editors of the two cities:

The Buffalonians are much annoyed about Ericsson's propellers; at least we should judge so from the tone of some of their papers. And well they may for this valuable improvement in the application of steam power will transfer the forwarding business from Buffalo to Oswego. Within less than three years nineteen twentieths of all the goods destined to the upper lakes will pass through Oswego, despite the young or old lion of the West. The City of Buffalo will then stand "solitary and alone", far removed from the great thoroughfare between the Atlantic and the "Far West". This is sad and gloomy prospect for our neighbors—they have our deep and lasting sympathy. There is one way, and only one, in which this great calamity can be averted from our sister city, and we hasten to point it out to our neighbors so that they can

72

avail themselves of ot before it is too late. It is this—abandon, destroy, and annihilate at once the great Buffalo Humbug, which is the greatest of all humbugs, the enlargement of the canal west of Syracuse, and apply a portion of the ten or fifteen millions of dollars which it will cost to dig this big ditch along the banks of Lake Ontario, in constructing a steamboat canal from Lewiston to Buffalo; this will keep the Buffalonians "on the right track," and nothing else can do it.

It should be realized that the Welland Canal could not be used by the side wheel steamers of the day because the locks were too narrow to pass these vessels. Oswego's trade was therefore limited to the use of schooners which could pass through the Canal locks between Lake Ontario and Lake Erie. In view of the foregoing importance of the screw propeller to the City of Oswego is apparent as the screw propelled vessels could easily clear the Welland Canal locks, permitting steamers to go from Lake Ontario ports to the Upper Lakes without breaking cargo.

The Messrs. Hollister of Buffalo examined the *Vandalia* on her first trip to that port in the Spring of 1842. As a result they arranged for the rights to install propellers on two vessels, the *Samson* and the *Hercules*, each vessel being about 400 tons displacement. The *Hercules* constructed in 1843 was a famous steamer of the time.

New vessels were constructed at Sackets Harbor and other points on Lake Ontario; many existing vessels were built to accommodate the new propellers, until in a very short period the propeller driven steamer had become a common sight on the Lakes.

The schooner *Chicago* was built at Oswego in 1842. The *Palladium*, in its issue of June 1, 1842, states:

This beautiful and staunch vessel which has just been completed at the shipyard of S. Doolittle and propelled by the Ericsson improvement, leaves this port for Chicago—she was built with particular reference to this route—has handsome and convenient accommodations for sixty cabin passengers, and of sufficient capacity for 150 tons of freight. She is to be commanded by our fellow citizen William S. Malcolm, whose nautical skill, experience and gentlemanly deportment, eminently qualify him for that post.

We learn that the enterprising proprietors, Messrs. Bronson and Crocker of Oswego, intend to dispatch a steam vessel of the above class for Chicago, on the 1st, 10th, and 20th of each month, touching at the intermediate ports on Lake Erie, Huron and Michigan, thus affording unusual facilities for the conveyance and transportation of passengers and freight. It seems to us, that travellers, particularly families, moving with goods, will find this line of boats admirably adapted to their wants. The price by this line is much less than by any other steam conveyance, which is a consideration in these times.

In 1843, Sylvester completed the building of the Propeller *Oswego*. The Erie Observer, in a june issue of 1843, contained an item which gives some information concerning the *Oswego*. The item follows:

A boat bearing the name *Oswego* and propelled on the Ericsson plan touched here on Wednesday last. She left Oswego a few days before, came through the Welland Canal, and is bound for Chicago.

In appearance, the *Oswego* partakes equally of the qualities of the schooner, canal boat, and steamer. She was very heavily loaded with freight, and had nearly 300 passengers. Owing to the small amount of fuel required to supply the engine, and the cheapness of the machinery, passengers are carried at prices far below those charged on the side-wheel-type of steam boats. The steerage price from Oswego to Chicago, a distance of 1,300 miles, is only six dollars. We understand that there are several large boats being built on this plan, and we have no doubt that the enterprise will be successful".

The *Palladium* of July 12, 1843, carried an account of the return of the *Oswego* from the run described by the *Erie Observer*. The account reads:

The steam schooner *Oswego*, under the command of Captain Davis, arrived at the port on Saturday, from Chicago, with 900 barrels of pork consigned to Messrs. Bronson and Crocker. This vessel had performed the trip from this port to Chicago and back, discharging and receiving freight at nearly all ports on Lake Michigan and at Cleveland and Detroit, in 23-1/2 days, being the shortest passage ever made. The distance traversed during this time by the *Oswego* is about 3,000 miles—equal to a voyage across the Atlantic.

In 1844 and 1845 Doolittle built the *Racine* and the *New York*. Bronson and Crocker were associated with him in the construction of all the above vessels. George S. Weeks of Oswego built the *Syracuse* a vessel of 300 tons in 1845 and the *St. Lawrence*, 340 tons, in 1848, Moses Merrick & Company were the owners of both vessels.

During the 10 years from 1845 to 1855 the population increased from approximately 10,000 to almost 16,000, a growth more rapid than that of any city in the state. Seventy-one Oswego owned vessels, including steamers, propellers, and schooners rode in and out of the port.

Thousands of persons were making their way by the "all water route" through Oswego to settle in the West. Capitalists invested large sums of money in the construction and operation of steam-propeller passenger ships. In 1847, twenty-six vessels slid down the ways of Oswego shipyard into Lake Ontario, each one a symbol of Oswego's commercial superiority and the craftmanship of her builders.

Regular passenger service between Oswego and Chicago became a reality. There were sailings in either direction each day of the week except Sunday. Records show that they were loaded to capacity with passengers and freight. The vessels were advertised as having commodious cabins, handsomely fitted, with special arrangements for the accommodation of families. Emphasis was placed on the improvement of steerage accommodations. The quarters were enlarged so as to furnish at least 75 passengers with good comfortable berths between decks. Most of the advertisments stressed the fact that steerage passengers would not have to sleep in the hold.

Some valuable and interesting data relating to these ships had been collected from the local press. Quoting from these sources:

The fare charged for passengers from Oswego to Detroit was $7.50 per passenger with "found" [food] provided and $5.00 "without found." Steerage fare was $4.00 between Oswego and Chicago. The cabin passage and found was $14; a cabin without found, $10; steerage, $6.

Freight rates were quoted by the bulk barrel. The barrel bulk was estimated at 7 cubic feet. Four chairs were called one barrel. The charge between Oswego and Chicago was $1 per bulk barrel.

Children between two and twelve years of age traveled at half fare; those under two years of age were carried free. On half of a barrel bulk of furniture or luggage was allowed each

75

full passenger without cost. A cooking stove "not exposed to the weather" was provided for the use of those who wished to board themselves."

From 1855 on, there was a gradual but persistent decline in ship building at Oswego.

This story would not be complete without a short commentary on the men who were instrumental in the construction and operation of the *Vandalia*. This momentous event led to the abandonment of the side wheeler steamboat on open waters and eventually to the sailing vessel itself.

Oswego and Chicago.
STEAM PROPELLER LINE,
For Milwaukee, Racine, Southport, Chicago and Intermediate Ports.

1845.   **1845.**

The Six New Steam Propellers
will leave OSWEGO as follows :

RACINE,	NEW YORK,	VANDALIA,
R. Hawkins,	*T. Cornwell,*	*J. S. Warner.*
Wednesday, April 30,	Saturday, May 3	Saturday, May 10
" June 4,	Tuesday, June 10,	Tuesday, June 17
" July 9,	" July 15,	" July 22
" Aug. 13,	" Aug. 19,	" Aug. 26
" Sept. 17,	" Sept 23,	" Sept. 30
" Oct. 22,	" Oct. 28,	

CHICAGO, OSWEGO, SYRACUSE,

W. L. Pierce,	*D. H. Davis,*	*William Williams.*
Saturday, May 17,	Saturday, May 24,	Thursday, May 29
Monday, June 23,	do June 28,	do July 3
do July 28,	do Aug. 2,	do Aug. 7
do Sept. 1,	do Sept. 6,	do Sept. 11
do Oct. 6,	do Oct. 11,	do Oct. 16

This popular line of *Steamers* carry freight and passengers. All have commodious Cabins, handsomely fitted up, which have been altered with special reference to the accommodation of families, and the Steerage sufficiently enlarged to furnish 75 passengers with good comfortable berths between decks, avoiding the necessity of carrying any in the hold; and as a new propeller has been added to the line this spring, furnishing the means of shipping every six days, the passengers will have more room than heretofore.

PRICES FOR PASSAGE AND FREIGHT.

From Oswego to Detroit, Michigan.

Cabin passage and found,	$7,50
Cabin passage and not found,	5,00
Steerage do do	4,00
Furniture and luggage, per barrel bulk,	62
Two Horse Wagons,	4,00
One Horse Wagons,	3,00

From Oswego to Milwaukee, Racine, Southport and Chicago.

Cabin passage and found,	$14,00
Cabin passage and not found,	10,00

Holland Land Office Museum, Batavia

Aaron Van Cleve

Captain James Van Cleve (1808–1888) was born in Lawrence-ville, New Jersey. When he was one year old the family moved to Batavia, New York, where he acquired a common school education which was later rounded off with two years at the pioneer academy at Middleburg. At the age of sixteen he began his career as a clerk in a Lawrenceville store. It is hard today to imagine that there was a time when boys went to work on such jobs working from six in the morning until 9 at night, just for the opportunity to learn the cal-ling. Fortunately, for us, young James realized that as he put it, he was "drifting onto a lee shore". He quit his store job and became a clerk on the steamer *Ontario* and later became her master. The *Ontario* was built at Sackets Harbor in 1816 and put into commis-sion the following year. A description of her maiden trip to Oswego and her subsequent difficulties is described in a work by the writer entitled *Oswego: Hamlet Days 1796–1828*. He became associated with the shipping industry at an early age, and during his life time commanded most of the finer vessels on Lake Ontario. At the time of his meeting with John Ericsson he was a young man about 32 years old. His was a long and useful career.

Van Cleve in later years made his home in Lewiston where he became a civic leader and was connected with many local enter-prises. He was the chairman of the board of the company that was responsible for the building the first suspension bridge across the Niagara River at Lewiston in 1850.

Captain James Van Cleve died April 20, 1888, at his home at

Sandwich, Ontario, where he apparently lived just prior to his death.

In 1877, Captain Van Cleve presented to the City of Oswego his book written or printed by hand on the ships of Lake Ontario. He was skilled water color artist as well as an historian, and his book is illustrated by sketches of Lake Ontario harbor entrances, shipyards and of vesels. This book is a thing of rare beauty. The history was dedicated to Alvin Bronson in this fashion:

> To Alvin Bronson. A Pioneer in the Commerce of Lake Ontario, and for more the 50 years an active participator and keen sympathizer of all things pertaining to its advancement and the posterity of Oswego this volume is respectuflly deidcated.

Alvin Bronson (1783–1881) was a ship-builder, naval store keeper during the War of 1812, flour-miller, manufacturer, commercial forwarder. His name was connected with practically every worthwhile undertaking during the early days of Oswego. He served as State Senator, first president of the village in 1828; first president of the Oswego & Syracuse Railroad. For a biography of this remarkable man, see F. Hosmer Culkin, "Alvin Bronson, A First Citizen Of Oswego", Yearbook, Oswego County Historical Society, 1951.

Sylvester Doolittle was a ship-builder of rare skill. His shipyard was located at the east end of West Cayuga Street. John C. Churchill in his Landmarks Of Oswego County had this to say of Doolittle:

> Sylvester Doolittle was born in Whitestown, Oneida County, January 11, 1800. While a young man he went to Sodus Point, where he learned the ship carpenter's trade. In 1822 he removed to Rochester and built there the first boat that went through the canal to New York. Through the influence of Mr. Abraham Varick, Mr. Doolittle settled in Oswego in 1836. Here he had a shipyard and built several vessels advancing and carrying capacity of lake craft. Late in life he erected the Doolittle House [stood on the site now occupied by the Pontiac Hotel] at an expense of more than $200,000 and also expended a large sum in the developing and placing on the market the Deep Rock Spring Water. Mr. Doolittle died October 11, 1811.

Hotels

The civil history of Oswego began with the evacuation of the British from Fort Ontario on July 15, 1796. In that year Neil McMullen packed on his barge at Kingston a disassemled house to be erected at Oswego. This so-called frame house was actually a beam and plank house. It was one and one-half stories (15x20 feet) and located on Lot No. 7 on the southeast corner of West Seneca and Water Streets. With an addition of logs, the whole constituted the first tavern. In those days almost every man kept a tavern who had two rooms in his house. For men who traveled, a tavern was a needful thing, even in Oswego. It was moved several times, eventually to 182 West Second Street.

Sharpe's Tavern

Peter Sharpe came to Oswego in 1798. He built a two-story frame house, large and roomy for the time and place, on Lot No. 1 on the southeast corner of West Schuyler and Water Streets. Here he accommodated travelers and boatmen, stored goods detained on their passage. Mr. Sharpe left Oswego about 1806 and settled near John Van Buren, near the mouth of Black Creek which is north of Fulton. It should be noted that Mr. Sharpe took his slave with him.

The year of 1808 was one which relations of this country and England were seriously menaced and that there was a possibility of war. Lieutenant Melancthon Taylor Woolsey was selected to superintend at the constructuion of, and to, command a war vessel [*Oneida*] to be built on Lake Ontario. He brought with him to Oswego, Messrs. Thomas Gamble and J. F. Cooper. James Fenimore Cooper related how, in 1808, Oswego was a mere hamlet of some twenty houses that stod near the water. The arrival of a party of officers, together with a strong gang of ship carpenters, riggers, blacksmiths, etc., made a sensible change at that place. Lieutenant Woolsey, and his party, hired a house, Sharpe's Tavern, and commenced housekeeping. Balls, dinners, and suppers were given to the better portion of the inhabitants.

Z. SMITH,

EAGLE TAVERN,

No. 65 EAST FIRST-STREET.

This House is pleasantly situated in the immediate vicinity of the

STEAM BOAT LANDINGS.

☞ It has been thoroughly repaired and newly furnished. The travelling community are respectfully invited to call.

Z. SMITH, PROPRIETOR.

AMERICAN HOTEL,

T. W. SMITH, Proprietor,

WEST SENECA, BETWEEN FIRST AND SECOND-STREETS.

The Sharpe House was kept by Colonel Eli Parsons of the Shay Rebellion notoriety presumably from 1810 on. Deacon John B. Parks kept a select school in Parson's tavern during the winter of 1816–1817. School was dismissed so that the children could welcome the first visit to the port of the steamboat, the *Ontario*. Shortly thereafter the tavern was destroyed by fire. Mr. Parsons relocated his tavern on Lot No. 45, being the southwest corner of West First and Cayuga Streets. It was removed in 1828 to make room for the Welland Hotel.

Washington Hotel

In 1803 Bradner Burt erected a frame house on Lot No. 1 on the southwest corner of West Schuyler and Water Streets. The building with the Dutch or hip roof and clapboarded, was originally the residence of the Burt family, and was considered the most pretentious mansion west of the Albany area in its day. It was later known as the "Washington Hotel." It had been somewhat enlarged by additions and stood until mid-century when it was destroyed by fire.

In the same block, on West Seneca Street, stood an early and old tavern, the Center House. Because of the style of the exterior painting indulged in by the artist called to paint it, the name Checkered Tavern was given to it and appropriated by the owner. Later it was known as the Frontier House which was consumed by fire. On the site a large hotel was built by Myron Pardee and others, which was never completed for occupancy. The latter was torn down to make room for a building for the Herrman Lumber Co., constructed by Thomson Kingsford. The brick building known as the Wright & Boyle, door, sash and blind factory was razed in 1979.

Lake Tavern

An interesting view of an early business, the oldest cafe in the community, is especially noteworthy. In 1805, Isaac Shepard opened the Shepard House, later known as the Lake Tavern, in lower West First Street, and conducted it until his son, William J. took over. It was then transferred to the American Hotel, 18–24

HOTELS.

WELLAND HOUSE,

Corner of West Cayuga & First-Streets.

(Within a few rods of the Rail-Road Depot, Steam-Boat Landing and the Postoffice.)

A. BRONSON,

PROPRIETOR.

This long established and popular Hotel, under the direction of its present proprietor, has undergone a thorough repair within and without, and with its additions and improvements—new, rich and elegant furniture—in point of comfort and convenience now offers inducements to the traveling public not surpassed by any other house in the city.

Mr. B. has had the pleasure of serving the public in other establishments since his residence here, and flatters himself that to the citizen it will be unnecessary to solicit patronage—to the stranger he would merely say that no exertions, on his part, shall be wanting to give entire satisfaction. Indeed his daily increase of business affords sufficient evidence of the popularity of the Welland House, and the proprietor repeats the assurance that he will never slacken his efforts to please while he shall have charge of the same.

His tables will at all times be furnished with the choicest viands and luxuries of the season ; and his bar will be supplied with the purest and best of wines and liquors.

AN OMNIBUS & BAGGAGE WAGON

always in readiness to convey Passengers to and from the Cars and Steam-Boats free of charge.

☞ A Livery Stable is adjoining the premises, where Horses and Carriages of the first class, may be obtained by those who may desire to take a ride round the city and its environs.

West Seneca Street. He was succeeded by his son, Frederick J. Shepard. It was an uninterrupted business, 115 years duration, that terminated on January 16, 1920. National prohibition, as a great social experiment, closed out the business that had been carried on through three generations from father to son and grandson. Mr. Shepard continued his residence at 16 West Seneca Street. The buildings on Seneca Street were demolished to make room for a lumber yard operated by Neal & O'Brien. The yard was also consumed by fire.

Henry Eagle

Henry Eagle built a tavern on Lot No. 7, on the southeast corner of West First and Seneca Streets, facing First Street in 1817. This spacious tavern was rented to Mr. Giteau. Many social functions and public meetings took place here. This location, First and Seneca Streets was the center of town at that time. The road from the south ended at Fort Oswego and the road from the west ended at the foot of Seneca Street. The ferry was the only means of crossing the river.

Welland Hotel

In 1828 anticipating the opening of the Welland Canal, the famous Welland Hotel was built, and owned by Joel Turrill. The name was presumably taken from the canal. The builder was Francis Rood. It was a three-story brick structure fronting West First Street with a wooden extension in Cayuga Street. It was a celebrated hostelry, known throughout the land. To the business man it was a Chamber of Commerce, Board of Trade and a place of meeting evenings for social enjoyment. There was a spacious hall in the upper part of the hotel where the elite of the village held dancing parties.

In the *Oswego Free Press* of August 4, 1830, under the heading "Opening Of The Welland Canal," it expressed the joyous feeling of the inhabitants:

> "Blow the trumpets—beat the drums—
> Lo! the gallant ERIE comes!"

SENECA-STREET HOUSE,

WEST SENECA-STREET,

Near the Steam-Boat Landing.

This House has been lately fitted up and

FURNISHED THROUGHOUT

WITH

GOOD & CONVENIENT FURNITURE,

so that all who may favor it with a call will be served in

GOOD STYLE.

The subscriber is ready at all times to supply his friends and the Public.

BAGGAGE

taken to and from the boats and cars

FREE OF CHARGE.

☞ *Boarders accommodated on liberal terms.*

GOOD STABLING & CARRIAGE ROOM

for the accommodation of Citizens and Travellers who may travel with their own conveyance.

GEORGE F. ROGERS, Proprietor.

The article continued to say:

This day must be considered a proud day for Oswego, and will long be remembered by her inhabitants, and all who take an interest in her welfare. This morning about 7 o'clock the schooner ERIE, Capt. Bouquet, arrived from Cleveland, Ohio, through the Welland Canal. [By passing the Niagara Falls and Buffalo, Oswego's commercial rival.] All was activity celebrating the event. All turned out to meet her with a hearty welcome. At 12 o'clock a field piece that once waged war against us was brought forth from its hiding place and spoke distinctly and forcibly. The old 18 pounder fired a national salute with ringing bells. An excellent dinner was prepared by Col. White of the Welland House.

A week later, August 11, 1830, the same paper described the festivities in greater detail. "We had the high satisfaction in our last paper of announcing to our fellow-citizens the arrival at this port of the schooner *Erie*, Capt. Bouquet, from Cleveland, Ohio. By this important event, we were apprised of the opening of the great navigable communication between Lake Erie and Ontario, in a manner entirely satisfactory to all interested in its final success, and in the rising prosperity of this village. (In 1830, population was 1,962.) The arrival of the schooner was greeted by the ringing of bells, by a national salute of 24 guns, by a display of all flags of the village and harbour, and by cheers and congratulations of our citizens. The corporation of the village, animated by the public sensiblity, invited its citizens to celabrate the event by a civic feast at the Welland House. Entertainment was got up by Col. White.

Guests included Capt. Bouquet, Gerrit Smith (who was on a visit here), Theophilus S. Morgan, George H. McWhorter, Alvin Bronson, Judge (Peter D.) Hugunin, Judge (John, Jr.) Grant, James Cockran, D.(avid) P. Brewster, H. P. Edwards."

Standing on the hotel steps in 1836, Martin Van Buren, 8th President of the United States, (also a large land owner in Oswego), spoke to a concourse of people that filled the thoroughfare, the hotel windows and the buildings opposite. Mr. Van Buren was entertained at the G. H. McWhorter residence, corner of East Sixth and Mohawk Streets.

A visitor from Syracuse had this favorable comment as reported in the *Oswego Daily Commercial Times* of July 18, 1849:

As far as hotels I can't say anything, so far as construction is concerned. The Welland House, kept by Capt. Stewart, is the largest and most convenient. He is an excellent landlord, attentive to all the wants of his guests, and provides for their bodily necessities like a man acquainted with the whole subject. His table is therefore supplied with the very best, and his beds are comfortable and clean, though as for sleeping in the most elegant apartments, this hot weather, that is out of the question. As a mark of estimation, I may add that the Welland House is crowded all the time.

On May 11, 1857, the building was destroyed by fire. A large barn standing on the corner of West First and Bridge Streets caught fire and a brisk southerly wind carried sparks into the cornish of the building and in a short time the famous hostery was destroyed. It was not rebuilt as a hotel.

Oswego House

In 1828 Gerrit Smith built a hotel of wood and brick on the southeast corner of East First and Bridge Streets. It was formally opened the following year. The hotel portion was originally on the second and upper floors with the stores below. The east end of the block were offices. Eventually the hotel, known as the Oswego House, Fitzhugh House, Munger House, etc., occupied the entire block. John B. Edwards, Smith's business manager, most persistent problem was the rental of the hotel, since a hotel of Gerrit Smith's was a temperance house, and proprietors of temperance hotels who could pay rent were a rare breed. In 1835 Moses P. Hatch purchased the hotel for $25,000, built verandas and added a cupola; with other improvements he sold it the following year to a Mr. Baldwin for $120,000. The sale was not perfected, and the property again passsed to Mr. Smith. About 1855 he sold it to O. G. Munger, an experienced landlord, who had previously kept Niagara House (West Bridge between First and Water Streets).

Wiliam Metcalfe Clarke, of Syracuse, a nephew of Dr. Deodatus Clarke of Oswego, in his autobiography (Onondaga Historical Association) described a visit he made to Oswego at the height of the land boom in the following language:

MUNGER HOUSE,

Corner of East First and Bridge-Streets.

O. G. MUNGER,

PROPRIETOR.

This Hotel is more pleasantly located than any other in the city, commanding a fine view of the Port, River and Lake, which, together with its large and airy rooms, render it the most desirable house for travellers and parties of pleasure. During the last season an addition has been made larger than the original building, and which is finished and furnished in a manner that will suffer nothing by a comparison with the

FIRST CLASS HOTELS

of the East.

The subscriber has long been engaged as " mine host," and he hopes his exertions to please, which have received such flattering testimonials in times past, will still secure to this establishment a support commensurate with his outlay.

He has always had the name of

SETTING A GOOD TABLE,

and it will be his ambition to retain the reputation.

His LIQUORS have been selected with reference to purity rather than price.

AN OMNIBUS AND BAGGAGE WAGON

always in attendance at the cars and boats to convey passengers and baggage, *free of charge*, to and from the House.

From Syracuse I went by packet to Oswego for a visit, and found the village like a seething caldron. Every one was wild, in speculation in village lots, and whenever it cropped out it was contagious to an alarming degree, and no one was safe, although he may have had the desease the natural wasy before. But it was unlike small pox in that respect. For instance the Oswego Hotel on the east side of the river was sold for $100,000 really worth less than $10,000. This price was given with the expectation that an area fool would be found in a short time. But that fool did not turn up.

After describing other incidents of speculation, he continued:

In 1836, the Oswego House, was sold by Moses P. Hatch, the proprietor for $100,000 of which $10,000 was paid in cash. At the time this hotel was sold, it was not in too good condition. Before the purchaser had made further payments the land boom bubble burst and no futher payments were made, the property reverting to its original owner.

Henry Clay once visited Oswego and addressed the citizens from the wide balcony that extended on the Bridge Street side. Clay was entertained at the residence of Mr. Philo Stevens.

The *Syracuse Journal* of April 15, 1859, gave this visitor's impression of a visit to Oswego: "We had a pleasant and social visit to our neighboring city, Oswego, on Wednesday last." Then he described the economic situation (there was a financial depression or panic about that time) and other things, the visitor continued to write:

The Munger House is a well kept and popular hotel, just such a place as travelers like to find. Everything about the House is in complete order, and the tables are loaded down with all the good things that appetite can relish. O. G. Munger is the proprietor, and a right, good landlord; he is too polite and attentive to the wants of his guests. We predict that no one ever puts up at the Munger House once but that he decided that that is his place to stop ever after, especially so long as MUNGER is the governing spirit. Success to the Munger House.

The Fitzhugh House, known for many years by that name, was demolished on August 22, 1877, to make room for the new building of the Second National Bank. This building in turn was demolished recently, leaving a vacant lot owned by the Columbia Bank.

HAMILTON HOTEL,

East First, between Bridge & Cayuga-Streets.

THIS IS AN

ENTIRELY NEW EDIFICE

from basement to garret, just finished in the best and **most** modern style, **w**ith the latest improvements for convenienc**e** and comfort, and fitted up every way with reference to **the** accommodation of the traveling public. The furnit**u**re **is** also new, and of the richest and most approved style **and** finish. In short, no pains nor expense have been spared **to** make it

ONE-OF THE BEST ARRANGED HOTELS

in the State ; and the subscriber feels confident from **his**

LONG EXPERIENCE IN HOTEL KEEPING,

of giving satisfaction to all who may favor him with **their** patronage.

His table will at all times be supplied with the

BEST THE MARKETS AFFORD,

served up in a style which cannot fail to please, and tho**se** who may desire, will be furnished with wines and liquo**rs** of the choicest brands.

☞ Passengers and baggage conveyed to and from **the** Steamboats and Cars, free of charge.

Z. SMITH, Proprietor.

Hamilton House

There were several hotels on the site, 67–71 East First Street before the block was demolished to make room for an urban renewal project. There were references in the early history of Oswego to an Eagle tavern on the east side of the river. Unfortunately, the tavern was consumed by the great fire (1853) that spared very few buildings in an area from the Oswego River to East Sixth Street and from East Bridge to Schuyler Streets. It was rebuilt in 1855 by Hamilton Murray, a prominent Oswegonian. A new hotel was built on the site in 1892 by Max B. Richardson. It was a design of Mr. Richardson to lodge the many show people that would come to Oswego. He felt that Oswego deserved a good theater and built one in 1895 on the northwest corner of East First and Oneida Streets. (The Academy, on the top floor of the Doolittle Block, located on Water Street, was condemned in 1892). The Richardson was the best theater in northern New York. Many famous stage personalities lodged in the 42 room Hamilton Hotel, among them the renowned Lillian Russell. For many years the hotel had been used as a meeting place for local politicos.

In 1909 M. C. Hammond sold the hotel for $12,000 to Joseph E. Danio. After two months of intensive remodeling, the hotel was equipped with the latest style furniture, each room provided with steam heat, electric lights and other conveniences. The hotel was run both on the American and European plan, and was noted for its fine grill room. But above all, it was known for its rooms that were kept immaculate condition and a hotel that always gave absolute satisfaction.

In 1921 the Danio Hotel was sold at auction to John J. McGinnis of Fulton for $10,550. Prohibiton was given as the reason for Mr. Danio going out of business and wanting to devote his entire time to the serving of Welsh Rarebit. Danio was one of the best known chefs and caterer in northern New York. He was a member of the United States Life Saving Station at Oswego in 1880, and for many years steward on private yachts. Mr. Danio made it a specialty of catering to wedding, automobile and theater parties. He was a most interesting conversationalist and courteous man. Mr. Danio died in 1936.

Martin F. "Barney" Lannon was a proprietor at one time and the hotel was named after the proprietor. After the death of Mr. Lannon, the hotel was unoccupied.

The hotel was reopened on September 12, 1958, as the Oswego Hotel. There was fire damage in June which resulted in renovation and refurbishing the hotel. The hotel was jointly owned by Robert J. McGann and his wife, Estelle. Mr. McGann was a former city democrat chairman, city Chamberlain, Commissioner of Public Works and for six years Democrat County Chairman. "I have the distinction of being the most thoroughly trounced candidate for mayor this city has ever seen."

The buildings in the whole block were demolished in 1965 for an urban renewal project.

This is the Home of The Danio's Famous Welsh Rarebit and the Home of the Traveling Public in General. Oswego N. Y.

The Danio Hotel

NIAGARA HOUSE,

S. P. JOHNSON,

PROPRIETOR.

This house is situated on the

GREATEST THOROUGHFARE
IN THE CITY,

being at the west end of the lower bridge, and being more convenient to all the business, as well as to the different points of egress and ingress than any other hotel in the city.

During the last few months large additions have been made to the main building, affording as much more capacity as the old establishment, and other improvements have been superadded, giving it rank among the

First Class Hotels in the Country.

The proprietor has long been engaged in the business, and flatters himself that by his attentions to his customers, he will merit and receive the liberal share of patronage hitherto bestowed upon him. His tables will always be

WELL FURNISHED,

and his bar supplied with the

BEST OF WINES & LIQUORS.
OMNIBUS & BAGGAGE WAGON

constantly in attendance to convey passengers to and from the Steamboats and Cars, free of charge.

American Hotel

The American Hotel, a wooden structure erected at an early date, occupied the site on West Bridge Street between First and Water Streets. The sitting room was at the east end of the building fronting Bridge Street. In front of this room, in the side walk, grew three large cherry trees, very attractive when in blossom. The Hotel was also called the Rideau, Franklin, and Niagara. Fire consumed the building on August 30, 1859, while in the possession of Mr. A. P. Grant. A building, known as the Grant Block, was erected on the site. This building in turn was razed in 1957 and the present Green building, with added space to the south, now occupies the space.

93

Oswego Harbor

1860 Gazetteer of New York State

Drawing was made on West First Street about the present site of the Pontiac Hotel, looking north towards Lake Ontario.

Revenue House

In its early days Oswego grew rapidly. From a village of 1,962 people in 1828, it became an incorporated city of 12,000 in 1848. The Oswego & Syracuse (later the D. L. & W.) Railroad was just completed. The railroad station was on West Utica between First and Second Streets (demolished in 1953); its freight house (still standing) also on Utica between Second and Third Streets. Passengers came and left the harbor for the West on steamboats daily. In midcentury Oswego began to experience a "Golden Age". A movement was started for a "good" hotel. In 1849 a local paper, in an editorial, asked, "Why can't Oswego have a good hotel as Syracuse, Utica, Rochester, Buffalo?" It could and did have good hotels.

The Lake Shore Hotel or the Revenue House was located on West Utica Street between First and Second Streets. The four story building, built by Myron W. Pardee in 1858, faced Utica Street. It had stores facing the three streets. It was also across from the Oswego & Syracuse Railroad depot. Some time later the Rome, Watertown & Ogdensburg Railroad constructed a branch of 29 miles from Pulaski to Oswego, the tracks and depot were on Utica Street. Thus it was in a favorable position to accommodate rail travelers. Unfortunately, the building was destroyed by fire in 1904. The present building, a Spanish design, was built in 1907, and served as a ticket office and depot for the New York Central Railroad. When all passenger service in and out of Oswego was discontinued, the building was converted into a supermarket.

State Normal School—1907—Built as the United States Hotel

United States Hotel

In 1836 Mr. White erected a handsome building of cut limestone on West Seneca Street between Sixth and Seventh Streets. It was four stories high -with East and West wings of wood. This building, with its wide verandas and fluted columns, was one of the most pretentious hostelries. It was built at a time of real estate speculation (a financial panic in 1837 burst the bubble). Times and location were not propitious for profitable conducting of an hotel, and for three years it was used as a barracks for United States troops under Colonel E. J. Worth. They were brought here because of a disturbance on the border between the United States and Canada, known as the "Patriot War". During the Seminole War the soldiers were ordered to Florida in 1840. On December 23, 1841, the building was partially destroyed by fire and the destruction would have been complete had it not been for the determined work of the "bucket brigade". A line of men and women formed a line leading to a well on the opposite side of the street. The men passed the buckets filled with water from one to another until they were dashed upon the burning building when the empties were sent back by the women, and the hotel was saved. Shortly thereafter the structure was rebuilt. In 1845 the Braman Sisters established a female seminary there which flourished for some time. In 1857 it was opened as the United States Hotel. (That year the Welland Hotel was consumed by fire). In 1865 the Board of Education purchased the hotel for use as a normal school. It paid $11,500 for the building, with $14,500 for additional improvements. In 1866, the United States Hotel Building housed the Normal School, the practice school, and two model schools, devoted to observation. The following year it also housed the high school. In March 1867 the Oswego Normal School building and grounds were accepted by the State. By the 1880's the State's appropriations to Oswego had increased from $3,000 annually to $25,000.

The Welland House

NORMAL SCHOOL BOARDING HOUSE.

The New Welland

The "'New Welland" still standing at the corner of West Second and Cayuga Streets, was built by Dr. Hard for his residence and office in 1850. It was built of limestone. After Dr. Hard removed from the city, it was, with appropriate changes turned into the hotel New Welland. Afterwards other changes were made. It will be recalled that the first Welland Hotel burned in 1857. The following year the new Welland Hotel emerged and it was thought it would have considerable success because of its location but that was not the case.

It was purchased in 1867 for $25,000 by a syndicate to provide non-profit housing for students. It was a dormitory for young women attending the Oswego Normal School. Women living there were governed by very strict rules and men calling for the first time had to meet the preceptress of the house before hand. Dorothy Rogers in her *Oswego: Fountainhead of Teacher Education* devotes considerable space to the life in the dormitory.

With the closing of the Oswego Normal School on West Seneca Street and the opening of the new school in 1913, the Welland ceased to be a dormitory. Again it became a hotel. It was sold in 1936 and, after a few improvements were made and the porches closed off, it became an apartment house. In 1952, fire struck the Welland. Two people died in what was believed to have been the result of a careless cigarette tossed into a waste basket. After this tragedy, a new sprinkler system was installed with a fire escape. It changed owners several times through the years and in October 1978, tennants were evicted because the building was declared unsafe. Due to financial problems of the current owners, the building has not been repaired and its fate is uncertain.

99

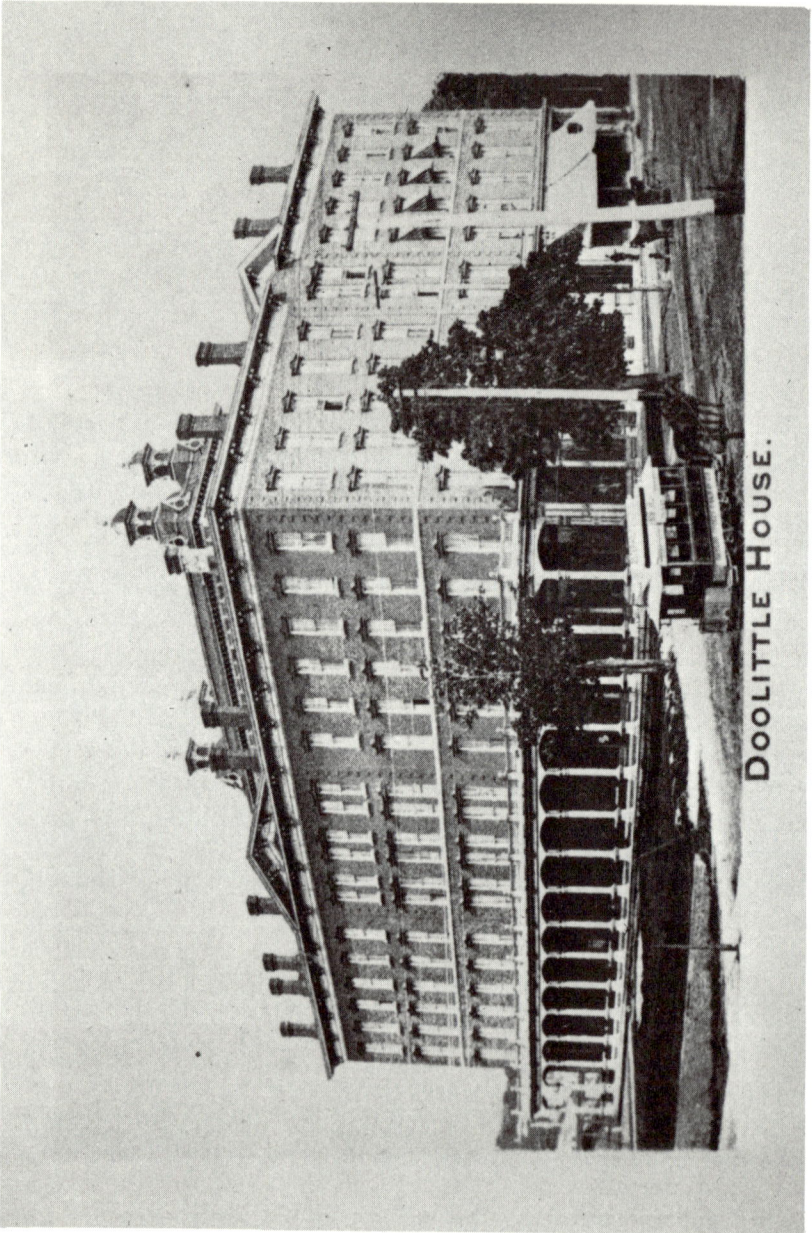

DOOLITTLE HOUSE.

Doolittle House

In 1816 "Judge" Nathan Sage, known as Captain Sage to the early settlers, built his residence on the southeast corner of West First and Oneida Streets, being Lot No. 19, block 45. At that time Mr. Sage was the customs collector and postmaster. This dwelling was one of the most pretentious in the village. Moses P. Hatch was the next resident; he sold the building in 1869 to Sylvester Doolittle. It was moved southward (north of the Oswego Candy Works and moved again to make room for the State Armory) to make room for the Doolittle House.

The Doolittle House was opened to patrons in 1874 and continued in service until demolished in 1910 to make room for the Pontiac Hotel. The hotel was not a financial success since it was too large for the patronage it received.

DOOLITTLE HOUSE

COR. WEST FIRST AND ONEIDA STS.,

OSWEGO, N. Y.,

House Heated by Steam!!

PASSENGER AND BAGGAGE ELEVATOR,

FREE OMNIBUS TO AND FROM ALL TRAINS AND BOATS.

THE CELEBRATED

Deep Rock Water Free to all Guests.

165 WELL LIGHTED & VENTILATED ROOMS.

House open all night. Special care will be given to families wishing day board.

JAMES IVES, Proprietor.

Deep Rock Spring

In connection with the hotel is a history of a famous spring.
While the big stone wall in the middle of the river was under
construction and the channel was being deepened so as to allow
vessels to pass above the Lower Bridge (the D. L. & W. planned to

102

build a coal trestle and load boats), indications of mineral water were found. The mineral spring was discoverd boiling up through the rock of the then dry bottom of the river bed. This was in 1869. Sylvester Doolittle, one of the most enterprising citizens in those days, who owned property along the river bank opposite the point where the discovery was made, began an investigation. He traced the vein to a point on his property. After a large expense, with much labor, he secured what was known as the Deep Rock Spring. He went through solid rock to a depth of 100 feet. Everybody grew discouraged except Mr. Doolittle, and his faith finally began to weaken. One day, on going down into the excavation, the man in charge endeavored to persuade Mr. Doolittle that further blasting was useless.

"Well", said Mr. Doolittle, "let's try one more blast and make it a good one."

The blast was prepared and it was a big one, too, shaking the town from the center to circumference when it went off and startling all the people. There was a great commotion around the spring a moment afterwards. The final blast had penetrated the hidden cavity and lo! the water gurgled up in great quantities, filling the monster hole near to the top. This happened in 1870, and the cost of the work was nearly $40,000.

The discovery was heralded far and near and in 1871 the water was first placed on the market. Since its introduction it had gained great popularity both as a beverage and a remedial agent. Thousands of gallons were sold throughout the eastern and southern states through agents. Sales ceased when transportation costs became prohibitive.

The spring became the property of the Deep Rock Spring Co. The company produced a beverage, "Whistle", a popular Summer drink, enjoyed a tremendous sale throughout the East. Mr. D. B. Cooper, a well known insurance man of Syracuse, purchased the spring in 1921 and had kept the well in first class condition and kept the property up. One of the propositions at that time involved marketing the water under the same agencies used for the distribution of "Whistle", and another was that of water itself might be used in the manufacture of that beverage.

The *Palladium*, August 13, 1924, announced:

Purchase of the former Deep Rock Spring Co. property, south of the Pontiac Hotel, from Albert Richheimer and Neil

Currie, who acquired the property from the Jermyn estate six weeks ago, will be consummated Saturday by the Oswego Hotel Corporation, owners of Pontiac Hotel. Action in taking up an option on the property, which had been secured by George Campbell, Vice-President of the Hotel Corporation, was confirmed by the directors of the Corporation at a meeting held Monday at the hotel.

Again the same paper, on April 16, 1925, mentioned that the stockholders of the Oswego Deep Rock Spring Co., Inc., voted to reopen the Whistle-Deep Rock bottling plant shortly.

Some time thereafter the bottling of the beverage was discontinued and the building razed. About 1975 the engineer of the Pontiac Hotel asked the aid of this writer to locate the well. The purpose was to use it to make a profit and for advertising the hotel. The well was traced to its source. When the heating plant of the hotel was converted to the use of oil as fuel, it was found necessary to install large oil tanks in the basement of the building. The space selected happened to be in a room over the well. The water was found to be contaminated and nothing further was done.

Pontiac Hotel

In the spring of 1909 three Oswegonians met in a downtown business place. They were Frank E. McCormack, Superintendent of the New York Central Railroad, Neil Gray, Jr., Oswego industrialist and Frederick W. Barnes, Oswego furrier. The discussion led to an agreement to start a movement for a new hotel. Shortly afterward, the Chamber of Commerce became interested and named a hotel committee, composed of Messrs. McCormack, Gray and Barnes, with the president of the Chamber as ex-officio member. Later Chauncey Place, another business man, was named to the committee, taking the place of Mr. McCormack, who in the meantime, had been transferred to Corning by the New York Central.

After a year of investigating during which plans were formulated for action and interest in the project created among citizens of the city, The Oswego Hotel Corporation was launched, with former Mayor John D. Higgins as President and Messrs. Barnes and Gray, Vice-presidents; William V. Burr, secretary; and Mr. Place, treasurer. Directors named were Messrs. Higgins, Barnes, Gray, Place, Burr, David D. Long, James P. Doyle, Elliott B. Mott, Louis C. Rowe and Thomas F. Gleason.

The company was incorporated with a capital stock of $150,000 and with a view of making the project as much as possible a civic undertaking, the purchase price of shares was placed at $10 each. The belief of the officers that many citizens would participate financially in the movement, was justified, for after the stock selling campaign was completed, the names of more than 500 citizens were recorded on the Company's books as stockholders.

After the financial organization was completed, the question of a site for the proposed hotel was next in order. After careful consideration of every angle, it was decided to purchase the Hotel Redstone, formerly the Doolittle House, raze the building and have the product of "New Oswego" rise on the ground where had been located the "pride of the past".

It was considered the ideal site, centrally located as to railroad stations, trolley lines and business sections of the city. It was explained that it was not a sentimental reason that prompted the decision of the hotel company officials in making the choice. The price paid for the old hotel was $25,000.

On July 14, 1910, a building committee composed of Elliott B. Mott, chairman, John D. Higgins, Chauncey C. Place, Frederick W. Barnes, Neil Gray, Jr., William V. Burr and Frederick A. Emerick, was named. Later it was announced that George B. Post & Sons New York architects, had been engaged to prepare plans for the new hotel.

So careful was the building committee to get the best arrangements possible, it accepted plans only after five different sketches had been prepared by the New York firm, considered experts in the designing of hotels, and after consultation with experienced hotel men from various parts of the State.

The contract for the construction of the hotel, was awarded on April 14, 1911, to the Amsterdam Building company. Meanwhile, the old brick hotel had been removed and the site cleared under separate contract.

With the building of the new structure under way, there was a long public discussion over a suitable name for the hotel. The name Pontiac was presented by Frederick O. Clark, an esteemed Oswego gentleman, who had devoted a great deal of his life to the study of history. The reason for the choice of Pontiac was that it was the name of a famous Indian Chieftain of the Ottawas nation, who came to Oswego in July 1766. On behalf of the western Indians he signed a treaty proposed by Sir William Johnson representing the British Crown which put an end to warfare which raged along much of the frontier. Contrary to popular belief, the treaty was signed on the south side of Fort Ontario and not on the hotel site.

On the occasion of the formal opening of the new hotel on March 18, 1912, the local press praised the splendid services of John D. Higgins and Thomas P. Kingsford (financial support), officers, and stockholders. The hotel was a fitting tribute to the loyal citizens of Oswego. The hotel cost in the neigborhood of $265,000.

The Hotel Pontiac was the first hotel to come under the operating supervision of the American Hotels Corporation founded in 1923. After the first ten years, during which the corporation was bringing other hotels under its management, the Pontiac was leased outright by the AHC. This arrangement continued until 1942 when the Choueguen Hotel Corporation was formed to purchase the hotel.

Instrumental in forming the new corporation was Gen. J. Leslie Kincaid and associates in the AHC. There were eight stockholders in the Choueguen, none of them being a majority stockholder. It was said the stock was about evenly divided between the holders. All the stockholders were members of the board of directors. Purchase of the hotel property by the Choueguen had not changed the status of the Pontiac, the AHC had continued as operating supervisors. A change in ownership came in 1964.

The *Palladium-Times*, March 5, 1965, had an item in its paper about the hotel:

Refinancing of the property comprising Hotel Pontiac and other details have been completed in connection with a general remodeling of the hostelry. The changes indicated by papers filed in the County Clerk's office yesterday include the sale by Edward F. Butler of East Seneca Tpk., Syracuse, to Rocco M. Vivenzio of 639 Dewitt St., Syracuse, of the former's interest in the hotel property which was held by them jointly since they became owners more than a year ago.

106

The Pontiac "THE PLACE DIFFERENT," OSWEGO, N. Y.

The Pontiac

Mr. Vivenzio sold the hotel to Robert McGann and Orlando Testi, announced on May 7, 1974. Upon the death of Mr. McGann, the hotel closed its doors. In the meantime a realty company with the aid of a government agency restored the hotel for apartment occupancy. The grand re-opening was announced in the Spring of 1983.

Let us quote from *The Oswego County Messenger* of August 2, 1982:

In only two months, the newly renovated Pontiac Terrace Apartments are expected to be ready for occupancy.

That's the word from Conifer Realty Vice President William Durdel, who is overseeing the restoration of the Pontiac Hotel.

The 'Grand Staircase' with its wrought iron railings and marble stairs will be restored to its original appearance. Existing plaster on columns and beams will be maintained as well as other ornamental plaster work.

Workmen are preserving the old 'Governor's Suite' with the original, although inoperable fireplace, to reflect historic flavor. Lower levels will be used for laundry facilities, tennant and building storage and other uses.

The restored Pontiac will contain 63 one-bedroom apartments, along with seven efficiencies. Six of these apartments are designed specifically for the handicapped or disabled.

Along with the 70 apartment units, the renovation will also include approximately 4,000 square feet of commercial space. This space will be located in the lower level of the building and will be available for rent in mid-October.

Pre-applications are being mailed out to all persons expressing an interest in the apartments, Durdel said. Conifer is financing the restoration of the Pontiac under a mortgage loan agreemnet with the New York State Housing Finance Agency (HFA). Conifer has received approval from the U. S. Department of Housing and Development (HUD) which will provide rental assistance payment for lower income persons.

To be eligible for assistance, prospective tennants must be 62 years of age or older, or if younger, handicapped or disabled as defined by federal law. Income limits established for HUD are $14,900 per year for one person and $17,050 per year for couples. Some apartments will be equipped for persons who require wheelchair facilities. Eligible persons will pay slightly less than one-quarter of their monthly income.

State Normal School

The Struggle for Free Public Schools in Oswego

The Yellow School House

The first school in Oswego was taught in a log cabin near what is now the corner of West First and Seneca Streets, about 1898, by Miss Artemisia Waterhouse, of Oswego Falls. Captain Edward O'Connor taught in 1802 in a log building erected for a shop by Captain Augustus Ford near the bank of the river between what are now Cayuga and Bridge Streets. A permanent school building was built in 1805 by Bradner Burt. Mr. Burt stated that funds were provided by public subscription. Among the contributors were Joel Burt, the customs collector, Matthew McNair, shipper, William Vaughn, lake captain, and others. It was a 35 feet square structure, with a cupola on top of its four-sided roof. A coat of yellow paint completed the outward adornment. Inside finishing and furnishings were useful rather than ornamental. The structure was fitted up with a pulpit to serve itinerant preachers of various denominations. It was used for other types of gatherings, including those by the County Court. The building was situated on the corner of West Third and Seneca Streets, on what was formerly known as "Court House Block" (Block 10). When the block was sold(1817) and the proceeds applied to the erection of a court house on the east side of the river, the building was removed to the opposite block on the southwest corner of Second and Seneca Street, then the corner of the public square. Later it was used as a wagon shop until it burned in 1865. At times it was referred to as the "Old Yellow School House."

As more people came to make their homes in Oswego it became necessary to build more one and two room schools. In 1848, the year Oswego became a city of 12,500 people, there were 12 individual school districts, each governed by their own set of trustees. Each district school was supported by payment of tuition or rate fees ranging from $1.50 to $4.00 per child. In addition to these "common" schools, private schools flourished.

The Old Academy

While Oswego, along with the majority of other New York State communities, had long placed emphasis on common or grammar school education, high school opportunities were slow in coming. Agitation by a number of leading citizens of the community for an Academy began in the late 1820's. Specifically, a meeting of subscribers was held at the Welland House (West First and Cayuga Streets) on Friday evening on June 25 at 8 o'clock for th purpose of adopting a measure for the erection of a building. A Board of Trustees was incorporated and Alvin Bronson was its first president. Mr. S. F. Swift was the first principal in the new Academy.

An Academy was built in 1831 across the park on West Third Street between Cayuga and Seneca Streets (present site of the Salvation Army building) but not used for school purposes. Some citizens objected to this site because of its close proximity to a primary school. They did not believe that two schools widely different in character was a good idea. The Academy building was sold and school trustees purchased a home on West Fourth Street (between Seneca and Schuyler Streets), converting it into a high school. It was occupied until 1851. At that time the West Fourth Street school was sold and the original Academy building, long used as a boarding house, was purchased and refitted for its original purpose. The Academy continued for two more years when it was absorbed by the Public High School.

Let us place ourselves in the period of time, so distant, by examining a few items taken from the local press. One item on June 16, 1841, is thus expressed:

Thanks of the subscribers are gratefully presented to the citizens of Oswego and its vicinity, for their liberal support of the Academy for young gentlemen, during the present term. (Right above is a long advertisement of a young ladies school). It is now believed that this institution is permanently established and the continued patronage of the public is solicited.

The Quarterly Examination will take place on Monday and Tuesday, the 26th and 27th instants. The friends of the school, and those interested in the causes of education generally, are respectively invited to attend.

The next term will commence, after a vacation of two weeks on Wednesday, the 11th of November next.

Thomas S. Myrick, principal.

Wednesday July 10, 1844, Oswego Academy:

J. B. Wasson, Principal, and teacher of Latin, Greek, and German languages, mathematics, &c.

J. B. Scantlebury, Teacher of the French Language, Instrumental Music and plain ornamental Penmanship, &c.

Miss Eliza Bright, Teacher of Drawing, Painting, Astronomy, &c.

The Principal, encouraged by the very liberal patronage extended to him heretofore, by the citizens of Oswego and its vicinity, has secured and neatly fitted up the whole Academy buildings for the accommodation of a large number of students. In connection with the Academic, there will be a juvenile department, including those studying spelling, reading, writing, and mental Arithmetic.

The following are the tuitional charges per term:

for Juvenile Studies—$2.50

Arithmetic, English, Grammar, principles of general grammar, geography, botany, history, natural, moral and mental philosophy, astronomy, rhetoric and logic, surveying, linear and solid geometry, and plain and spherical trigonometry, etc.—$4.00

Conic sections, algebra, Greek, Latin, German, French, drawing and painting—$6.00

Music—$12.00

Full charges made invariably for those entering before the expiration of the half term—half for those who enter after that time.

The next term will commence on Thursday, the 25th Inst. It is very desirable that all those who intend entering, should come on the first day, that the classes may be immediately organized.

Dr. Edward A. Sheldon

FREE PUBLIC SCHOOLS

Beginning in 1848, the year Oswego was incorporated as a city, a movement was initiated to establish free grade schools. Edward Austin Sheldon became the voice for the Free School Party in Oswego. He was forced to leave Hamilton College in 1847 because of illness. He came to Oswego in the fall of that year to go into partnership with J. W. P. Allen in the nursery business. The nursery on the corner of East Tenth and Utica Streets was not a financial success. He then focused his attention on the condition of the poorer class. His investigations showed that 1500 could not read of write.

Mr. Sheldon's concern for the plight of the poor people brought about the first meeting on October 31, 1848. A committee was appointed to take into considerations the expediency and importance of making some provisions for the education and care of the poor children of Oswego. A week later, November 7, the Orphan and Free School Association of Oswego adopted the following resolution:

Resolved, That in the judgment of the Committee it be deemed expedient and important to organize an Orphan and Free School Association, with a view of providing for the establishment of Free Schools for the benefit of the poor children of the city that cannot be gathered into other schools.

An adjourned meeting, held on November 9, for the further consideration of this subject, at which the Committee reported a constitution and a plan of operation for the Association. Objectives of the Association, as stated in the Constitution, were:

Article 1. The object of this Association shall be the intellectual and moral education and improvement of such poor and orphan children in this city as are otherwise provided for in these respects.

A second meeting was held on the 26th; and the third on the 30th. At this meeting Cheney Ames was appointed President, and B. Randall, Secretary, and other officers. Appearing in the audience was a respectable number of prominent Oswegonians. It was reported that over 400 shares were taken. The movement enlisted the sympathy and cooperation of all churches, clergymen and philantrophic gentlemen. The ladies, through the aid of sewing societies, prepared clothing for the childern. Mr. Sheldon, without his intention or desire, was pressed into becoming the teacher of the "ragged school" as it was first dubbed. He solicited and collected funds, visited the families of the poor, distributed clothing and taught the school. About 125 children (Irish and French, boys and girls) of all ages, most of whom rarely, if ever, had seen the inside of a school, came to the first free school. It met in the basement of the old "Tabernacle", later called Franklin Hall, a building on 156 West Second Street, owned by Gerrit Smith. Incidentally, the Orphan's Home or Orphan Asylum came into being as a result of this movement for free schools.

"I sometimes tremble at the responsibilty I am taking upon myself", Sheldon wrote at the time, "for it is all new, entirely new business for me. I put my trust in God, who alone can give me wisdom to direct and strength to perform.... This was a strange school, with no less strange teacher. None such had ever been assembled in Oswego."

To fully understand and appreciate the noble undertaking, Sheldon's Report to the quarterly meeting of the Orphan Asylum and Free School Association, July 1849, is presented. His report reflects not only the depth and breadth of his humanitarianism and his faith in education as a moral force, but also the appalling conditions among the recently arrived Irish and other poor in Oswego. The Temperance movement was making rapid strides at this time. There were organizations for men, women, and children. The report:

Since our last quarterly meeting little of peculiar interest has occurred. The last report contained a brief history of the design, rise, progress and success of the Association. What was reported in regard to its success then, still holds true. We are fully satisfied that an incalculable good has been and is still being accomplished. Not as much has been done during the 1st, as the previous term, in the way of clothing and providing places for destitute children, nor has the demand been as great. A few have been provided with homes, and other clothes. The number of children at school, and for the most part the regularity of their attendance, particularly during the latter part of the term, has been good as could have been expected. The present number of regular attendants is 52; although the number of different scholars during the term has been much greater. A majority of these are small children. The older ones having found places

114

to live, or work to do. A great number of boys are to be seen about the streets, peddling various articles, others, in part at least supporting themselves. The progress of the children during the past term has been very good, though not as marked as during the former term. But comparatively few of those now in school can read intelligibly, being for the most part new comers. Each child has two exercises each day in spelling and reading, aside from their testament lesson in the morning, also in mental arithmetic, geography and various and miscellaneous exercises in concert. Wednesday afternoon is devoted to teaching them to sing. We find manifested in them, a general desire to learn, and a readiness to receive moral impressions. Nor is this influence entirely confined to the children, but either directly or through these scholars it is brought to bear upon their friends. We have in mind a very interesting instance of this head.

During the progress of the first term a little Temperance Society was formed, and the names of nearly all the children attached to the Temperance pledge. Among the number was a little girl, seven years old, who had an intemperate father.

Although the most part a kind husband and father, and an industrious man, his habits of intemperance were fast gaining ground; and drowning every better feeling of his nature. We shall never forget on our first visit at his house, the earnestness with which the wife pleaded with us to do something to save her husband, and anxious countenances of their interesting group of children. Said she, "He has always been a good provider and a kind man, but unless he is saved soon, we are all ruined." He was repeatedly urged to sign the pledge or join the Sons of Temperance, but all to no purpose. The poisoned cup had charmed his appetite and he seemed deaf to reason. For a long time we had not heard from him, not having inquired after him, when one morning, (a few days after the circulation of the pledge in school) this little girl coming up and clasping the hand of the teacher in both of hers, her eyes sparkling with delight said, "Pa says if I will sign the pledge and bring home the paper he will sign it too, and give me a new pair of shoes and a new dress." Both their names were accordingly prepared and she made her mark on the spot, and at night took home the pledge for her father to make his. We called on them a few days since and found the mother and children at work in the garden and the husband out employed in his daily labor. She assured us that they were again happy and prosperous, as he was faithful to his pledge. In repeated instances these children at work, as soon as able to read had been anxicus to receive testaments that they might read them to the parents. Invariably they express great delight at the thought of thus being able to read to them.

Thus we see that a powerful influence may be brought to bear upon the parents which could not be otherwise effected. There are hundreds of these parents in our city who are almost as ignorant as the Hottentots of Africa; not knowing one letter or figure from another, and having no correct idea or knowledge of matters or things either as connected with the present or the past. Accordingly we find them exceedingly bigoted and superstitious, and as a matter of consequences a dead weight upon every enterprise or improvement.

The greatest encouragement for doing good among them, is in the influence that may be thrown around their children. At least we hope by this means, to save the rising generation, who are soon to become fellow-citizens with us, and to a greater or less extent form the character of our city.

Nearly every abode of poverty and wretchedness has been visited since the opening of warm weather, and for the most part the children have been gathered both into day schools and Sunday schools. In these respects a great change has been produced since November last. Then there were hundreds who were not in school—had no prospect of going to school, and who never under any wholesome moral influences, now scarcely a child can be found over the age of five years, if not usefully employed, but is in some day in school and Sunday school. We find that in this respect a great good has been accomplished. We shall regret to see an institution that has already effected, and promises still to effect so much for the welfare of this class, nipped in the bud. But without the means it is impossible to go on. Enough has been pledged to meet all the expenses of the year, but we find a great want of promptness in the fulfillment of their pledges; which is a fair indication that there is a lack of interest in the effort. This constitutes the only discouraging feature in the case. We hear the tale of poverty, wretchedness and degredation coming from distant shores of Ireland, and we open our granaries, our wardrobes, our purses and send relief to the half famished inhabitants with a liberal hand. We send our missionaries to instruct them, and feel that our money is well expended and

116

every effort amply rewarded; and so they are. It is a good noble work; and should have aid and prayers of every Christian and Philantropist. These same half-starved, wretched and deluded creatures are continually crowding to our shores by thousands, and although thrown under far more favorable circumstances, for being aided and benefited, we once give them up in despair, as a race for whom every effort to do good is worse than wasted, and thus leave them neglected and uncared for. It is a painful fact that while we are sending missionaries at a great expense half way around the globe to educate and reform a degraded heathen people, we make either or no provision for the thousands in our very midst who are as absoulute heathen as the world ever saw, although every encouragement for doing good is vastly in favor of the latter. We would not for a moment discourage any effort to do good abroad; but while we are sending our money away, to relieve and educate the poor and ignorant, let us not slight the imperious demands that are upon us at home. There is spread out here within the sight of our own eyes, a broad field for doing good. Let us then one and all, as we value the credit and morale of our city, as we value and avoid crime, misery and degradation, improve the opportunity afforded us. Let us do what we can to enlighten the ignorant, reform the immoral, reclaim the wanderer, feed the hungry, clothe the naked, and we shall at least, be entitled to the blessing in store for Him, who careth for the poor.

The report made the citizens of the city conscious of the plight of the poor. Government concern and social responsibility was to come much later.

The effort to raise money to meet various expenses of the school and necessities of the poor, began to abate, and the general interest to cease. As Mr. Sheldon saw these tendencies, he urged the members of the committee to realize the importance of making all the public schools of the city free. This met with a hearty response. Persons outside of the Orphan and Free School Board were consulted. It was evident that sentiment was in favor of such a movement. It was decided to call a public meeting to discuss that question. He took it upon himself to circulate the call for such a meeting, and to explain to the individual citizens the advantages of a free school system. All this ground work covered many months. The meeting was called for December 15, 1849, to consider the condition of the public school, and probable effects of the Free

117

School Law and to see what changes were necessary. The call had 63 signers. At that meeting a plan for the consolidation of the schools under a free school system was presented and discussed. For the most part the plan was accepted.

Opposition was immediate. One man, Thomas Bond, a politician, objected to the plan appealing to the religious prejudices of the audience by representing it as a Protestant movement. Others fought it on the ground of expense while some people felt that it would take away from them the direct control of their schools. At this meeting a decision was reached to appoint a committee to draw up a definite plan, draft a school law, and submit the same to a public meeting to be called. Three days later a general meeting was held with Hamilton Murray as the chairman. A. H. Dunham, city Superintendent of School, stated that one-third of the children of the city, entitled to public education, could be accommodated. Resolutions were passed to adopt some system of greater efficiency, appoint a committee to procure statistics of the number of children, also the number and condition of the school houses. The press reported on November 13, 1851, that the committee presented a detailed report. Briefly it stated that the whole number of children in the city entitled to public money was 3,886. The school houses could accommodate 1,390, leaving the balance of 2,496 to run the streets. The daily average attendance was 1,037. In the meantime Mr. Sheldon taught in the United States Hotel building, then located on West Seneca Street between Sixth and Seventh Streets. Then he accepted a position of Superintendent of Schools in Syracuse.

It became evident, as a result of these public meetings, that if Oswego was to have a system of free schools, it must be secured in some other way. It must be accomplished in a more quiet way. During the winter of 1851–1852 an effort was made to pass a bill through the State legislature to organize a free school system in Oswego. For some reason it failed to become a law but the following winter(1852–1853) with Hon. Dewitt C. Littlejohn in the Assembly and Hon. Robert C. Platt in the Senate, friends of the new educational movement, the proposed bill became a law on April 5, 1853. Under this act the first Board of Education was organized May 11, 1853, and, quite unsolicited by him and greatly to his surprise, Mr. Sheldon was elected secretary to the Board, as the superintendent was called, at a salary of $800, "with the prospect of an advance."

Thus out of the humble beginnings of the "ragged school" came the Oswego system of free public school. The movement, filled with opposition and strife, marked one of the noblest achievements of the citizens of Oswego.

Oswego High School—West First Street

The Free Public High School

Edward A. Sheldon reorganized the districts and their schools, and provided for a free public high school as the "crowning glory" of his system of free schools. "This school", Sheldon said, "shall be a thorough academic institution." Later he was to report that the high school "has given a high tone and character to the whole system". However, in his Annual Report of 1864, he said, "We regret to learn that objections still exist in the minds of some of our

119

worthy citizens to the maintenance of this school as a part of our system of free schools."

The first principal of the high school was Mr. Delos Gary, who was assisted by Miss Mary T. Howe and Mrs. Davies. The school was opened with about fifty pupils, and twenty more were added during the year. Mr. Gary retired at the end of the first year, and was followed by Mr. Emerson J. Hamilton, who held the principalship until September 1872. During this time he was assisted at various times by Mrs. Hamilton, Miss Mary T. Howe, Miss Eliza Morgan, Miss Z. G. Wright, Miss T. C. Staats, Miss E. S. Edwards and Professor Herman Krusi. Under Mr. Hamilton the pupils were classified, and the three years' course of study was arranged. In 1856, the first class, numbering only three graduated. The second class did not graduate until two years after the first. The time of the course had been changed from three to four years. The class of 1858 was the first to be publicly awarded the diploma.

By 1872 Sheldon's methods introduced under his tenure came under fire in the City of Oswego. On September 5, 1872, the Board of Education offered the following Resolution:

> Whereas, The taxpayers demand a reduction of school expenses, and the Common Council has refused to levy a sum sufficient to carry on the school; therefore, Resolved, That the High School be discontinued, the teacher of music be discharged and the annual appropriation to the Orphan Asylum be discontinued.
>
> (Ayes 8, Noes 5)

On the 20th the Board resolved to abolish the Object Method of teaching because the extra teachers and added expense. Letters to the editor in the newspapers charged that pupils did not easily pass from grade to grade in lockstep. Teachers and parents wanted text books instead of oral lessons. Some parents were against text books because of the cost. Objections were raised to taxing everybody for free public school education so some children could "take botany, geometry, or Latin". Gymnastics should be done away with. Mr. Sheldon was accused of building up fortunes of "Book Publishing Rings". Some letters advocated that the teaching of only the three R's and Geography should be carried on. Even the number of teachers employed in the system came under fire.

Charles W. Richards
Principal of the Oswego High School, 1872–1910
Superintendent of Oswego Schools, 1910–1920

The High School was discontinued from September 1872, until February 1873. Missess Staats and Edwards, however, held together about twenty pupils, graduating seven and sending a few pupils into advanced classes of the school after its reorganization in February 1873. At this time Mr. Charles W. Richards was appointed principal, assisted at first by Miss Staats alone. Soon after Miss Edwards was added to the staff.

The old Academy Building located on the site of the old high school on West Third Street was purchased and fitted up for a high school. This institution was maintained on this site until it was temporarily removed to the Normal School, then located on West Seneca Street. In February, 1868, the old academy or the first high school building, was destroyed by fire. During the succeeding summer a substantial brick structure, 88x89 feet, accommodating 600 pupils and costing $22,223 was erected on the same site. For more than thirty years the high school occupied the third floor only, with the second and first floors by other students. Due to overcrowding, the school was discontinued in January 1923 when a new high school on West First Street was completed. This was used until 1971 when it became the Middle School. A new Middle

School was in turn built on the former Kingsford Farm on West Fifth Street. It was found that the old High School on West First Street was no longer suitable for school purposes. Other uses were explored. After some adjustments were made to conform to local zoning laws, a private company turned the building into a condominium in 1981–1982.

No history dealing with these formative years would be complete without placing the proper perspective the part that the first free high school played in the founding of the Oswego Normal School, currently known as State University of New York at Oswego. In 1854, Dr. Sheldon (Principal of the Normal School 1862 on; Doctor of Philosophy by the Board of Regents of the State of New York in 1875) set the process in motion by designing a subject for the last year of high school entitled "The Theory and Practice of Teaching". An integral feature of this course was that the students be "sent at regular intervals to lower grades and engage in the actual duties of the school room under the direction of the most skillful teachers". So successful was this venture that a Training Class for teachers was established as a regular department of the high school and property was acquired by the Board of Education to provide a separate site for a Teacher Training School. When, in 1866, the City of Oswego transferred control of this property to the State of New York, it marked the emergence of the Training School as a state institution. "This institution", noted Dr. Sheldon, "may be fairly considered an outgrowth of our public system; and of this, as also the honorable reputation our schools have achieved, we have a right to be proud."

The Oswego Method

Edward Austin Sheldon soon came to the realization that school work was too formal, too much of a memorizing process. He wanted something that would wake up the pupils, set them thinking, observing and reasoning; it must be objective. In the matter of discipline, his tendency at first was to restrain the activities and impulses of children; in short, it was toward repression. He soon realized the folly of his thinking, and changed his mind. He now would encourage and cultivate the children by giving them proper direction; give them the greatest liberty possible believing that freedom tended to give growth and vigor. The better to understand this great man, his idea and philosophy of practical instruction is herewith noted:

In this plan of studies the object is not so much to impart information as to educate the senses, and awaken a spirit of inquiry; to this end the pupils must be encouraged to do most of the talking and acting. They must be allowed to draw their own conclusions, and if wrong, lead to correct them. The books should only be used as references, and as models for the lessons to be given. The children should be allowed to have two short recesses for ten minutes each, morning and afternoon, and gymnastics and singing exercises should be frequently introduced, to give change of position and rest to the children, and keep up an animated and pleasant state of feeling.

Dr. Sheldon sought more information about the objective method of teaching. In 1859, he visited Toronto schools. He spent $300 for a collection of objects, pictures, charts, of colors, form, reading charts, books for teachers, giving full directions as to the use of these materials. These were mostly the products of the Home and Colonial Training Institution of London.

Thus the Object Teaching—The "Oswego System" of teaching in primary schools was born. No better description of the system can be found than in the Remarks of C. T. Richardson, President of the Board of Education at the public exercises of the High School (1861):

LADIES AND GENTLEMEN: As the Board of Education has decided upon some changes not only in the organization of the High School, but in the system of teaching to be pursued in the other schools of this of the city, it has been thought best that at this time I should make some explanation of those changes, of the reason for them, and their cost, that the Board may not be accused of innovating rashly, or of trying experiments from which no good may be expected; or the taxpayers be afflicted with those qualms to which they are liable.

From a partial trial during the past year in the Primary Schools, which has been very satisfactory, and from information obtained from various sources, the Board has decided to introduce as far as parcticable the system of teaching known as Pestalozzian, the basis of which is Object lessons.

It might be necessary to make a brief explanation of the system. A Swiss philantrophist of Italian extraction, who first, about one hundred years ago, introduced among the children of Switzerland its distinctive characteristics. Since his time it has been modified and improved, and his ideas have been established and developed, until under one name or another they form the basis of all truly philosophical mental culture. The central ideas of the system are as follows:

First—That all education should be according to the natural order of development of the human faculties.

Second—That all knowledge is derived in the first instance from the perceptions of the senses, and therefore that all instructions should be based upon observation of real objects and occurrences.

Third—That the object of primary education is to give a harmonious cultivaion of the faculties of the mind, and not to communicate technical knowledge.

The development of the faculties of the mind in the natural order is in this wise. First, the power to receive impressions; after that the power to conceive thoughts; after that the power to reason. In other words, the Sense, the Understanding, and the Reason.

The proper method, then consists in presenting to the child's mind the quality of knowledge suited to its state of development. The ordinary method disregards this principle and frequently, just the reverse of this practice. In arithmetic for example, the children are taught to repeat rules. Now a rule is a generalization from many simple facts, and to a child ignorant of the facts convey no idea whatever, although it may repeat it by an effort of memory.

By the new method the idea of number is made familiar to the child by appealing to the faculties that are already developed, that is by showing them objects, marbles, pebbles, etc. When the idea of concrete number is obtained, they are led to dispense with objects and deal with figures which are symbols and rules which are abstract.

How many children can repeat the ordinary tables of weight and measure, but how few have any real conception of what constitutes an inch or a pound?

Usually a child is taught as a vessel is laden at the wharf, in bulk; facts are thrown in loose without regard to the fitness of the child's faculties to receive them, and when a certain amount has been committed to memory the child is considered educated. The true course is to present no other facts, and those no faster than can be assimilated and organized into the mind. By this method, education answers its own definition; it is to lead out the faculties. It is organic—it is growth from within, not an addition from without. It is the difference between knowledge chemically combined with the child's mind, and knowledge mechanically held in solution.

Take the growing plant putting forth in all directions its roots and fibers seeking food. But put the right elements in its way and the plant will organize them into its growth, varying its demands according to its different stages, obstinately refusing at a later period what it obstinately demanded at an earlier, and vice versa, till we have first the blade, then the ear, then the full corn in the ear. So with a child's mind. If when it requires simple impressions on the senses you feed it with complex obstructions, it pines and withers, or at best attains but the development of one faculty at the expense of the rest. But if you place it the right elements, it absorbs them, organizes them, each faculty taking what it needs, till the simple elements reappear, in the leaf, the flowers, the ripe fruit of vigorous healthy mental growth.

It is simply placing in the child's way the knowledge suited to its natural requirements that the art of Teaching consists. The Teacher must furnish the material at the right time. The child must educate itself.

The most active opposition to the movement sprang up in the State and National Educational Conventions. The first attack was made by Dr. Wilbur, Superintendent of the State Asylum for Imbeciles, at Syracuse, New York. It was at the New York State Teachers' Association at Rochester in 1862. The second attack by Dr. Wilbur was before the National Educational Convention at Ogdensburg in 1864. A committee was appointed to report on the subject. Professor Green came to Oswego, examined the system and gave his report to the National Education Association at Harrisburg, Pennsylvania. The favorable report is attached to this story.

Dr. Sheldon resigned as the Secretary of the Board of Education in September 1869. About the same time or soon after, the character of the Board began to change and the opposition to the object method of teaching increased. The discussion got into the press with considerable animus. In 1872 the "big fight" began, culminating in the discontinuance of the High School as already noted.

Henreich Pestalozzi

Heinrich Pestalozzi, Zurich, (1746–1827), was born before the middle of the Eighteenth Century, belonged in spirit, and largely in activity, to the Nineteenth. With little learning, and less system, but with an overwhelming faith in the people and love for children, this warm-hearted, devoted man may fairly be said to be the father of modern popular education. Above all he insisted that education should be extended to the whole people, that its methods should be kindly and considerate, and that it should relate to things rather than words, to facts rather than rules. He aimed to cultivate not merely the intelligence, but also, and still more, the affections, the moral judgment, and the will. He insisted that children should learn not only to think, but also to do, and hence that education should consist largely of manual labor.

Pestalozzi demanded that children should be made acquainted with the glories of nature; he insisted that the worth of the individual soul should be realized and recognized. It was education for freedom, not for subordination.

Horace Mann, Massachusetts, (1796–1859), was more like Pestalozzi, with all Pestalozzi's human sympathy, democratic interest, and moral enthusiasm, but with a practical sense and talent for organizing. It may be fairly said that Horace Mann is the father of American education.

126

REPORT OF THE
NATIONAL EDUCATION ASSOCIATIAN,
AUGUST, 1865, HARRISBURG, PENNSYLVANIA,
as reported by the *Oswego Commercial Advertiser & Times*,
August 23, 1865.

THE "OSWEGO SYSTEM" OF TEACHING IN PRIMARY SCHOOL. As we have frequently referred to it, our readers are probably aware that last week there assembled at Harrisburgh, Penn., the most important convention of teachers and professors, which has ever met in this country. It was made up of Presidents and Professors from the various colleges, and teachers of various grades from all parts of the country.

There are many things of interest connected with the proceedings of this eminent body, which we shall be glad to dwell upon, but our limited space forbids. It had been understood for some time, that the Pestalozzian method of instructing primary schools as pursued in this city would receive the attention of the Convention, and for that reason the friends of that system have felt much interest in the deliberations.

A special committee was appointed last year to investigate the objects and claims of this system, and report to this body. Rev. Dr. Sears, President of Brown University, was the Chairman of this Committee, which was entirely composed of eminent practical teachers from different parts of the country. The report was presented by Prof. T. S. Green, of Brown University. It will be remembered that this distinguished scholar spent much time here in early summer ostensibly for the purpose of giving lessons in Language and English grammar to our teachers. His subject was to investigate and become fully acquainted with the merits of the "Oswego System". His report was all that the most ardent friends of the system could desire. He proceeded to inquire how far knowledge may be taught by the presentation of external objects, by shape, form and depicture. Says the Rev. Dr. Hill, "It is the thought of God in the object that stimulates the child", and the great object to teach the child more than you can teach in words. With such a text, the report fully investigated the manifold claims of object teaching - it is the only effective method by which the child can readily acquire the fundamentals of analogy and analysis, the education of perceptions, and derive, indeed, the ideas and conceptions. The spontaneity of language in the young, is also one of the results of the observation of externals; and nature itself, with its verse of types, shapes and forms, is only one great language, besides which mere words, texts and dry formulas of the schools are barren. Languages and texts are indeed only the conveyances of objects. How vastly more advantageous to the teacher if the objects themselves can be conveyed: The report which, we believe, was partly written by Dr. Sears, was an emphatic and very thoughtful indorsement of the system, which has been introduced with so much success in this city.

The report of this eminent Committee was fully sustained by the sentiment of the Convention. It was a complete triumph of the Pestalozzian system of instruction as elaborated, reduced to practice and Americanized in this city and it is taught in the Training School of the State, located here.

The special reporter of the *New York Tribune,* sent out to report the proceedings of this Convention, on this topic says:

Object teaching, as pursued at Oswego, appears to have gained the general voice of the Convention. It was suggestively illustrated by Miss Cooper of Oswego, with a random class of young children resident in Harrisburg, the object being an apple, which was resolved into shape, color, parts and constituents, to the quick apprehension of the pupils. Professor Sheldon, Principal of the same school, replied at length to the objections assailing this system, in last year's address of Dr. Wilbur of the asylum at Syracuse. Professor Northrup of Massachusetts described object teaching as the cultivation of the senses and of expression, and declared the indebtedness of the teachers of the whole country to the system pursued in Oswego.

The time has come when not only Mr. Sheldon, whose ability and indefatigable industry and perseverance has perfected the system, but the intelligent Board of Education, whose good sense and appreciation of his labors have sustained him, and our citizens generally, may congratulate themselves upon the fact that the system so modestly introduced into our schools, and which in doing so much for our own youth, is appreciated and extolled by the nation.

Ned Lee — City Missionary

Introduction

The life of Ned Lee reminds the writer of saints like Augustine of Hippo who was born in North Africa in 354. His Confessions "show how worldliness and carnality can be transmitted into a life of dedication to the service of God." Unlike Ned Lee, St. Augustine received the classical education of a young pagan but they were similar in that both were tireless preachers. St. Augustine's exceptional talents were recognized and he was consecrated Bishop of Hippo, North Africa, in 395. Similarly Ned Lee's talents were recognized and accepted by the whole-hearted response of polite society as evidenced in testimonials included in this story.

Around the middle of the 19th century there was born in Oswego, New York, a boy whose life was remarkable because of the contrast between the early years—what he called "the wicked years"—and the later years when he became an evangelist and missionary to the down-and-out, whose hardships and temptations he knew so well from experience. He was a "living epistle, known and read of all men". He was a natural orator, he spoke his message in his daily life.

Those who remembered Ned Lee described him as straight, sinewy, well-built, keen blue eyes, brown curly hair with glints in it that often went with a lively, quick temper. Quick, that was the word for him; quick in temperament, in action, in sympathy. Gifted with a pleasant, resonant voice, he lifted it in song and in exhortation. He loved music. He loved flowers, but above all he loved people, from little children to old timers, and delighted to be of service to any one in trouble, need, or adversity. Nothing of a writer himself, he was persuaded by his friends to tell the story of his life to Mr. Charles Dunning Clark who at that time was connected as a reporter with the *Oswego Palladium* and also at one time for the *Oswego Times*. He wrote the "Beadle Dime Novels."

Long before there was any radio Ned Lee chose for his theme song the rousing militant gospel hymn, "Hold The Fort":

129

Ho, my comrades! See the signal
Waving in the sky!
Reinforcements now appearing!
Victory is nigh!

Chorus:
Hold the fort, for I am coming,
Jesus signals still.
Wave the answer back to Heaven,
By thy grace, we will!

Another gospel hymn he liked was "Pull for the Shore, Sailor, Pull for the Shore." This was a favorite with the crowds at the City Mission in Oswego. He was also fond of "Throw Out the Life Line." The songs were those much used by Ned Lee in his work as an evangelist.

While traveling on his missionary work, he stopped long enough to make a fortunate and happy marriage. Dates were rarely mentioned but he spoke in this manner: "I was married to Miss Ella Sever, at Wolcott, N. Y., September 5, 1883" adding, "the people of Oswego would not have known it so soon, but some one caught me buying white gloves at Massey and DeForest's." (A well known Oswego department store which was located in West First Street, south of Bridge).

Mrs. William Brown, a daughter of Mr. Earl, remembered Mr. Lee, his lovely wife and his little daughter, Ella. Every Sunday the three came to have dinner with the Earls and they were always welcome guests. Mr. Lee was full of fun and a most interesting talker. "He was the kind of man no one who met him could forget." Mrs. Brown also remembered going to play the organ for services Lee held at the old jail on East Second and Schuyler Streets, and she recalled her dread of the place. Attached to this story is a brief history of the county jail.

The story of Ned Lee ends with his return to Oswego near the end of 1888, where he took up his old duties. But not for long. There came a call for his services from Davenport, Iowa, and he resigned his work as a city missionary April 10, 1893. Once more the deciding influence was the welfare of his wife and little daughter. Again and again he brougnt his family to call upon old friends in Oswego, but he remained in Davenport and made that city his home for the rest of his life. He died there August 30, 1927, at his home

515 Kirkwood Boulevard. His body was buried in Oakdale cemetery in that city. At the head of his grave stands a G. A. R. marker that flies the American flag each Memorial Day. His widow continued after his death his settlement work in Davenport until June preceding her death, July 2, 1932. Her remains were placed in the grave alongside of that of her husband. Their daughter Ella M., the wife of A. K. Reading, continued to make their home at 402 East Rushholme Street.

Edward Lee

NED LEE

The life and times of Ned Lee, City Missionary, was written by Charles Dunning Clark. Although Ned had a gift of talking to a certain kind of audience, he felt that he did not have the ability to write a story. It was the desire of Ned that "polish" and "finish" should be appropriate style of the written work. But the editor "respectfully declined" because Ned Lee polished, would not be Ned Lee. Therefore he told the story of his life, in his own plain way, not to cover or conceal the errors of his early years, but to show to all what a man could do. This, then, is a condensed story of Edward Lee, edited by Charles Dunning Clark.

He was born in the First Ward of the city of Oswego, New York, on May 2nd, 1846. The locality where he was born was in a section then known as "The Flats." There was no portion of the town (about 12,000) which had sent out so many toughs, or had been the birthplace of so much riot, confusion and crime. People in other parts of the town have fancifully named Seneca Street, near which he was born, "The Dead Line", because there was a time when no officer of the law, or respectable person from another ward, dared to cross it after nightfall; and, if he did, it was at his own peril.

Water Street, in the days when Oswego was one of the most thriving ports along the lakes, was a busy mart. It was crowded with sailors, night and day. Every other building was a dance house or saloon. With the advent of the railroads, and the subsequent decay of the shipping interests of Oswego, this street lost its glory and in his time was filled with tumble-down rookeries, and the buildings began to be demolished. The population was a strange mixture of all nations, and it was in such surroundings that he first saw the light.

His father was a Scotchman, and his mother of Irish descent. His father died when he was five yearts old, and shortly after, his mother passed away. He was taken into the family of Edward Degan, and took his name; and after a time, it was forgotten that he had ever known any other. At that time, many people believed that Edward Lee was an assumed name, when it was, in fact, the only name to which he had a legal right. He was put into a family where there two girls and a boy—Kate, Mary and James Degan. He was treated as one of the family, and as well as the children of the poor

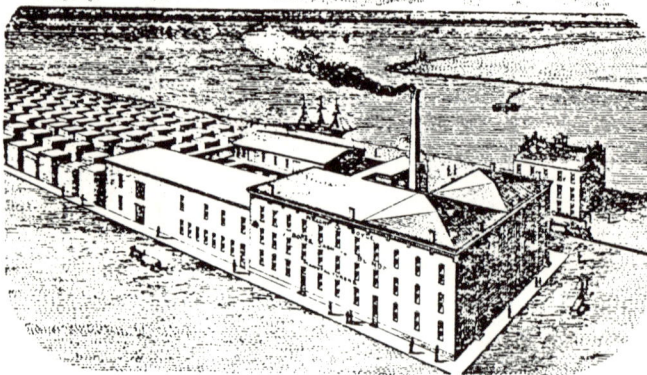

132

could be treated, but he was allowed to run wild, and was more upon the river than anywhere else. The place where they lived was known as the Murray Block (a building and not a street block), which was afterward burned, and the site was occupied by a large hotel (Checkerboard Tavern, later known as the Frontier House— Myron Pardee and other built a large hotel which was never completed for occupancy) and the building was torn down to make room for the Wright & Boyle sash factory (and torn down in 1979). It was a tough place, containing many good, honest people, but more of the other kind, and hardly the place to educate a boy, who was, perhaps, naturally inclined to go a crooked path.

He used to have a boat upon the river, and to work in association with Captains "Jack" and "Bill" Preston in ferrying people across to the East side. He remembered that M. J. Cummings (a prominent ship owner), at that time, kept a junk shop in the upper part of an old building south of the Northwestern Elevatror (West Schuyler Street between Water Street and the river; burned February 1922), and one of his early pranks was to roll a coil of rope out of his shop on to the wharf, in the rear, and then bring it back to sell it to him. He bought it and paid for it, and it was some time before he caught the trick. About that time they were driven out of the Murray block by fire, and a large building was being put up on the site. The boys used to vie with each other in seeing who could smash most windows. He was in it, of course, and, doubtless got his full share of the windows. The result was that there was a warrant out for his arrest, and Officer Betts undertook to serve it. He got sight of him, and then came his first race with the police. He was a

133

pretty good runner, and Ned saw that capture was certain if something was not done, so he let the officer come upon him, and then dropped suddenly in front of him, falling over him, barking his hands badly, and Ned got away. It was his first introduction to the police, although they were beginning to know him as a lad who needed watching. He ran away and hid in a swamp near Sheldon's point, the low ground near the works of the Oswego Manufacturing Company. After the affair had blown over, he came back home.

On The Road To Mischief

Ned in the meantime had fallen in with bad companions and was obliged to leave Oswego, by ruse, to Canada, but in a short time returned. After several "scrapes" in Oswego, he was sent to the House of Refuge (Industry) at Rochester, staying there one year. Shortly after his return, he again was into mischief, and again was obliged to change his residence. He stowed away on board a boat where a tough gang polished his education. He passed counterfeit bills, stole chickens, shoplifted a variety of goods—anything that he and his companions could "lift". It was a matter of time when Chicago detectives "chucked" the group into jail at Joliet.

He made a successful escape from jail; he managed to avoid the law in Chicago for a few days and then skipped to Milwaukee. He soon fell in with crooks who robbed stores. Again he was caught, tried but somehow managed to escape confinement in jail. He then went to Cheboygan, Michigan, but had to leave for Manitowac; from there to Chicago, and then to Toledo..

No matter where he traveled, he had an unusual instinct or maybe misfortune, to "fall in" with crooks of the first magnitude. At Toledo he worked with a crook until caught but escaped to Chicago. Again, the detectives made life uneasy for him. While in jail he was recruited (March 2, 1862) into the navy and shipped to New York.

At New York he was sent on board to Hatteras. He participated in actions at Roanoke Island, Elizabeth City, North Carolina; at Fort Macon, and Beaufort, South Carolina, on blockade duty.

At the expiration of his term in the navy, and upon his discharge, he returned to Oswego. While there he gave the Provost Marshal and his soldiers a merry chase. After several escapades he was caught and was released when he produced his honorable discharge. He soon tired of inaction and re-enlisted in the 147th New York Volunteers. He received a bounty of $850 for enlisting. From Elmira the contingent was sent to Washington; then to Culpepper; and on May 5, 1864, into the Battle of the Wilderness. He was captured by the Confederates and sent to the notorious Andersonville. He suffered with the rest from May 22nd to September 12th. With the coming of General Sherman, the prisoners were transferred to another prison pen. On the way an escape was made but capture came 250 miles later at Camden, South Carolina; then to a stockade at Florence; then to Augusta, Georgia. He escaped to the Union lines at Savannah, Georgia. In all he was a prisoner eleven months and twelve days. From that place he was sent by steamer to Annapolis and then on to New York reaching there that day after Lincoln was assassinated. He returned to Oswego; he gave Mrs. Degan $335 of a sum of $700 he managed to trick from some "tricksters."

A person with a bad reputation was always watched with suspicion by the police. It was not long before he left for his old haunts in Chicago. It got to "warm" there for him and he decided to travel again; this time to Toledo and on to Milwaukee. He resisted arrest by the police and was indicted for assault with a deadly weapon; found guilty; sentenced to a five-year term in state prison at Waupon. After three unsuccessful attempts at escape, he was finally released from prison after three years and ten months confinement.

Ned was constantly on the move. He left Milwaukee for Chicago, then on to Detroit. There he again got into mischief; was tried; found guilty, and was sentenced to serve two years in prison at Jackson. At Erie, Pennsylvania he was able to escape from the police to Oswego. Here he was pursued by police officers (William) Grant and (P. W.) Slatterly and captured in a barn at the Forks of the Roads. He was returned to Erie where he beat "the rap". At Buffalo he was charged with assault with intent to kill. The Erie County Penitentiary was escape proof but not to Ned. He made his way to Buffalo; from there he "back tracked" on country roads to Cleveland and then on to Chicago.

135

As he stepped off the schooner *Platt* at Oswego, he was not well received. He decided to take a "tour" through the South. As usual he got into mischief everywhere he visited. He returned by way of Washington, New York to Oswego in 1874.

It was a bad time to be in Oswego; for, a number of burglaries and robberies were committed. Continually watched by the police, it was a matter of time before Ned, half full of spirits, got into a row. He spent six months in the Syracuse Penitentiary.

The Change

Ned's conversion is best presented in his own fashion:

It was while I was in the penitentiary that the change in my life came. It was a simple thing that changed me—just the kind act of a noble woman—and I have always loved flowers for the sake of that lady. I don't know who she was—I never knew—but she was a lady of culture and came to the penitentiary and brought me a bouquet of beautiful flowers. Before she came in I was brooding over my wrongs, a sullen, desperate young man, thinking of nothing so much as revenge upon the men whom I thought were persecuting me without cause. When the fragrance of those flowers filled my cell, it seemed to me that they changed my nature in a moment. my heart was softened, and I set to work and picked a piece of pine apart and made a sort of frame which would hold the bouquet, and set it up, and I looked at it and wondered what had put it into my heart of that lady to bring flowers to me. I felt all malice and hatred go out of my heart at once, and said to myself: "That lady is what they call a 'Christian'." I would sit on my cot for fifteen minutes at a time, with my arms folded, looking at that poor decoration and with my heart full of wonder that this lady whom I did not know, and whom I might never see again, should be kind to a poor prisoner. Perhaps it was my bad fortune, but in my prison life I have never met with any such, and it was a surprise to me that any one would think it worth while to be kind to a prisoner. I thought of my life in the army, of the three years and five months I had served under the Union banner, and it seemed to me almost like decorating a soldier's grave. She made me three or four visits and before

136

they ended I had made up my mind to quit drinking—to be a man. I made no profession of religion then, and did not intend to. I simply made up my mind to do better. I did not even talk to the Chaplain, and that good man did not know what was passing in my mind. I remember that the day I was released a young man was going out, and his mother and sister came to the prison to meet him and take him home. It cut me to the heart to think that I had no kindred to meet me, and I said to the Superintendent Williams: 'There goes a man who has friends to help him along, and I have to go out alone'. But for all that, I was determined to fight the battle by myself, and when they opened the door from the office into the main corridor and I stepped into light and freedom, I felt strong in the hope that I could make a good battle before I gave up the fight.

The Missionary

He started out in his new life with a high resolve. Knowing that to carry out his good resolutions, it must be some other place than Oswego; he set out for Albany. In brief, he was befriended by Rev. Charles Reynolds, Chaplain of the Albany penitentiary, and Super-intendent of the Tract and Mission Society. He and his wife earn-estly wished for Ned to live at their house, even though he insisted that he was "unfit" for the society of people of culture. With training, he learned the knack of speaking readily; and, in one year's time he was albe to talk freely, if not smoothly, before any audience. But these people, if met in their own way and spoken in their own language, were easily accessible. Vice had a language of its own and understood nothing else. Ned felt that he was fitted for missionary work and wanted to go into it. He would say with pride, that no person could be better fitted than he was to face a howling mob; for, he had faced them under circumstances not much to his credit, if for nothing more than having bull-dog courage and being ready to face any danger. On many occasions the toughs stormed the meet-ings; an iron poker in the hands of a husky man, often averted danger of physical harm. A wholesome dread of cold iron often deterred a howling mob. A man needed to be a muscular Christian then; for, he had to fight while preaching meetings were being held.

Thus Ned aided in the establishments of missions in tough locations where gambling dens and houses of prostitution abounded, and the owners did all they could to break them up. He became the assistant superintendent of the "Tract and Mission Society." He also organized "Reform Clubs"—men who had been drunkards. He worked in slums. This type of work required such a man as Ned to go down into the depths of iniquity and speak to the abandoned men, women and children with which they swarmed. He could speak to their hearts, because the story of his life was the story of their lives and the lives of hundreds more whom they knew.

Unfortunately Ned overtaxed his strength and became ill. He was very weak, "near the gates of death", and was not expected to live. He managed to gain strength, and as he grew better he began to think of Oswego. He wanted to go back there to show people that he, Ned Lee, who had been hunted through the streets like a tiger in his native jungle, had made a man of himself.

Ned left Albany May 1, 1876, reaching Oswego that evening. He stayed at the Merchant's Hotel, later known as the Ringland House (southeast corner of East Bridge and Second Streets, replaced in 1904 by the present building), until October 1st. He went to Albany to avoid the severe winter. His health did not improve as rapidly as he hoped, but he was bound to hold meetings.

He arranged to use a building on Water Street, near his old haunts. He rented an organ, organized a Sabbath school at once, and held meetings on Sundays in the Methodist Chapel, on the Orphan Asylum hill (southwest corner of West Fifth and Tallman Streets–314 W. 5th). As expected, he had two or three fights (being way laid once) before things settled down, but determination won the day at last. The first help he got from the ministry was from Rev. Mr. Traver of the East Baptist Church. Chief Joel Baker and the police backed him up well. Unsolicited aid came from several members of the Y. M. C. A.—they paid his board as long as he remained in this city. His work in Oswego may be summed up in the following letter to his good old friend:

Oswego, N. Y., May 22, 1876.
Rev. Charles Reynolds, Albany, N. Y.

DEAR BROTHER—Brother Edward Lee requests me to write to you of his work here in Oswego. He came here two weeks ago to-day, and from the minute of his coming he has been at his work for the Master. To say he has created a sensation is faintly to express the results of his labors. He met me from the very first opposition and persecution, but the Lord has been with him, and his opponents have been covered with shame at their every move. He has held meetings in the Water street Mission rooms several evenings, and they have been crowded, and a large number have signed the pledge. Altogether the happiest results are coming from his Mission among us. He is the very man Oswego needs. Not only the classes to which he is carrying the gospel needed him, but the churches needed him. Religion had put on so much of the Laodician type here in this city that the advent of Brother Lee is like the coming of another Paul, and we have not a few Felix's who say that he is mad (not for his learning) but yet insane. Would that this land had a hundred thousnad men insane after the same way.

We are satisfied that his coming is of God and have no doubt that many will be glad through all eternity that Edward Lee came to Oswego.

Respectfully,
W. F. HEMINGWAY
Pastor of First M. E. Church.

To depict the many conversions under the most trying circumstances would be futile. In his travels one or two incidents would be of interest. From Albany he traveled to Syracuse; he visited communites along the Erie Canal from the east as far as Canastota and to the west as far as Buffalo. He noticed that Baldwinsville and Weedsport were especially troublesome. The bullies and their gangs sat in the front seats, and Ned knew they came to make trouble. An instance at Weedsport was intended to frighten people. Ned received some threatening letters; he was determined to stop that. He borrowed a revolver to be used at the next meeting. After the singing he pulled out his weapon and laid it on the desk and said quietly: "There are a lot of fellows in this town who have been sending skulls and crossbones to the house of Mr. Donovan, where I am stopping. There must be an end to that. I will put some of them in their coffins if it continues." Then he put up the weapon and had a peaceble time at meetings.

139

He then returned to Oswego to carry out another idea, the organization of a "Band of Hope" in Grace Church. Mr. Kingsford gave him the use of the chapel on West Bridge Street, and he got 400 hoodlums together and organized them into a school. He held there three months, and then the gang announced that they were going to come over and "bust" him. A tough he had helped came to him and told him what they were going to do, and he was ready for them. He did not say a word to anybody but got a big poker from the stove and set it up near the pulpit. He opened the bible and gave out his text, and then said: "You have come here to fight, and you have got just the right kind of a preacher to handle you." They kept quiet for a while, and then began to kick on the floor. He spoke to them twice, and the third time he sang out to Will Cole (an aid) to open the door and then he went for the crowd with the poker and banged them in a lively fashion and cleaned out the gang. It was quite a while before they stopped running, and they never made him the least trouble after that. One of the papers had an article headed: *Ned Lee has a Full Hand—The Only Time He Has Played Poker in Years.*

Ned again took to the road. This time he met some audiences that were somewhat queer to him. There he met spiritualists, atheists, skeptics, and other prejudices. From Oneida he traveled the shores of Oneida Lake with success and eventually to Oswego where he spent ten months. Proceeding northward towards Watertown, he toured the northern shore of Lake Ontario through Canada to Cleveland, Ohio. He had a particular object in working that direction; for, he was heading for Oberlin, where he intended to go to college for one year. He felt that he needed polish and to improve his theology. He was persuaded to continue his work for which he was so uniquely fitted because the polish would apt to spoil him. It was perhaps for this reason that he was a rough diamond and had such good success. He returned by way of Buffalo to answer a call to come back to Oswego. A review of his work in the city of his birth is appended to this story. He left the city in answer to call to take part for a time in Mission Work in the city of New York.

The Bowery needs no description—all sorts and conditions of man were to be found there. Every type of evil man congregated on that street. It was a hard and dangerous task; threre was indeed a for Missionary work. There was one class of people whom

140

Missionaries had to avoid—gangs who worked the churches. Frauds were discovered and dealt with; he soon learned how to cope with those numerous tricks. Every quarter of the United States and every portion of the globe was represented. To say he was in personal danger from individuals and mobs should be understood. He had bad experiences; it required nerve to face these gangs but they soon left him alone.

Ned was grieved at being obliged to give up his work in New York for various reasons. His was a peculiar work and it began to wear upon him. He questioned the justice of subjecting his wife and child by remaining in the city. He knew well that it would be a short time when he must give up that arduous work; for, his health was failing. He longed for the bracing breezes which came off the lake, and for the shaded streets of his native town. Thus he returned to the city of his birth where other work, more congenial, was given to him through the kindness of his friends.

Ned was instrumental in forming the for the Prevention of Cruelty to Children, and the twin Society for the Prevention of Cruelty to Animals. He devoted his time to this work; scarcely a day passed when some complaint came of a father neglecting his children. It was sad to state that the mothers were also guilty of the same cause, the love of liquor. A part of his work, and one which he took a deep interest, was his daily visit to the city lock-up. He believed that a prisoner, though perhaps guilty and deserved punishment, was yet a man; he was capable of reformation. He did, however, believe that young men were born evil and were natural criminals. He did admit his time was wasted on them.

[The writer will admit to teaching in a Reformatory in New York State. He also worked with a missionary clergyman in Georgia. Visits were made twice a week at the State penitentiary at Reidsville and Vernon. From the writer's experience, rehabilitation was possible—only if the prisoner desired it. Unfortunately very few inmates possessed that desire. All this work was done without compensation.]

REPORT OF NED LEE IN THE CITY OF OSWEGO

From December 1, 1886 to September 25, 1887:

Held 41 meetings in jail; 17 professed religion; 78 signed the pledge; 2,500 papers distributed to jail prisoners; helped 23 persons to employment.

Held 18 meetings in City Mission; 28 professed conversions; 125 at different times signed the pledge; 45 had lodgings and breakfast, five of them women; 1,327 cups of coffee given away; 178 children given ice cream and cake in one evening; received $23.78 for charitable purposes and distributed the same; helped 13 families to provisions; gave away *Harper's Weekly* and *Magazine* and religious papers and tracts to the number of 4,323; helped 11 persons out of town; gave 23 children toys, etc., given to him by the West Baptist Sunday School children; opened the Mission every evening from 7 to 9 o'clock; had 11 meetings in the country, driving out and back; daily visits to Police Station No. 1, except when sick; 227 pieces of clothing received and given away; supplied firemen at Oulds & Klock's fire with coffee and cakes, the latter supplied by Mrs. J. C. Churchill.

Testimonial Letters

COMMITTEE ROOM OF THE OSWEGO COUNTY COMMITTEE OF THE N.Y. CHARITY AND AID ASSOCIATION

Oswego, Sept. 22, '87.

Mr. Edward Lee.

DEAR SIR: I have the pleasure of transmitting to you the resolution adopted by our Committee at its meeting held Sept. 21, 1887, and beg to assure you that the Committee fully appreciating the value of your work among us, earnestly hopes and believes that you will be successful in your new field of labor.

Respectfully your obed't servant,
Geo. C. McWhorter, President.

Resolved: That we have learned with much regret that Mr. Edward Lee has determined to remove to New York to engage in work similar to what he has been employed in Oswego; that, in view of Mr. Lee's approaching departure, we record with sincere pleasure our appreciation of the capacity, zeal, industry and devotion displayed as City Missionary, and as a member of this Committee; and that in his new work we bid him God speed, and invoke in his behalf that grace which is an ever ready help in time of need.

MAYOR'S OFFICE, OSWEGO,
Oct. 10, '82

FROM MAYOR MORRISON

To Whom It May Concern.

The bearer hereof, Edward Lee, is well known to me as a christian gentleman, and in every way worthy of confidence and respect.

Clark Morrison, Mayor

GRACE CHURCH:

We, the minister, the officers, the members of Grace church, Oswego, together with all who are accustomed to worship here, or are worshipping with us at this farewell service, desire to record our regret that so good a man, so efficient a worker, so true a friend, is about to leave us.

We feel bound to concur in Mr. Lee's decision, because we believe his marching orders are from the Captain of this salvation.

We would testify our cordial appreciation of what Mr. Lee has done, the work he has done and in many ways, and the spirit of it all during the nine years of his residence here.

We claim to know the man. And we unhesitatingly endorse him as a thoroughly consecrated person.

We commend him to the ready confidence and christian sympathy of all those among whom he may live and labor.

We bid him good-bye with a hearty God-speed.

And this we pray: That his love may abound yet more in knowledge and in all judgment; that he may approve things that are excellent; that he may be sincere and without offense till the day of Christ; being filled with the fruits of righteousness which are by Jesus Christ unto the glory and praise of God.

Henry H. Stebbins
Minister of Grace Church for himself and all concerned.
Sunday evening, Sept. 25, 1887.

The following was handed to him on his departure:

OFFICE OF CITY CHAMBERLAIN, OSWEGO

I am pleased to recommend the bearer, Edward Lee, to any community to which he may go. During nine years we have daily seen evidence of his work.

Charles North, Mayor.
N. W. Nutting, Congressman.
B. Doolittle, Police Commissioner.
James Doyle, Chief of Police.
M. P. Neal, Ex-Mayor and Merchant.
A. H. Failing, Ex-Mayor and Merachant.
W. D. Smith, Commissioner of Works.
D. M. Irwin, Commission Merchant.
Elisha B. Powell, City Attorney.
James Gibbs, Police Commissioner.
A. N. Beadle, Sheriff.
C. N. Bulger, Recorder.
E. J. Hamilton, Sec'y Board of Education.
D. H. Judson, Ex- Mayor and Merchant.
Cyrus Whitney, Ex-County Judge.
John T. Mott, Pres. First Nat'l Bank.
James Sloan, Oswego Shade Cloth Co.
Swits Conde, Manufacturer.
S. B. Johnson, Com. Merchant and Miller.
O. F. Gaylord, Com. Merchant.
Theo. Irwin, Jr., Com. Merchant.
John A. Barry, Editor.
W. A. Richardson, Cap't of Police.
W. A. Poucher, Ex-Assemblyman.
R. J. Oliphant, Printer and Bookbinder.
T. P. Kingsford, Oswego Starch Factory.
D. C. Littlejohn, Ex-Member of Congress.
Gilbert Mollison, Local Normal (School) Board.
James Dowdle, Ex-Mayor.
Edwin Allen, Ex-Mayor and Lawyer.
Jules Wendell & Sons, Jewelers.
I. B. Poucher, Collector of Customs.
N. M. Rowe, Deputy Collector of Customs.

W. H. Corregan, Merchant.
E. A. Sheldon, Principal of Normal School.
P. W. Cullinan, Ex-Assemblyman.
Clark Morrison, Ex-Mayor.
M. L. Wright, County Judge.

The following Ned Lee treasured as one of his jewels:

Oswego, N. Y., April 22, 1887.

I have the pleasure in writing this letter because it relates to a gentleman who has my earnest respect and admiration. That gentleman is Mr. Edward Lee, for several years a resident of this city, and for the past nine years the incumbent of the office known as City Missionary.

Mr. Lee is a notable example of what a man may do himself in the intellectual and social scale if he has the desire and the will to do. From the most unpropitious conditions in early life Mr. Lee has speedily builded up a good name until that name has come to stand for a reputation most creditable and not a little remarkable.

As a result of this Mr. Lee can count troops of friends in this community who thoroughly believe in him and confide in him. They know him to be worthy of their best support and confidence, because they know of his usefulness in conserving the morality of this city and the cause of religion he preaches and consistently practices. Universal regret is therefore felt at his departure, but since it is known that he goes to a wider field there is general concurrence in the wisdom of his going. It is perhaps superfluous to add that Mr. Lee carries with him the benedictions of all who know him, and most surely he deserves them all, and more.

Geo. B. Sloan.

To whom it may concern.

[George B. Sloan was a powerful figure in the State Senate, and a wealthy grain merchant. His home, still standing, is located at the corner of West Schuyler and Eight Streets.]

Just before he took the train to New York, Mr. Neil Gray (Oswego Shade Cloth Co. Home on West Fifth and Bridge Streets, now the Elks Building) met him on the street and asked him to step into Corregan's store a moment. There he met Mr. Charles H.

145

Bond, who thrust a big envelope into his hand, and got away before he had time to understand what had happened. It contained $75 and the following:

We believe it our duty, as it is our pleasure, to bear witness to the efficient, fearless and untiring manner in which Mr. Edward Lee has performed his duties as City Missionary in this city. We believe the amount of good he has done cannot be properly estimated. We regret that circumstances cause him to leave us. He carries with him our best wishes for his success in his new field of labor, and for his prosperity. As evidence we mean what we say, we bet he will accept the accompanying amount, which we take pleasure in subscribing.

Signed:

Neil Gray,	C. H. Bond,
James Sloan,	Gard. T. Lyon,
Swits Conde,	T. W. Walpole,
D. P. Fairchild,	John Stoddard,
J. B. McMurrich,	C. C. Buel,
A. Cooper,	Charles Ott,
D. C. Loomis,	E. Monen.
E. A Van Horne,	

There were several more accounts of the beneficences of his good friends in Oswego, but these mentioned will do.

The Oswego County Jail

Stone walls do not a prison make,
Nor iron bars a cage.

Richard Lovelace.

Ever since Oswego County was formed in 1816 it had the distinction of having two county court houses, one in Pulaski and the other in Oswego. A law was passed on March 12, 1818, authorizing the levying of $1,500 in taxes to be used to construct a court house in Pulaski. The court house was built on Bridge Street on land donated by Benjamin Wright, the cornerstone being laid in 1819, with additions made in 1858 and 1887. In those days there was a jail in the basement of the building. A deputy sheriff for many years continued to live in the annex at the rear and meals for prisoners were cooked on a woodburning stove in the cellar. Later the jail was moved to Oswego and the old Pulaski "lock up" was only used occasionally.

The Court House in Oswego was begun in 1818 but the building was not completed until 1822. Lacking funds in 1822 to permit the completion of the Court House, previously started, the Board of Supervisors had to petition the state legislature in that year for authorization to raise additional funds to complete the structure. In the clerk's record book of the Town of Oswego there is recorded a petition from the freeholders and inhabitants dated March 6, 1821, to the New York State Senate and Assembly remonstrating against a law authorizing the Supervisors of Oswego County to levy a tax for the purpose of completing the court house building in East Oswego. It was reasoned in the petition that the building should be in West Oswego because of convenience, the distance, the river and the county clerk's office was already in Scriba. The legislature did not heed the petition of the Oswegonians; for, it passed an act (Chap. 81, laws of 1823) authorizing the County to raise money for the sale of lands granted by the State for the purpose of completing the court house. The act provided the sum of $750. The court house was completed in 1822.

The first court house, located in East Park, was a modern structure of modest dimensions which soon proved inadequate for the growing needs of the courts. In the basement of the Court

House was the county's first jail. In 1838 the Board of Supervisors rented cells in the Market building (the Village City Hall) on Water Street. A description of the "Black Hole," taken from the local press follows:

In describing the status of the City Hall in the 1850's, the north end of the basement had been fitted up in a cheap manner for the purpose of lodging persons who made application to the Police, and also to secure in a comfortable way, such vagrants and others as may be found in the streets at unreasonable hours, without having any place of abode. The room next south was leased for storage. The next room was used by the Police as the "Lock Up," or known as the "Black Hole." The next two rooms were also leased for storage purposes.

In the jail of Oswego are three cells for males, and one for females. Each cell occupies a space of about eight feet, running back about twenty feet. They are located in the basement of the City Hall—damp—unwholesome and filthy, with no ventilation or light except what is admitted through the gratings of the cell doors. The cells are all open into a hall or area, of about ten by twenty-four feet. Here the prisoners are detained under sentence, prisoners detained for trial, prisoners detained on civil process, and those detained as witnesses all occupy apartments in common.

Adjoining the cells for males, is one for females of the same dimensions and only separated by a board or plank partition, where they have constant communication with the male prisoners.

This "Black Hole" is justly a subject of public reproach, that an aprtment so miserably mean and unhealthy is the present Jail, should be permitted to be used for the temporary lodgement of citizens destined simply on charges what Humanity. The Law is designed to protect Society from depredations, punish and reform offenders against it—not to endanger their health and destroy the constitutions of those answering the penalties it inflicts, and finally set them at liberty a prey to disease and a charge upon our public institutions of charity.

An outrage more aggravating in its character and shocking to the feelings is to be found in the practice of confining persons detained as witnesses in criminal cases, in the same unhealthy, dismal and revolting burlesque on a County Jail. It is enough to mantle the cheek of every citizen with shame, to know that in this enlightened age of progress and improvement, when the condition of the

148

unfortunate, the degraded, the abandoned are every where receiving the sympathy and aid of the benevolent in their effort to better their condition -that here in the enterprising city of Oswego, the old "Black Hole of Calcutta" should be completely eclipsed and thrown into the shade!

With the above public outcry against the treatment of prisoners, the County decided to build its own jail. In 1848 the new jail was located in East Park; at the same time abandoning the Court House. The Board of Education then rented the court house building to house Junior School No. 5 and Senior School No. 3. When the Fourth Ward School was completed (East Fourth Street between Cayuga and Seneca Streets) in 1857 this use was discontinued. It was then moved in 1859, with the consent of the Board of Supervisors, from the site of the present court house to a lot across the street owned by the Church of the Evangelist and became a part of the church property.

Almost forgotten, in the history of Oswego County, was a movement to divide the county. This movement was started in 1841 by leading business and professional men of Oswego. While the argument lasted, it created much ado, but terminated, as such agitations many times do, in much ado about nothing. The county remained with two county seats and two county court houses but most of the county buildings and county clerk's office are in Oswego. Mexico has today, however, the offices of the County Social Services (formerly Welfare) department, County Extension Service, and while it existed, the County Home (Poorhouse). The City of Oswego constructed and presented to the County a Clerk's Office which had cost $2,000 (and received special permission to raise the money from the State Legislature). In 1853 a county jail, (45 X 75 feet, two stories) was constructed on the southeast corner of East Second and Schuyler Streets.

One of the most destructive fires that ever took place in the city of Oswego broke out about half past ten o'clock in the morning of July 5, 1853. The section of the town consumed was bounded on the west by the river, on the south by Bridge Street, east by Sixth Street, on the north by Fort Ontario grounds. The heat across the river, a distance of 700 feet was so great that it was feared the opposite side would catch fire, but the wind blowing strong in the oppostie direction prevented it. Several minor incidents kept citizens in a state of uneasiness, one of which involved the jail.

149

The jail, a stone building, came very near set ablaze. A cinder flew into the window and set some straw on fire and it spread with great rapidity in the rooms. The prisoners were liberated and took hold with energy and saved the building. The jail was replaced after it was used thirty-five years.

In 1888 a new county jail was built at a cost of $30,000. It was built upon a unique principle which proved to be such a bane of existence to many Oswego County Sheriff and his staff, that finally the jail had to be abandoned in 1909. A new one was constructed to put an end to the series of "incidents" which the peculiar cell arrangements of the jail invited. It was equipped with a turntable upon which were supported all the cells of the jail. When the sheriff wished to gain access to a particular cell, he touched a button and the table would turn in response until the cell he wished to enter swung opposite the door of the sheriff's office and there it would stop until the sheriff had entered and transacted his business. After he lodged his prisoner in the cell, if that was his purpose, he would cause the turntable to function once more until the next cell to which he desired to gain access came up opposite the landing door. But there were times when the mechanism would "strike" and fail to function. These times were hard on both sheriff and prisoners until the cause of the trouble could be located and repairs made. There was no way of getting food into the cells, or men in and out when the turntable was on "strike" several days at a time. As a result of a series of such incidents, it was finally determined that the county would have to have a new jail. This resulted in 1909 after the State Prison Commission had condemned the jail for further use. The present jail was erected on the East River Road just inside the city limits of Oswego at the cost of $85,000. The old jail was purchased from the county by the Ames Iron Works for $10,000.

On January 27, 1975, the Oswego County Sheriff's Department officially began operations from its new offices adjacent to the Oswego County Jail on Route 57. Sheriff Ray T. Chesbro had announced the opening of the new facility and at the same time closing the offices of the Sheriff's Department in the County Court House. "We have centralized all the operations in the new, modern and fully equipped building," said Chesbro concerning the recently completed structure. The Sheriff elaborated, "We will now have ample office space to carry out the many functions of the department under one roof, along with a fully equipped garage for making repairs to our own vehicles."

The one-story, sand-colored brick building was begun in the spring of 1974 with the plans for the building having been formulated by architect Allen Kosoff of Syracuse in late 1973. Construction of the newest county building was under the direction of the Reddick Construction Co. of Gouveneur.

151

Oswego Harbor circa 1850

The Civil War

I would like to see truthful history written. Such history will do full credit to the courage, endurance and soldierly ability of the American citizen, no matter what section of the country he hailed from, or in what ranks he fought.

General U. S. Grant.

The Draft

At first both North and South relied on volunteers to fill the ranks of their armies, but before long both resorted to conscription. The confederacy, with less than a third the manpower of the North, started drafting men in April 1862. In March 1863, the United States Congress passed a Conscription Act that provided for an incomplete and unfair use of the draft. A draftee was permitted to avoid military service by paying $300 or by hiring a substitute. Naturally, those without money to buy their way out resented this arrangement, which made it "a rich man's war and a poor man's fight." Opposition to conscription caused the terrible draft riots in New York City in July 1863. For four days, mobs of men and boys terrorized the city, killing and plundering.

Besides the draft, the North also used a system whereby enlistees were paid a lump sum when they joined the army. Bounties offered by federal, state, and municipal governments sometimes totaled $1,500 for a single three-year enlistment. This led to the practice of "bounty jumping", whereby a man would enlist, collect his bounty, and then desert only to re-enlist elsewhere. Nevertheless, bounties proved an effective means of luring volunteers from northern farms and factories and even from Europe.

The Draft In Oswego

The draft in Oswego began on August 5, 1863, at 2 o'clock P. M. At 1:30 o'clock the crowd began to assemble which soon increased in proportions, thronging the street in front of the Grant

153

Block, in which Provost Marshal Scorr had his office. The Grant Block (a block then referred to a building) was located on the south side of West Bridge Street between First and Water Streets.

At half-past one o'clock a detachment of the Invalid Corps (stationed at Fort Ontario), numbering 37 men, under the command of First Sergeant George H. Hawley, marched up the stairs and took their positions in the main hall, adjoining the Provost Marshal's office. The Enrollment Board consisted of Addison L. Scott, Oswego, Provost Marshal, James B. Murdock, Oswego, Surgeon, and Daniel Q. Mitchell, DeRuyter, Madison County, Commissioner.

Mr. John D. Taylor, a man well known in the city, a resident of the Fourth Ward (at this time there were only four wards), was selected to draw the names from the wheel. Mr. Taylor was entirely blind, and hence there could be no suspicion of unfairness in the matter of the drawing.

At 2 o'clock the Marshal's office was filled with men, among them representatives of all parties, including several prominent Democrats (those Democrats who opposed the war were called "Copperheads"), and also quite a large number of foreign-born citizens. All these gentlemen had the opportunity of witnessing the drawing, and it was believed that all concurred that the drawing was conducted with perfect fairness. Seated at the table where the drawing took place were Bartholomew Lynch, Captain John D. O'Brien, Dr. Robert Scott, James Bickford, Senator, Joseph Owen, William Randall Avery, of Madison County, C. C. Petty, John Andrews, L. Garson, Captain Dykeman and Captain Morris, U. S. A., Michael Hennessy, H. C. Benedict, Major Townsend, Chief of Police Hawkins, Collector Perkins, Deputy Provost Marshal Scorr, and the clerks of the Marshal. At five minutes past two the wheel was placed in position by the Provost Marshal, which was the signal for considerable agitation among the crowd. The Provost Marshal then proceeded to read the order for the draft in this district for 2,068 men, and fifty percent in addition, from Abraham Lincoln, President of the United States. The fifty per cent in addition made the whole number to be drawn 3,102. For the First District (First and Third Wards; that is, the West Side) the number was 310; for the Second District, (Second Ward) 117; for the Third District, (Fourth Ward) 89. One thousand thirty-seven names on slips of pasteboard, being the names enrolled in the First District, were then

154

placed in the wheel, from which 310 were to be drawn. The blind man was then blindfolded, according to law, and took his position. The wheel revolved and the drawing commenced. The drawing recommenced the following morning at 8 o'clock until it was concluded. The local press took notice that not a single incident had occurred that day to mar the general good feeling which characterized the proceedings. The press offices were crowded the following day by persons from the surrounding towns, anxious to ascertain whether they had drew a prize in the National lottery. Not a single remark expressive of dissatisfaction from any one who discovered he had suddenly been converted into a soldier was heard. The names of the men drafted were recorded in the press.

Incidents of The Draft

Many incidents occurred during the draft for the city, which served to keep the good humor of the multitude assembled around the office of the Provost Marshal:

The name of John Fitzgerald, the enrolling officer for the first district, was received with loud cheers, as also were the names of Parker Wright and Theodore W. Brown, one of whom had lost an arm and the other a leg in the service of their country.

The name of Julius Biggsbee was drawn in the 11th district. As the person who bore that name had died since the enrollment was made, the chances of the fifty per cent surplus was decreased by one.

William H. Gardner, Warren D. Gardner and Washington A. Gardner, brothers and partners in business were drawn.

The Senate Chamber was represented in the person of Hon. Richard K. Sanford, of the town of Volney.

All trades and professions were represented in the city. The name of William Tiffany, lawyer, was received with prodigious shouting and cheering; two more names were furnished from that profession. The medical profession furnished two persons of S.F. Whited, and F. W. Potter.

The Mechanics Sax Horn Band came in for its full share, five out of thirteen of its members received a "ticket."

155

Editorials

The draft progressed quietly. The proceedings had been marked with perfect order, and no riotous demonstration of any kind occurred. The suppression of the mob in New York, where if anywhere a mob can be successful, has demonstrated that in this country there will be no resistance to the law, provided the authorities use ordinary diligence in preparing to vindicate them. In Oswego there were some men whose passions had been inflamed by the appeals of political demogogues, who might have created a disturbance had there been any chance of success. But the Provost Marshal had prepared for any emergency, and hence the public peace had been preserved, and life and property had been saved. It was thought it may be assumed that all danger of a riot in our city was at an end.

Another editorial under the heading "The Draft—Its Justice And Necessity" expressed the feeling and temper of the time. The following clear and proper statement of the nature and necessities of the draft, and of the action of the Government concerning it, it was asked:

Is the draft illegal? It has been ordered by an act of Congress, and is demanded by the exigencies of the hour. Is it oppressive? Every provision that humanity or justice can suggest has been made. The widow can retain her boy—the father is permitted to provide for his children—the sole male may remain at home. Has it been enforced in a secret or oppressive manner? We all know the contrary. Has it been resorted to needlessly or in wanton, reckless spirit? *We know that the Administration has omitted and postponed and hesitated and done everything to avoid the draft.* We know that citizens have contributed munificently to fill our regiments to the full quota. Indeed, if any censure is to be made, we think it should fall upon the Administration itself, for having been too lenient and kind in its dealing with the people in this matter of the conscription.

Conscription at this time was not an innovation. A letter to the editor, signed by An Old Democrat, revealed a previous instance where the draft was ordered. Among other things the letter said:

156

Mr. Madison, our Democratic President. with a Democratic Congress, declared war against England in 1812. The patriotic Tompkins was then the Democratic Governor of New York. In compliance with a requirement of the General Government, he ordered a draft from the militia of the State. It was then known to be a Democratic measure, and was considered by the Government necessary for carrying on the war in which it was engaged. I was at that time an enrolled militiaman in a regiment in Saratoga county, commanded by Colonel Gates. We were all warned to meet by companies to make the draft. I attended with the rest, and the draft was made. No one thought of resisting it any more than he would to resist the collector when he called for his annual tax. It was my fortune to draw a blank, while others had a prize of six months' soldiers's life. Some of them hired substitutes. From $30 to $50 was the usual sum paid. A neighbor of mine went for $40. No one would have considered it a privilege to have been exempt for $300, because they could get a substitute for so much less. The drafted men were organized into regiments and sent to Sacket's Harbor. The next year Governor Tompkins ordered out the main body of the militia in Saratoga county, and they went to New York and were encamped on Brooklyn Heights about six months.

Was this Democratic usurpation? It was under a Democratic Governor and Government, and was submitted to and approved by every good citizen, including many who bore the name Federalists. But we of that day well remember the excitement which a company of "blue lights" in New England created; but that soon passed away, effecting little but to leave a lasting stigma upon their political character.

I mention these things that some of my young Democratic friends may see from whence they are fallen, and not by future conduct disgrace themselves, and prove themselves unworthy of their political ancestry.

The Jollification of the Conscripts

That evening the conscripts drawn in the city of Oswego formed a procession under the lead of W. I. Preston, one of their number and had a regular jollification. The Mechanics Sax Horn Band headed the motley crowd, and all seemed to enjoy the sport immensely. The jokes were numerous and the fun decidedly exciting. After marching through several of the principal streets, the conscripts halted in front of the Provost Marshal's office, where they called for speeches. Hon. Henry Fitzhugh, Colonel S. R. Beardsley, and W. I. Preston made stirring and patriotic addresses, which were loudly applauded. There were cheers for the Union, for the President, for the draft, for the army, and divers other things.

All the speeches were practical and effective. That of Mr. Preston, one of the conscripts, was exceedingly patriotic and loyal, advocating a cheerful obedience to the laws of the land by all classes of citizens, and urging the paramount duty of putting down the rebellion in order to secure our liberties.

The conscripts were furnished with roman candles, and there was a prodigal display of fire works which added to the general enthusiasm. The fun was kept up till a late hour, and everybody went to bed apparently in good humor.

So ended the draft in Oswego County.

Skedaddlers

It was reported that one day from one hundred to one hundred and fifty persons were prevented from escaping to Canada at Suspension Bridge (Niagara Falls), to avoid the draft. The United States officers at that place refused passage across the lines to all persons who were supposed to be escaping from this country to avoid the conscription. They obtained a miserable greeting from the Canadians. The *St. Catherines Journal* spoke of the draft dodgers in this manner:

The skedaddlers are being greatly increased in number. As fast as possible these gents of nimble-heels but feeble courage are leaving Uncle Sam's territories and coming over to Canada. The Canadian mechanics and working men, who have taxes for years, and who are, always have been, and always will be, loyal to their government and country, are beginning to feel the efforts of the large influx of these emulators of Bob Acres, for they agree to work for small wages, are employed of course, and thus throw out of employment for at least a portion of their time, are own 'good men and true'. A large number of our mechanics, sooner than go idle, have provided themselves with certificates that they are British subjects, and have gone over to Yankee land, to supply the places of these skedaddlers. We don't think much of the trade, but suppose it must be endured. Those who employ the skedaddlers will have a serious account to settle with their consciences 'when this cruel war is over' and the last act of life is about being performed. They actually encourage cowardice, one of the meanest and lowest and most useless elements of human character. There is an old fellow 'down below' who can, and no doubt will, take charge of all skedaddlers; and that thought causes many brave men to sleep easy.

WHAT OSWEGO COUNTY DID IN THE WAR

Address by H. H. Lyman, late Adjutant 147th N.Y. Volunteers, at Oswego County Veterans' Reunion At Pulaski, N. Y., August 24, 1895.

    I have been requested by your Committee to make a brief statement as to what Oswego County did for the Union Cause, as a sort of introduction to the more interesting exercises.

    To many, this may seem unnecessary and perhaps a tedious part of the program, but it must be remembered that a full generation has elapsed since those terrible times, and that more than one-half of the people to-day only know of the War of the Rebellion by hear-say, tradition and history.

    I see in this little gathering, people who were not born when their fathers enlisted, and yet today they are here with their children, some of whom are almost men and women, to do honor to the old veterans, who have now mostly reached that point in life where age, if anything else, should command veneration and respect. Other things being equal, all prefer to hear a matter discussed by those who have had experience, and personal knowledge of their subject. This is especially true of the old soldier, who takes but little pleasure in hearing the scenes of war discussed by those who do not know a ramrod from a lanyard.

In this respect, we are particularly fortunate to-day in having with us two veteran soldiers, both of whom are not only able and eloquent orators, but also comrades of our own local regiments, who will talk to us as friends and brothers having a common experience, and from whose patriotic lips many of us have before, and oten, heard the grand old story of freedom, union and loyalty,—men who in our country's darkest days, with us risked their lives to uphold its flag and its principles, and who since the war have stood with us shoulder to shoulder up on the solid ground of fraternity, loyalty and charity, always ready and willing to defend the weakest, and honor and assist the poorest and most humble comrade of the Grand Army.

The population of Oswego County at the outbreak of the Rebellion was 75,600.

It was excelled by no county in the State, in promptly and fully responding to its country's calls, and is credited with having furnished 12,500 men for the War, as shown by the records of our War Committee. Many of these, however, were re-enlistments of men who had served in short term regiments; and some even, who deserted, repented of their foolish action, and again entered the service.

As to the exact number of individual men furnished, I am unable to state, but in round numbers, not far from 11,000, or fifteen percent of its whole population, and seventy five percent of its voting population.

These figures will seem almost incredible, until you know that nearly as many enlisted who were under the voting age as those who were over,—the average being about twenty-three years.

We had five regiments of infantry and two batteries of artillery, composed mostly, and some of them entirely, of Oswego County men, namely, the 24th, 81st, 110th, 147th and 184th Infantry and

160

Ames' Battery and Barnes' Battery. The 24th Cavalry was also called an Oswego Regiment, but actually had but three Oswego Companies, and they were largely re-enlistments from the old 24th Infantry.

We furnished a battalion each for the 12th Cavalry and the 189th and 193rd Infantry. We sent 300 men into the 1st Artillery and 241 into the United States Regulars, and being a lake country, with at that time a large sailor population, sent hundreds into the navy, besides many to the Engineers and other branches of the service.

I have given considerable time and study to this matter and have traced out and looked up 80 separate organizations, in the field rather than to form new ones.

Many of our men served four years and some even five, and upon adjustment and final settlement, it was found that Oswego County had furnished in excess of her quota, when reduced to years of service, an equivalent of 5,000 years of service.

The law gave us re-payment for this at the rate of $300 per year or a total draw-back or refund due from the State in cash of $1,500,000; but the State disputed and repudiated its liability for excess of men and service furnished after July, 1864, and finally compromised by paying into our County Treasury $552,700, for this excess of 5,000 years service.

After furnishing the full quota of men required by the government and State, and doing their whole duty in the field and on the sea, they actually earned for our Country a million and a half of dollars, in what might be called as over-time, over half a million of which was actually accured to its treasury, and it was not the soldiers' fault that the balance earned was lost to the County.

So much for the raising of Oswego County men for the struggle: Let us now briefly glance at what they did.

Oswego County was present, and helped open, the great struggle for the Union; and her "Old 24th Regiment," that stalwart contingent of the "Iron Brigade," covered itself and its native county with glory through all the early campaigns of Pope, McCleean, Burnside, and Hooker from Bailey's Cross Roads, through Sulphur Springs, Bull Run, South Mountain, Antietam, Fredericksburg, and Chancellorsville; making for itself and us a record which will grow brighter and more glorious so long as mankind read history.

161

Oswego County was at the seige of Yorktown, and through all the weary marches and bloody batteles of McClellan's Peninsular Campaign. Under Grant, it lead the charge at Cold Harbor, where Oswego men of the gallant 81st went down before rebel masked batteries and double lines of intrenched infantry like grass before the Mower's scythe.

The remnants of this brave regiment, after a full score of desperate battles, was the first to enter conquered Richmond; and Oswego County boys were the first to raise and unfurl the old flag over that spiteful and rebellious Capitol City, for the possession of which so many thousand of lives had been sacrificed.

Oswego was there when the grand and final assault was made up on Port Hudson, that strong fortress which had so long successfully blocked the Mississippi against the Union Armies. She not only gave Banks and Farragut efficient aid in opening this great water-way, but for a long time did important and valuable service in the lower Mississippi Country.

Day after day, and month after month, her brave sons faced dangers more terrible than batteries, and more deadly than bullets; campaigning in a hot, malarious climate, to which they were unused; scouting and skirmishing through miasmatic bayous, swamps and low lands; doing coast and guard duty in the fever stricken districts of Florida and the Gulf, with men sinking down to their death daily, helpless and hopeless; conditions which could only be faced, a strain which could only be endured, without demoralization, by men of the mental, physical and moral stamina of Oswego's 110th Regiment.

July 1st, 1863, Oswego was represented and made glorious at Gettysburg, where partly on the lands of freedom's great champion, Thaddeus Stevens, she opened the great and decisive battle which marked the turn of the tide in America's great war for human liberty.

Here 380 Oswego County boys desperately battled with a whole rebel brigade, with no immediate support for thirty minutes, stubbornly holding their ground although flanked and nearly surrounded and tenaciously holding the position assigned them, until ordered to retreat.

At a cost of 72 killed and 144 seriously wounded, in that brief course of time, they had delayed and broken Lee's advance division, broke up and rendered possible the capture of a large portion of

"The Boys Have Gone to Gettysburg."

The boys have gone to Gettysburg, the boys of sixty-three,
  With hoary heads and grizzled beards, and hearts that keep
    aglow,
Again they've gone to Gettysburg, historic sights to see,
  Made glorious and immortal just forty years ago.
When life was in its rampant prime, and when the country called
  For volunteers to save the flag, they nobly marched away,
Then death they faced in every shape with bosoms unappalled,
  And that is why these young old men are honored here today.

The boys have gone to Gettysburg, the few who yet survive,
  The halt and lame, with crutch and cane, and empty pants and
    sleeve;
They've gone to view those olden sights, those heroes yet alive,
  And thankful to the Power above who gave them such
    reprieve;
They've hobbled off the sights to mark where hell's artillery played,
  Where blood in crimson rivers ran from slaughtered friend and
    foe,
Where breast to breast in deadly strife, with bosoms undismayed,
  They won the field and cheered the flag just forty years ago.

They'll soon return from Gettysburg; they'll tell of Round Top's
  sights,
  Where Nature hides the boody clay with verdure from her
    breast;
Culp's Hill no longer shows the scars of great heroic fights,
  But stands in silent grandeur still above the braves at rest.
And soon Oswego's little band, that yet of life can boast,
  Will join the ghostly army for review with freind and
    foe;
They'll be assigned the honored place amid the deathless host,
  Front rank, right flank, like where they fought just forty years
    ago.

From: *Random Rhymes and Rhapsodies of the Rail* by Shandy Maguire. Cleveland, Ohio: Cleveland Printing Co., Imperial Press, 1907.

two rebel brigades, and, what is of greater importance, gained valuable time, which secured to Mead the advantadeous field of Gettysburg upon which to fight the greatest battle of the war.

On this identical spot, the people of the State of New York, in grateful remembrance "of what they did there," have erected a noble granite shaft, which not only recites the facts above stated, but bears in large letters across its tablet, the legend "147th N. Y. Vols. Oswego County, N. Y."

The handful of its survivors did not rest upon their Gettyburg laurels, but recruited and reinforced, followed the blood red moon,—that famous standard of Wadsworth, of Doubleday, of Reynolds, of Newton and of Warren,—by day and by night, wherever it lead, from Gettysburg to Appomattox.

Again we find Oswego at Harrison's landing and Bermuda Hundred during the eventful seige of Petersburg; and in the Shennadoah Valley at Fisher's Hill, and the famous battle of Cedar Creek, where our boys of the 184th were not like their glorious commander, Phil Sheridan "Twenty miles away," but on the front line, where they helped to turn back the strong tide of battle upon which Early was riding up this historic Valley, winning much praise for their cool bravery and soldierly conduct although this was their first engagement.

Our County was not only in the very first campaigns and battles of the War, but was nobly represented in Grant's closing campaign from Petersburg to Appomattox, and the famous AppleTree.

The 24th Cavalry, mostly old re-enlisted veterans, took the field with Grant in the Spring of '64. During their one year's service they were in 35 skirmishes and battles, and wound up their eventful service by opening the last day's work of the Army of the Potomac at Appomattox.

They were on the skirmish line engaged with the rebel cavalry when orders were received to "cease firing". The white flag was advanced, and the shattered fragments of what was once Lee's proud and victorious army laid down their arms, while cheer upon cheer, that fairly raised the roof of the heavens, rolled up and down the Union lines.

In the brief time allowed me, I cannot follow details. There were over 2,000 battles fought for the Union, and in most of these were to be found some of Oswego's 11,000 soldier or sailor heroes.

Here men were present at the crucial test between the little *Monitor* and her powerful adversaries, the result of which revolutionized naval warfare. She had a representative on the *Kearsarge,* when she sent the piratical *Alabama* to the bottom of the sea; and a brave officer from the little village of Pulaski was with *Farragut* when he ran the batteries below New Orleans, and, as it were, tore open the mouth of the sluggish and sullen old Misissippi, and once for all cured her of her rebel lockjaw.

No words of mine can do justice to the patriotism and loyalty of our Oswego County people during those dark days; neither is the credit and praise all due to those who enlisted. Our people as a body were enthusiastically patriotic and loyal from the start.

Our women were especially noted for their hearty support of the cause and their liberal contributions and zealous work for the relief of the sick and wounded.

I could speak at length of the many kind acts and brave deeds of Oswego's noble and patriotic army nurse, Mrs. R. H. Spencer, who went with my own regiment, and who, for faithful and efficient service, was soon promoted to a wider field of usefulness, as New York State Agent, and later as United States Agent, for the relief of sick and wounded soldiers. "May God bless and comfort her in her old age," is the prayer of thousands of veterans who received kindness and relief at her hands in the days of their sickness and distress.

The many deeds of patriotism and acts of loyalty and devotion to the Union cause of numerous religious and civic bodies and citizens of our County generally, is a matter of record which will always be referred to with pride by Oswegonions.

Our Country was not saved by its men in arms, but by the unselfish patriotism of its whole people, who stood solidly behind its soldiers at the front, always ready to furnish needed means and material or, if required, to fill the depleted ranks, caused by the waste and ravages of war. In this, Oswego County was a marked example of zealous devotion. The results of their patriotic efforts and the part taken by the men representing them at the front, I have truthfully stated in the figures and facts already presented.

Oswego County, in the war, had reason to be proud of her veterans, and her veterans had equal reason to be proud of Oswego County.

Battle Hymn Of The Republic

Mine eyes have seen the glory of the coming
    of the Lord;
He is trampling out the vintage where the
    grapes of wrath are stored;
He has loosed the fateful lightning of his
    terrible swift sword;
His truth is marching on.

Julia Ward Howe.

Elmina P. Spencer
1819—1912

ELMINA P. SPENCER
Civil War Nurse

Elmina P. Spencer was born in the town of Mexico September 18, 1819. She first saw the light of day in a log cabin built from logs hewn in the virgin forest by her father, Darius Dunham Keeler, and a little party of French Canadians who had accompanied him into that region. Her mother was Aretha Powers, a native of Vermont. In this log cabin home, with its primitive surroundings, Mrs. Spencer spent the first six years of her life, and then with her parents who removed to Oswego.

From the age of six until ten, Mrs. Spencer attended the little public school on Seneca Street. After a time the elder Keeler went up the river, where Minetto stands, and operated a sawmill, the family going with him and making their home at that place.

In 1829 when she was ten years old she joined the Sunday School of the First Methodist Church here. This church was in the southwest corner of Franklin Square (West Park) and faced Cayuga Street. Methodists those days were thought a very peculiar people. They found closest fellowship among themselves. Quarterly meetings when communion was held, none were admitted except those who had a ticket, showing their character had been passed upon. Wordliness such as shows, cards, dancing and finery in dress was shunned and denounced. Mrs. Spencer told how when a young member was labored with because she appeared with a Quaker bonnet trimmed with fiery red cheapness and shirred with a cape. Rev. Sayer, the minister, was condemned for getting his wife a box of artificial flowers. Members were disciplined for not attending church, for Sabbath desecration and another for calling a sister Methodist, "A nuisance".

The young man, Robert Hamilton Spencer, whom she married had an interesting life. He was the son of Col. Abner R. Spencer of the U. S. Army who served in the War of 1812. He desired his son to study law. He entered the law office of Judge William F. Allen of Oswego. He was seventeen and finding the study of law rather dry, he ran away to New York City, where he shipped on a whale boat as a sailor. He shipped as a sailor before the mast, was promoted to be Mate, and finally was employed as Captain. He was away three years before he returned to Oswego. He sailed summers and taught school winters. Robert H. Spencer and Elmina P. Keeler were married at Oswego, N. Y., November 4, 1840, by Rev. C. L. Dunning, Methodist minister.

That winter Mr. Spencer taught school at Fulton where they lived. In 1841 Mrs. Spencer went with him on his vessel, *Kirvosha*, to Southport. The vessel was lost on the shores of Lake Michigan. His friends induced him to remain there and teach school which he did; and they remained there until 1844, when they returned to Oswego. He again took up the study of law and was admitted to the bar. He did not follow the profession much but continued as a teacher and kept a book store in Oswego. Mrs. Spencer wrote of him that "his only habit of dissipation was chewing tobacco and that moderately."

When the 147th Regiment, New York Infantry was organized, R. H. Spencer, aged 44 and past draft age, enlisted as a volunteer on August 30, 1862, in Oswego for three years as a Corporal in Company G. He was mustered into service September 23, 1862. He was dischaged February 10, 1864, to enlist as a hospital steward, U. S. Army. He was appointed ward master of the regiment. Elmina P. Spencer was also mustered into the service of the U. S. Army as matron of Hospital Department of that regiment. Together they left with the regiment. At times they were detailed at division hospitals, field hospitals and in 1863 the New York Legislature passed a law creating Agencies for the Relief of Sick and Disabled Union Soldiers in the Service of the U. S., appropriating $200,000 to carry on this work. His Excellency Horatio Seymour, governor, set up 14 agencies and appointed agents to carry on this work. Number 5 was the Agency in the Army of the Potomac under the charge of Rev. J. V. Van Ingen and Mrs. Robert Spencer. These agents were subject to orders from the Surgeon General of the Army, H. and held credentials from New York State, also from the military. General U. S. Grant issued to Mrs. Spencer an order permitting her to pass in and out of Union lines, in all places. The work of these agents was to see that wounded and sick were cared for; that articles of food, clothing, medicines etc., were theirs; that wounded were cared for on battlefields, in emergency camps, hospitals, etc.; that hospitals be visited and things for comfort of wounded be procured and distributed and the families of the soldiers at home be contacted and informed as to whether they were living or dead, and if wounded where they were and their condition. Also later on they did a great work getting soldiers in touch with their regiments so that they might obtain their pay, having not received any pay since they were separated from their military unit, in action, and their whereabouts became lost to their military units.

The regiment arrived in Washington October 1, 1862. She slept that night on a bench of the Soldiers Rest. Some of the men of 147th Regt. had sun strokes crossing Long Bridge and she cared for them. The next day she began service feeding from her stores wounded from the Battle of Antietam. The regiment moved to Arlington Heights but they remained in Washington in charge of hospital stores and caring for the wounded. Supplies and tents being sent to Acquia Creek, they volunteered to stay and take care of the wounded from Fredericksburg. These were brought into the hospital in the Patent Office. January 1, 1863, Mr. Spencer rejoined his regiment at Falmouth, Va., and she went to New York City for supplies. Returning she joined the regiment at Belle Plains and went to Wind Mill Point and was there six months caring for the wounded in Hospital of First Corps. Mr. Spencer was an attendant there. Transferred to Belle Plain and to Acquia Creek until June 13, 1863, when they rejoined their own 147th Regt. Mrs. Spencer was a good horsewoman and foraged for supplies for sick and wounded. By orders of Dr. Hurd, Medical Division, First Corps, she took with her, her mount and rode with the regiment on the march to Gettysburg. On this march they encamped a week at Broad Run. Mrs. Spencer's horse carried besides herself, her bedding, clothing, and 350 pounds of supplies for the sick. She had two knapsacks and two haversacks and materials to make tea, coffee and beef broth. She often took care of soldiers' coats when they went into action, or on forced marches, when they threw them off, but later sadly needed them. Many a cheer she received from the soldiers when after forced marches or falling back, from fighting. Mrs. Spencer made coffee for them, and cared for their wounds. The Battle of Gettysburg had begun on July 1, 1863; the 147th arrived and went into action, losing that first day 40 killed, 200 wounded and 30 missing. On this day the color bearer, Sgt. Hinchcliffe, was shot and fallen upon the colors. Sgt. William A. Wybourn, Co. I, volunteered to secure it and did so amid a storm of bullets. During this heroic act he was wounded.

The day before, an ammunition train attached to the regiment exploded; Mrs. Spencer tore up her comforter that covered her bed to get cotton to care for the driver's burns, and the calico for bandages. Mrs. Spencer remained to care for the man while she stayed alone with the regiment, spreading their rubber coats on the ground and with others making a tent, in the mud where she slept.

On July 2 she joined Mr. Spencer. They occupied a barn, where she made coffee for the soldiers. Wounded from the 11th Corps were brought in, and to get them off the field, they had to cross between two lines of artillery firing. Orders came to fall back but they moved forward seeking to regain their regiment. The surgeon of the 1st Div. hurrying past called her to help form a hospital. They found the men of the 147th were in the ambulance train. They crossed to White Church on the Baltimore Turnpike, four miles away, arriving there after dark. There 60 wounded were crowded into the small church. Wounded were placed on boards covered with straw, placed on top of pews. The supply train having been sent back many miles, she made coffee from her knapsack. The

Sanitary & Christian Commission sent supplies and here were cared for 600 wounded and 100 wounded prisoners.

By mutual agreement the supplies of the Sanitary Commission were available and could be drawn upon by Agents appointed by New York State for Relief of Sick & Disabled Soldiers.

Mrs. Spencer stayed in White Church Hospital. Some trips were made to New York City with wounded men. While there she secured supplies. Mr. Spencer was clerk in Medical Purveyors Office in Gettysburg Hospital and she remained there. From there they went to Brandy Station where Mr. Spencer was discharged from the Volunteer service of 147th Regt. and entered the regular army of the U. S. as Hospital Steward attached to the Medical Purveyors Dept. Mrs. Spencer went to Alexandria to care for wounded from Battle of The Wilderness. Then she went to Belle Plain until May 1864 and on to Port Royal. Mr. Spencer arrived on the Medical Purveyors boat; she went to the White House Landing where she was Superintendent on the Government cooking barge as well as agent for N.Y. State distributing supplies to thousands in distress and need. On June 18, 1864, she arrived at City Point. About one mile from the landing she got her kitchen set up and her station remained here until the end of the war. She visited General Hospitals to discover all N. Y. State soldiers and be of service to them. She rode horseback 20 to 40 miles a day about Petersburg and Richmond. One day with her black hat and feather, looking quite like an officers on her mount, a sharp shooter fired at her. The bullet lodged in a tree just back of her. She dug it out with a knife and carried for a souvenir. She said, "I never believed I would be harmed by shot or shell." At City Point when a boat blew up, she was struck in the side by a piece of shell and suffered temporary paralysis of her limbs. A small missile cut off the string of her hat. It was found the next day.

On April 8, 1865, Abraham Lincoln came to the hospital at City Point and went about shaking hands with the wounded soldiers. This was just one week before he was assassinated.

Mrs. Spencer stayed at City Point until all wounded were transferred. On May 31, 1865, she went on Medical Supply boat to Washington and offered her services. She stayed there until June 15, visiting the hospitals.

Mrs. Spencer's report of the New York State Agency at City Point, Va. is presented:

171

To Mr. John F. Seymour
General Agent N. Y. Soldiers Relief

Dear Sir: In Albany last Summer I said to you I would send you a report of my labors from the time I left Alexandria to find our wounded after the Battle of the Wilderness. My husband being Hospital Steward I made my home by consent of Dr. Brinton, Medical Purveyor of the Army of the Potomac with that Dept. Under orders of Surgeon General May 8th, cars were loaded and we left for Rappahannock Station with supplies to care for the wounded. We found no wounded and learned the enemy had intercepted our trains and the wounded had been taken elsewhere. We returned next morning to Washington. With monies supplied by Governor Seymour I had purchased such supplies of food and comfort as I needed, including a large supply of tobacco thanks to the generosity of Thomas Hoyt, 104 Pearl St., N. Y. On our way back we distributed tobacco to all soldiers on duty. Returning to Alexandria we were ordered to load two boats with supplies for Belle Plain. I stood on the dock with my basket and haversack filled with rations. We arrived in early morning. The Sanitary boat with her stores, delegates, and ladies lay besides us. Slightly wounded soldiers who had been able to walk from the field were moving slowly toward the boats with hungry anxious faces. These were fed with crackers and other food. As soon as I could land I went from the boat to the shore with my rations thinking I might make a litte coffee or tea for some of them. I met Dr. Babcock our State Medical Agent moving from one wounded man to another, dressing their wounds and cheering them with kind words. After feeding my rations I went to another portion of the field and found ten theological students delegates of the Sanitary Commission employed in making coffee in camp kettles. The kettles hung upon a pole over the fire each end of the pole resting in crotched sticks driven into the ground as standards for the poles. I offered my services to stir, dip or serve in any way. My services were gratefully received and we all worked with a will. Some cut wood and brought it, some brought water, some kept the fire, other with pails and cups to distribute to our hungry wounded men.

Elmina P. Spencer
Stone carving—Great Western Staircase
New York State Capital, Albany

We worked until dark and far into the night. We fed six thousand men including those brought in by ambulance with their drivers and attendants. In the afternoon it rained without ceasing. The rain descended in torrents. The wounded lay upon the ground surrounding us by the thousands; some under bushes for shelter; others without shelter except blankets; more with no covering of any kind. It was impossible to make shelter in such short time. We were thankful that we could feed them. Often when passing from one to another I have heard , a grateful 'God Bless You'. Often I passed a soldier lying in the mud and rain with his arm or leg off or a wound in his body he would say in answer to my inquiry, if he had tea or coffee? 'Yes, I've done well. Thank you. But you lady will get your death in this rain. How can you go through this mud to wait on us?' Their cheerfulness to me was surprising. I stood in the mud that day over the tops of my boots while preparing food for the wounded. The sanitary had but one tent erected. That sheltered their stores. At 11 o'clock it occurred to me I had no place to sleep.

One of the men who had been assisting me said he would go and ask a driver to give me a place in his wagon. One of the drivers readily assented and left his wagon for my use—finding room for himself with another teamster. I got into the wagon, wrapped my shawl about me, sat myself on the bottom of the vehicle, placed the mule saddle at my back and for the first time since morning settled myself for rest. I could not sleep, my clothes were saturated with rain and mud. My bones were aching with wet and fatigue, yet I did not feel discouraged. How could I? When I thought of the thousands lying around me, crippled, wounded, some dying. I found myself in prayer for my suffering countrymen.

At dawn I felt rested and ready for another days work. In going from the wagon to our cooking place I experienced the difficulties of walking through Virginia mud. I found many of our wounded lying in these beds mud mortar. The ambulances picked up all the wounded that they could and placed them on hillsides. The wounded continued to come and be cared for. Miss Dix with her lady nurses came and after a while passed to Fredericksburg. The government kitchen issued supplies to thousands furnished by the Sanitary Commission when short

174

of meat, bread, sugar, coffee, etc. I stayed here in charge of the cooking. There was so much suffering and need for my services. My shoes were worn out and needed clothes. But we were working in an emergency. On May 25th, we left Belle Plain for Port Royal. The wounded were arriving in large numbers. We found an old building with fireplaces but no wood. We tore off the outside of the building for fuel and started our fires and we worked all night distributing coffee. That day Col. Cuyler, Inspector General of the Army had stoves brought into the building and five cauldrons outside and sent 28 men to assist in the work. Two cauldrons were filled for coffee, one for soup, two for mest. With these facilities we cooked enough to feed all who came.

Just before leaving for White House Landing which was to be our next base, I met Mr. Fay, of the Sanitary Commission. He asked me if I was aware that the Commission did not employ lady agents and as their greatest need now was past, he advised me to join some hospital as a nurse. I thanked Mr. Fay telling him I could not do so as I was at present State Agent for New York, and that I could get passage on the Medical Purveyors boat on which my husband was a steward.

I reported to Col. Cuyler what Mr. Fay had said to me and he said he would place me in charge of the cooking on the government barge to oversee it and at the same time, see to my work as Agent for N. Y. From the barge we fed the first wounded that came to White House from the field. After a day or two our stoves and cauldrons were brought on shore and we fed our thousands again. We called it the Government kitchen and from it regiments including those from New York were supplied with nourishment. Mrs. Lyons of Williamsburg, L. I., and Mrs. Jenkins of N. Y., labored with us until both returned home sick sick from the scenes that they had witnessed. Their superhuman exertions and overtaxed strength gave out. Senator Bell of N. Y. visited us and helped us distribute coffee, meat, bread and tea to the Tenth regiment of New York, State Heavy Artillery, over 1500 strong, but worn and weary with a long march without rations of any kind. We fed them all they and they can testify to the benefit of having an agent on hand to give them help in their need.

We came to City Point June 10. Here again was plenty to do. The wounded were still coming in. The ground was covered with them and our labors were no lighter. Our hospital was finally established. Our Medical Purveyors boat moved around upon the the Appomattox River. The Government kitchen was kept in action and I stayed until the hospital kitchens were in good order, and our hospital ready to receive patients from field hospitals or battlefields. From that time my labors were mostly distributing to needy soldiers at the front, field hospitals and rifle pits. In general hospitals I am not needed so much although I visit them and distribute a portion of my supplies to them. They have their surgeon, ladies and ward masters while at the front have to struggle on alone with only their regimental surgeons. I have found many friends willing to assist me. Dr. Brinton of the Medical Purveyor has kindly given me of such things for the soldiers as do not belong to the Government but are classed as hospital stores. One reason being my husband being one of his stewards. Another he saw I did not grudge to any State soldier that I found in need.

General Grant has kindly given me a pass to visit the front with supplies where other ladies are not permitted to go. General Mead and Provost Marshal Patrick have shown great favor. I have been furnished transportation when in need of it. I think I have great need to be thankful to an over-ruling Providence for aiding and protecting me in this great work. I never felt more sensibly my dependence on a higher power than when the explosion of our ammunition boat at City Point. I sat on my horse about 65 feet from the boat. When it exploded pieces of shell, cannon balls, human flesh, and sticks of timber over and about me -no escape in any direction. I was hit but not seriously hurt. I felt in that moment of destruction that no power but the Almighty could save. I still feel that God in his great mercy protected me in that terrible time.

I could continue but my report is now too long. The money I have received for the soldiers has been faithfully expended and supplies distributed according to my best judgment. I have sent you the vouchers. Still with all you send and have sent I have not been able to reach every N. Y. Regiment. New York has an army of her own and immense

supplies are needed to give to all a mite. With much respect,
Truly yours,
MRS. R. H. SPENCER.

Archives of New York State, and daily papers of New York, Albany, Oswego and many other cities published during this war, contain letters from regiments of New York State troops in the field, expressing gratitude to Mrs. Spencer in her distribution of supplies from the state and her great services to the sick and wounded soldiers.

During the war Mr. Spencer's health failed and after they returned to Oswego he secured different employments but in none was he able to perform all the duties they entailed. His ailment seemed to be partial paralysis. Thinking Government land in Kansas might be available to them in 1872 her father, Mr. Keeler, and Mr. Spencer went there and took up some land. In May 1873 Mrs. Spencer followed taking with her their mothers, Mrs. Keeler and Mrs. Spencer. She sold her piano and earning money teaching music she built a small house. Robert Spencer's health continued to fail. He died November 27, 1873. Mrs. Keeler died July 17, 1874; Mr. Keeler died November 4, 1874, and on December 24, Robert Spencer's mother died.

In September of that year her home and contents was destroyed by a prarie fire. She then sold her land and bought a small house in town, Great Bend, Barton County, Kansas. She mortgaged the house, hoping to get a widow's pension from the Government. She went to Washington in her attempt to secure it. In her application she stated:

I worked faithfully for my country. I have given her my husband. I now ask that out of her abundance, she will give sufficient to sustain my few years in comfort. I will be 61 if I live to the fifteenth of next September. I submit this to your fair consideration hoping God will direct you.
Mrs. Elmina P. Spencer
Washington, D. C.

Her application was granted and she was awarded a pension of $8 a month on services of her husband in the Union Army.

In the early 1880's she returned to Oswego. Hon. N. W., Nutting of Oswego, our Representative in Congress, set himself to

the task of securing for her a better pension and was untiring to that end. At this time were recited her own services on the Union army, in the field, on the march, on battlefields and in hospitals. Mr. Nutting said in Committee: "Her pension of $8 a month is entirely inadequate for her support. She has no child, no home, no property. She is 65 years old, bowed down with poverty and pains of desease. She cannot at the most live long. She is an object of charity and the American people owe it to themselves and to her to increase her pension to $20 a month." Passed by Congress February 26, 1885.

In the 1890's every parade in Oswego in the place of honor escorted by military units, marched a great company of Grand Army of The Republic. At their head in carriage rode Elmina P. Spencer, always proud of the respect and love that the G. A. R. showered upon her. Some of these comrades would never have lived to come home only for her sacrifical service when wounded. She was a member of the Grand Army of The Republic and of the Womens Relief Corps, both of these organizations named in honor of Capt. John D. O'Brien, first Captain of Volunteers commissioned in New York State.

Thirty years after the Battle of Gettysburg July 1, 1893, the State of New York sent all survivors of the 147th Regiment to Gettysburg to dedicate the monument erected on the position held by that Regt. They also received the Gettysburg Medal from the State. 150 survivors answered the roll call. Major Nathaniel A. Wright presided, and called the roll of 76 killed in that battle. Horatio N. Berry a Drummer boy in the Regt. gave the oration. Mrs. Elmina P. Spencer made this trip and recounted her experiences there caring for the wounded.

In 1905 she lived in the Arcade Block (on the north side of Bridge Street next to the river). Failing health compelled her to give up living alone. She lived with Mrs. A. Vickery, 142 East Mohawk Street, Emiline E. Gray, West Bridge Street, and Ella H. Smith, 84 West Second Street where she died December 29, 1912. The ladies of the Womens Relief Corps for many years were very kind to her and she was provided for. For several last years of her life she was bed ridden.

179

DR. MARY E. WALKER
Civil War Doctor And Congressional Medal Of Honor

by Lorrie Arden-Sebold

Bunker Hill lies four and one-half miles west of the city of Oswego in Oswego Town. At the turn of the century, an eccentric but spirited old woman lived there on a farm. She had few friends and relatives to care for her. Her neighbors shunned her; Oswego residents ridiculed her. But that did not disturb her. She would boast of her earlier days: "presidents and cabinet ministers and great generals were glad to meet and listen to me."

She was known internationally for her manly attire. She appears in photographs dressed in her usual black dress coat, trousers, white shirt and tie, and most distinctly, a black silk hat. She was one of the few women physicians of the 19th century, as well as one of America's leading suffragettes. And she was the only woman ever to receive the Congressional Medal of Honor. Her name was Dr. Mary E. Walker, a name that brought recognition to Bunker Hill and Oswego.

Alvah and Vesta Whitcomb Walker came to Oswego in August 1832. They had four daughters; Vesta, Aurora, Luna and Cynthia. Alvah built a house and barn on 33 acres of land on Bunker Hill Road. A fifth daughter, Mary Edwards, was born three months later on November 26. Mary was considered a beauty as a young woman. She was petite, just five feet tall, and slender. She had eager, sparkling eyes and brown curls that hung down her back. Eventually, she would sell her curls, giving the money to a destitute woman in Albany.

Alvah Walker believed women should have an education and career. At his own cost, he built and equipped a school house on his property. His neighbors assisted in the erection of the building. Mary and her sisters attended their father's school, then went to the Falley Seminary in Fulton. Mary taught school in Minetto for two years, but her heart was set on medical school. In 1853, she was accepted to Syracuse Medical College, which had just opened two years earlier. She received her MD in June, 1855, the only woman in her class. (Elizabeth Blackwell graduated from Geneva Medical

Dr. Mary E. Walker

College in 1849, the only woman in her class). At 22 years of age, Mary was one of a handful of female physicians in the country.

Dr. Mary Walker tried unsuccessfully to establish a practice in Columbus, Ohio. She returned to Oswego and married Dr. Albert Miller, who she had met in medical school. Mary displayed her unorthodox view of dress by appearing at the wedding in trousers and a dress coat. Furthermore, she had the obligation to obey her spouse deleted from the ceremony. According to Charles McCool Snyder in his biography of Dr. Mary Walker, she later explained the omission: "How barbarous the very idea of one equal promising to be the slave of another, instead of both entering life's greatest drama as intelligent equal parties. Our promises were such as denoted two intelligent beings instead of one intelligent and one chained." Mary also insisted on retaining her maiden name. Occasionally, she signed her name Miller-Walker, but never Mrs. Mary Miller.

Albert and Mary set up a practice in nearby Rome, but Mary was again not successful as a physician. Women physicians were not widely accepted, and Mary's manner of dress did not help. She had adopted the bloomer fashion during her medical training. Mary wore a knee-length dress or coat over trousers because it was comfortable and practical. Her father had not permitted his daughter to wear corsets or tight-fitting dresses. He claimed they impaired women's health.

Mary's trousers became her mark of distinction. She spent her life crusading for dress reform and was constantly ridiculed by the press and public for wearing clothes "unbecoming of her sex." In an interview printed in the Worcester Daily Telegram in 1894, a reporter asked Mary why she wore her pants costume. "Common sense," she snapped at him, "Why should not a woman have the same privileges as a man of being comfortable and adapting herself to circumstances? I have worn this costume since before the war and I propose to continue wearing it!"

Mary's marriage lasted only a few years. When she received reports that Albert was unfaithful, Mary confronted him and he admitted the charge. She ordered him out of the house. Mary went to Iowa seeking a divorce, stayed a year and came home still married. She filed again in New York State in 1866, and three years later, the divorce was granted. The experience left Mary bitter towards Albert, who she referred to as "the villain," and cynical towards all men.

Mary continued her meager practice in Rome. She contributed regularly to Sybil, a woman's magazine. She wrote about dress reform and women's rights, which began her life-long campaign in those two areas.

When the Civil War created a demand for physicians, Mary set off for Washington, D. C. to seek a commission as an Army surgeon. The Surgeon General denied her request; women could only serve as nurses. This did not deter Mary. She volunteered her services in a hospital set up in the U. S. Patent Office. There she served as administrative assistant to the head surgeon, Dr. J. N. Green. Mary plunged into her duties with enthusiasm, although no evidence existe to prove she performed as a physician. She was assertive, which her biographer says contributed to Mary's effectiveness in a war emergency, but not in civilian life. On one occasion, Mary visited the Deserters' Prison in Alexandria. When the guard refused to admit her, Mary said emphatically, "I am Dr. Mary Walker of the Union Army. I command you to let me pass." The surprised guard stepped aside. Mary was convinced several of the prisoners were unjustly confined. She demanded the War Office to release one boy, who left his regiment to visit his dying mother. The boy was pardoned.

Mary was disturbed by the frequent amputations performed on injured soldiers. She felt surgeons were amputating for practice more than necessity, but could not risk her dismissal by complaining to a higher authority. So she convinced the injured to refuse surgery, and to use bodily harm if the surgeon persisted.

While in Washington, Mary helped organize and raise funds for the Women's Relief Association. They provided room for visiting families of wounded soldiers. Later, the Women's Relief Association also offered housing to all destitute women and children.

Even though Dr. Mary Walker had not one, but two medical degrees, her value as a physician was often in question by established doctors and members of the community.

After working in Washington where she helped organize and raise funds for the Women's Relief Association, Mary left the capitol for a while in the spring of 1862. She traveled to New York City and attended the Hygeia Therapeutic College. On March 31, 1862, she received her second medical degree and then visited her home in Oswego. She gave a lecture at the Music Hall about the war and her impression of President Lincoln and his wife, Mary.

In the fall of 1863, Mary arrived at Chattanooga, Tennessee. From there she was sent to the 52nd Ohio Infantry at Gordon's Mills where she became assistant surgeon. Dr. Perin, medical director of the Army of the Cumberland, called Mary a "medical monstrosity" and ordered an examination of her qualifications. The unfavorable report called her medical knowledge "not much greater than most housewives." Undaunted, Mary remained at her post. Everyday she traveled alone on horseback into enemy territory to minister to the wounded soldiers and civilians.

On April 10, 1864, Mary took the wrong turn and was captured by a confederate patrol. She was taken by train 700 miles from Dalton, Georgia to Richmond, Virginia. "News that a Yankee lady physician in bloomers was aboard preceded the train via telegraph," her biographer said, "and the curious turned out at the various stops." At one, Mary persuaded her guards to let her attend the theater. She bought the tickets for the seven guards who accompanied her.

Mary was imprisoned for four months in Castle Thunder in Richmond. She complained of the rats and poor quality of the food. Nothing was done about the rats, but, to Mary's surprise, vegetables appeared on the menu. On August 12, Mary was exchanged as a surgeon for a Southern major. She was the first woman exchanged for a male ranking officer by any Army, a fact she boasted of for years after. She continued to seek a commission as an army surgeon, but was denied. Finally, Mary appealed to President Lincoln. He replied in a week in his own handwriting—another rejection.

Finally, Mary's persistance paid off. In October of 1864, Mary was awarded a contract as Acting Assistant Surgeon, U. S. Army, with a salary of $100 a month. Another first for Mary - she was the first woman to serve the position. Mary's first assignment was at the Women's Prison Hospital in Louisville, Kentucky. After six months, the inmates accused her of cruelty, and Mary was transferred to an orphan and refugee asylum in Tennessee. Her duties ended in June of 1865.

On November 11, 1865, Mary received the nation's highest award, the Congressional Medal of Honor for meritorious service in the Civil War. It was signed by President Andrew Johnson, but the original citation was written by Lincoln on the back of an envelope, reported an article appearing in MD magazine. Mary wore the medal everyday for the rest of her life. In 1917, when Mary was 85 years old, the Board of Medal Awards ruled the award unwarranted. The names of Dr. Mary Walker and 910 others, including William "Buffalo Bill" Cody, were stricken from the roll of Medal of Honor holders.

A young officer was sent to Oswego to reclaim the medal. As the Boston Globe reported in a 1977 story, Mary sent him back emptyhanded, shouting, "You'll only get it back over my dead body, and then only if you can rescue it from rigor mortis!"

In 1977 the Army restored Dr. Mary Walker's medal. Today it is displayed, with the presidential citation, in the Oswego County Historical Society.

Mary spent the years following the war lecturing and writing on dress reform. By the 1880's, Mary's attire was completely mannish. She wore a man's coat and pants, a white shirt, stiff collar and tie, topping off the outfit with a high silk hat and cane. In June of 1866, Mary was arrested in New York City for "impersonating a man" when she attracted a crowd of onlookers. She stated in her defense that men's clothing was more healthful. Women's clothing was uncomfortable and inconvenient. Impressed, the Police Commissioner freed her, saying, "I consider, Madam, that you have as good a right to wear that clothing as I have to wear mine." He ordered the arresting officer never to arrest her again.

Two weeks later, Mary was in Syracuse to address the National Dress Reform Association convention and was elected its president. That fall she was chosen as a delegate to a social science congress in Manchester, England. This began a year-long tour in Europe, where Mary received a warm welcome, quite a change from her own country where people ridiculed her.

Returning to America in 1867, Mary found she was no celebrity here. Teaming with suffragettes that included Lucy Stone, Susan B. Anthony, Mary Livermore and Belva Lockwood, Mary later broke with the group when they accused her of "retarding the women's rights crusade" by her "bizarre" dress. While the suffragettes wanted the Constitution amended to give women the right to vote, Mary claimed they already had the vote as citizens of the United States.

"We the People" included women too. Florence Dennler, Oswego Town Historian, says, "The reason Mary opposed the 19th amendment was because men could not give women the right to vote. The right to vote was already theirs."

In 1920, one year after Mary's death, the 19th Amendment was added to the Constitution.

Dr. Walker wrote two books. The first, *Hit*, was her autobiography, published in 1871. In *Unmasked: or the Science of Immortality*, published in 1878, Mary gave frank treatment of sex. She discussed veneral desease, kissing, which she said spread germs, and marriage. She claimed the happiest marriages were those in which total equality existed between husband and wife.

Five days after Congress declared war on Germany, in April of 1917, Mary sent a cablegram to the German Kaiser. She asked him to stop the war and offered her Bunker Hill farm for a peace conference. She promised transportation, meals, typewriters and telephones, all without cost, although Mary had little money and many debts. The Oswego press printed the cablegram, with the headline: "No Information as to who Pays for the Cable."

In 1917, Dr. Walker fell on the capitol steps in Washington. She never recovered, and, in August of 1918, she was hospitalized at General Hospital 5 at Fort Ontario in Oswego. In September, Mary's long-time friend, Nellie Van Slingerland, rushed to Oswego and took Mary to the home of neighbor on Bunker Hill, Mrs. Frank Dwyer. As Mary lay dying, her eyes filled with tears, she told her friend, "But now I am alone with the infirmities of old age fast weighing me down and practically penniless, and no one wants to be bothered with me." But Mary was never one to grovel in self-pity and concluded, "But it is the same experience that have come to others, and why should I complain?"

Dr. Mary Walker died on February 21, 1919. The simple funeral was held at her farm; her casket draped with the American flag. Buried in her famed black suit in the Rural Cemetery, less than two miles from her farm. Her small headstone was simply inscribed, "Mary."

Although she left no will, she requested the farm be left to her nephew, Byron Worden. A few years later, a fire destroyed the Walker farm.

In the late 1960's the name of Dr. Walker returned to the news. People in Oswego Town appealed to senators and assemblymen to restore Mary's Congressional Medal of Honor. In 1977, when the medal was restored, the Oswego American Legion dedicated a new tombstone for Mary's grave. It was enscribed with the words, "Mary E. Walker, Medal of Honor, Surg 52 Ohio Inf. Civil War, 1832–1919."

Today, people like Florence Dennler, who has notebooks filled with letters, newspaper clippings and photographs on Mary, keep the memory of Dr. Walker alive.

Stories About Dr. Mary Walker

How "Bishop" Oberly Surrendered At Last to Dr. Mary Walker

John H. Oberly is the latest victim to the prowess of Dr. Mary Walker. Lately her ambition has been to secure as special examiner in the pension service. Several attempts were made by her to obtain interviews with Gen. Black. These foiling she determined to apply for examination by the civil service board and then confront the pension commissioners with a certificate properly authenticated. Having come to this determination she announced to some one that she proposed to call on Mr. Oberly and talk with him. He heard Dr. Mary Walker was to call upon him and determined to dodge an interview. Long ago he selected a den in the subterranean parts of city hall where the civil service commission has its offices, to avoid some of the calls that are made upon him. It took Dr. Mary Walker three days to track him to his den, but she finally did so. One day the "Bishop" was hiding in his place when a rap was made on his door. He opened it and there stood Dr. Mary Walker.

"Is Mr. Oberly here?" she inquired.

"No," said Mr. Oberly, while his face continued to bear those marks of Christian innocence which have gained for him the cognomen of "Bishop." "No, Mr. Oberly is not in, but I'm his messenger and will tell him any message you may wish to leave."

"I'll call again," replied the doctor.

Ten days afterward the scene was repeated. Dr. Mary called and was again told by this obliging "messenger" that Mr. Oberly was not in, but that any word left would be told to him. The next day Mr. Oberly was again disturbed by a gentle rap. He went smiling to the door, but was more than disgusted to find Dr. Mary Walker there.

"Good morning, Mr. Oberly," she said as she pushed her way into the room.

"But I'm not Mr. Oberly," declared the good "bishop," while the blushes that insisted in reddening his face on account of the prevaricaton even in self defense gave the lie to his denial.

"Oh, but I know you are Mr. Oberly," rejoined the imperturbable man-woman. "I thought you were fooling me, and I called on Mrs. Oberly before coming this morning and got her to show me your picture. I'm sure of you this time." The "bishop" was floored by the doctor. He surrendered then and there and gave her all the information about civil service examinations.

Washington Letter in *Chicago Tribune.*

One Sunday morning near the close of the 1st century I visited a Presbyterian church in Oswego, New York, and found myself seated next to—I looked with puzzled eyes, then looked away and back again—such an odd little man. Tiny, not much more than five-feet-two, and shriveled rather than slender, he sat with his black Prince Albert coat buttoned, his black trousers neatly creased, his little feet shod in low-heeled black shoes barely touching the floor. On his hands were white cotton gloves and at his feet lay a black cotton umbrella and a hat familiarly know as a stovepipe.

I ventured to glance higher. His face looked like yellow parchment, but was relieved by a pair of keen gray eyes that bore through me for a moment and then were turned toward the pulpit. Mislaying for a time my good manners, I frankly stared at his gray hair, which was neatly parted, but so long that it curled at his neck above his stiff linen collar and black tie;—my friend was leaning over and whispering to me—"Dr. Mary Walker." I almost gasped. So this funny little man was a woman!

Ina L.C. Lane in *MS*, September 1981.

EXECUTIVE ORDER

WHEREAS, It appears from Official Records that DR. MARY E. WALKER graduate of Medicine, of the Medical School at Syracuse, N. Y., has rendered valuable services to the Government, and her efforts have been earnest and untiring in a variety of ways, and that she was assigned to duty and served as an Assistant Surgeon in charge of female prisoners at Louiville, Kentucky—and upon the recom endations of Generals Thomas and Sherman; and faithfully served as a contract surgeon in the service of the United States and had devoted herself with patriotic zeal to the relief of our sick and wounded soldiers, both in the field and hospital to the detriment of her own health and has also endured hardships as a prisoner of war, four months in a Southern prison, while acting as a Contract Surgeon and

WHEREAS, by reason of her not being commissioned officer, in the military service, a brevet or honorary rank cannot be conferred upon her and:

WHEREAS, in the opinion of the PRESIDENT, an honorable recoginiton of her services and suffering should be made,

IT IS ORDERED
That a suitable testimonial thereof shall be made and given to the said DOCTOR MARY E. WALKER, and that the usual medal of honor for meritorious services be given to her.

Given under my hand in the City of Washington, D. C. this Eleventh day of November A. D. 1865.

ANDREW JOHNSON
PRESIDENT

Copy: The President
Copy: Edwin M. Stanton
Copy: Secty. of War.

[Copy of original Executive Order in the custody of the Oswego County Historical Society.]

The Photographic History of the Civil War

WILLIAM STEELE

WILLIAM STEELE

West Point,
Captain, United States Army
Brigadier General,
Confederate States of America
Adjutant General, State of Texas

Military History

William Steele, appointed by Joel Turrill, was admitted to the United States Military Academy as a Cadet July 1, 1836, and graduated July 1, 1840, standing No. 31 in a class of 42 members. He was promoted in the Army to Bvt. 2nd Lieut., 2d Dragoons on July 1, 1840.

He served: at the Cavalry School for Practice, Carlisle, Pa., 1840–1841; in the (2nd Lieut., 2nd Dragoons, February 2, 1841) Florida War, 18411842 being engaged in two skirmishes with the Seminole Indians; on frontier duty at Fort Jesup, La., 1842–1844; in garrison at Jefferson Barracks, Mo., 1844–1845; in military occupation of Texas, 1845–1846; in the War with Mexico, 1846–1848, being engaged in the Battle of Palo Alto, May 8, 1846.

(First Lieut., 2nd Dragoons, May 9, 1846) Battle of Monterey, September 21–23, 1846; Siege of Vera Cruz, March 9–29, 1847; Battle of Cerro Gorda, April 17–18, 1847; Battle of Contretras, August 19–20, 1847; Battle of Churubusco, August 20, 1847; Battle of Molino Del Rey, September 8, 1847.

Bvt. Captain, August 20, 1847, for gallant and meritorious conduct in the Battles of Contreras and Churubusco, Mexico; and as Acting Assistant Adjutant-General of Cavalry Brigade, 1847—1848; as Adjutant 2nd Dragoons, December 20, 1847 to April 10, 1849; in garrison at East Pascagoula, Miss., 1848; on recruiting service, 1848–1849; on frontier duty at Fredericksburg, Texas, 1849-1950; Fort Martin Scott, Texas, 1850; Austin, Texas, 1850; Fort Lincoln, Texas, 1850–1851; Fort Martin Scott, Texas, 1851; Austin, Texas, 1851; Texas (Quartermaster duty) 1851–1852; Fort Conrad, N. M. (Captain, 2nd Dragoons, November 10, 1851) 1852–1853; Scouting, 1852, being engaged against Apache Indians in a skirmish near Fort Conrad, N. M., July 28, 1853; Fort Craig, N. M., 1854; Fort Leavenworth, Kan., 1854–1855; Sioux Expedition, 1855, being engaged in the Action of Blue Water, September 3, 1855; Fort Leavenworth, Kan., 1855–1856; Fort Randall, Dak., 1856–1857; Fort Leavenworth, Kan., 1857–1858; in garrison at St. Louis, Mo., 1858; on sick leave of absence, 1858–1859; on frontier duty at Fort Kearney, Neb., 1859–1860; Kiowa and Comanche Expedition, 1860, being engaged in a skirmish near Bent's Fort, Col., July 11, 1860; Fort Scott, Kan., 1860–1861.

Captain William Steele resigned his commission in the United States Army on May 30, 1861, and joined the Confederate forces in Texas. He was appointed Colonel in the 7th Texas Cavalry and served in New Mexico in 1862 under General H. H. Sibley. During Sibley's New Mexico expedition he commanded in the Mesilla area and was promoted to the rank of Brigadier-General September 12, 1862. He was in command of Indian Territory in 1863 and in 1864 was assigned to command the defense of Galveston. He then fought under General Richard Taylor in the Red River campaign and was complimented for his conduct at Pleasant Hill. After the death of General Thomas Green at Blair's Landing, he commanded Green's cavalry division for a time, as senior brigadier, until superceded by Major General John A. Wharton.

Personal History

William Steele, the second son of Orlo Steele, was born on May 1, 1819, in Oswego New York. At that time the family home was located on East First and Seneca Streets. In 1821 the family resided in the stone house, still standing, (the light-house keeper's residence) on the Fort Ontario grounds when the light-house was on that elevation. When the new light-house was erected in 1837 in the harbor, the family removed to the west side.

He attended the old academy with Edwin Bronson, Peter Cockrane, Edwin Hawks, George Stevens and other sons of the community's leading citizens. William was "quite a favorite" with his fellow students and evidently well accepted. The same source essayed him as an exceedingly mild and gentlemanly person, doing his duty in a quiet manner in intercourse with the world, reserved rather than obtrusive, very domestic in his habits.

At the age of 17 he received an appointment to West Point from Congressman Joel Turrill, an Oswegonian. The local press made note of Captain Steele's visit to Oswego in 1848. It went on to say that he "being a native of this city, his military career had been watched with intense interest by many of our citizens, and it is a source of gratification to learn that no man in the army has established a better reputation as a brave, modest and intelligent officer, or as an honorable high minded gentleman."

His attachment to his family was doubtless the cause of his casting his fortune with the Confederacy. He, then Captain, married Annie Du Val, sister of Judge Thomas Du Val of the Supreme Court of Texas. They had one daughter, Lily.

After the Civil War, General Steele settled in San Antonio, Texas where he entered the commission business with Colonel T. G. Williams, under the firm name of Steele & Williams, at the corner of Navarro and Commerce Streets. He retired from that business and was appointed Adjutant-General of the State on January 20, 1874 and served until January 25, 1879. His record was a fine one, for he brought order out of chaos (by reorganizing the Texas Rangers) and at great pains and expense procured and published a list of all escaped convicts and other fugitives from justice, a copy of which he furnished the sheriff of each county.

General Steele returned to San Antonio shortly after he retired from the Adjutant-Generalship, where he lived in reduced circumstances. He lost his wife during his service there and she was buried in Oakwood Cemetery, Austin. When stricken with paralysis on January 12, 1885, he was alone, his daughter Lily, was in Chicago completing a particular branch of study. The remains were taken to Austin for burial; the General expressed a desire to be buried there by the side of his beloved wife.

"Peace to his ashes, and comfort be to those who mourn."

Family History

Orlo Steele, father of William, was born in Cornwall, Connecticut. He came to Oswego presumably for business opportunities. His wife was a sister of Colonel Seth A. Abbey & Bro., printers who came to Oswego in 1817. Mrs. Dr. Adkins and Mrs. John C. Hugunin were Mrs. Orlo Steele's sisters. William Steele's cousins were Calvin S. Sumner, Willis Sumner, William S. Adkins and D. Clark Abbey of Milwaukee.

Besides being the light-house keeper, Orlo Steele was a merchant on East First Street. When the State isssued a charter to the Oswego Bridge Company on March 22, 1822, the incorporators were Orlo Steele, Col. T. S. Morgan, Matthew McNair, Alvin Bronson, and William Dolloway. Again when the Oswego Canal Company was incorporated on April 23, 1823, Orlo Steele was the Secretary, Edward Bronson, Treasurer; others were William Dolloway and Peter O. Hugunin; in 1825 Steele became a director. Also on March 30, 1832, the Oswego Cotton Manufacturing Company was incorported by Gerrit Smith, William Dolloway, John Grant, Jr., Col. T. S. Morgan, Henry Fitzhugh, G. W. Woodruff and others. One of the others was Orlo Steele. It began manufacturing cotton fabric in 1834 with a capital of $25,000 and increased to $250,000 in 1836.

Orlo Steele served on the Board of Trustees of the village in 1828, 1829, 1833, and 1835.

He was a member of the Oswego Lodge, No. 127 F. & A. M. as early as 1825 and a charter member when it was officially chartered in 1847. He passed away on May 28, 1852.

194

Excerpts from *Personal Memoirs of U. S. Grant*, Charles L. Webster & Co., N. Y. 1894.

P. 115. Graduating in 1843 (Bvt. 2nd Lieut., 4th Infantry). I was at the military academy from one to four years with all the cadets who had graduated between 1840 and 1846 - seven classes. These classes embraced more than fifty officers who afterwards became generals on one side or the other in the rebellion, many of them holding high commands.

P. 38. In taking military possesion of Texas after annexation the army of occupation under General Zachary Taylor, was directed to occupy the disputed territory.

P. 44. Gradually the "Army of Occupation" assembled at Corpus Christi. When it was all together it consisted of seven companies of the 2nd regiment of dragoons (cavalry), four companies of light artillery, five regiments of infantry -the 3d, 4th, 5th, 7th and 8th - and one regiment of artillery acting as infantry - not more than three thousand men in all.

P. 62. The battles of Palo Alto and Resaca da la Palma seemed to us engaged as pretty important affairs ... about the same time, we learned that war existed between the United States and Mexico ... We then became the "Army of Invasion."

P. 67. On the 19th (Sept. 1846) General Taylor, with his army, was encamped within three miles of Monterey.

P. 78. Finally on the 7th of March 1847, the little army of ten or twelve thousand men, given General Scott to invade a country with a population of seven or eight millions, a mountainous country affording the greatest possible natural advantages for defense, was all assembled and ready to commence the perilous task of landing from vessels lying in the open sea. On the 9th of March the troops were landed and the investment of Vera Cruz, from the Gulf of Mexico south of the city to the gulf again on the north, was soon and easily effected. On the 29th Vera Cruz was occupied by Scott's army.

P. 80. Cerro Gordo is one of the higher spurs of the mountains ... and Santa Anna had selected this point as the easiest to defend against an invading army. The road, said to have been built by Cortez, zigs-zags around the mountain side and was defended at every turn by artillery. On either side were deep chasms

195

or mountain walls. A direct attack along the road was an impossibility. A flank movement seemed equally impossible. General Scott issued his order for the attack on the 18th of April 1847.

P. 88. The assault on Contreras was made on the morning of the 20th of August, and in less than half an hour from the sound of the advance the position was in our hands... and got on the causeway leading to Churubusco and the City of Mexico... but they did not succeed in this , and Churubusco proved to be about the severest battle fought in the valley of Mexico.

P. 91. Chapultepec is a mound springing up from the plain to the height of probably three hundred feet, and almost in a direct line between Molino Del Rey and the western part of the city of Mexico. It was fortified both on the top and the rocky and precipitous sides.

P. 92. The battle of Molino del Rey was fought on the 8th of September.

P. 93. The loss on our side of Molino del Rey was severe for the numbers engaged. It was especially so among the commissioned officers. During the night of the 11th batteries were established which could play upon the fortifications of Chapultepec.

P. 99. General Scott followed the troops into Mexico City on September 14, 1847 and took quarters in the "Halls of Montezumas"—the Palace—a mass of buildings in which Congress has its sessions, the national courts are held, the public offices are located, the President reside, and much room is left for museums, receptions, etc.

P. 100. General Scott invaded a populous country, penetrating two hundred and sixty miles into the interior, with a force at no time equal to one-half of that opposed to him; he was without a base; the enemy was always entrenched, always on the defensive; yet he won every battle, he captured the capital, and conquered the government.

P. 103. I would like to see truthful history written. Such history will do full credit to the courage and soldierly ability of the American citizen, no matter what section of the country he hailed from, or what ranks he fought.

General John P. Hatch
West Point — 1845

Military History

John Porter Hatch was admitted to the United States Military Academy as a cadet July 1, 1840, and was graduated July 1, 1845, standing No. 17 in a class of 41. He was promoted in the Army to Bvt. 2nd Lieut., 3d Infantry on July 1, 1845.

He served in the Military Occupation of Texas, 1845-1846; Siege of Vera Cruz (transferred to Mounted Rifles July 17, 1846), March 9-29, 1847; Skirmish of Puente del Medio, March 24, 1847; Battle of Cerro Gordo, April 17-18, 1847; Battle of Contreras, (Second Lieut. Mounted Rifles April 18, 1847) August 19-20, 1847; Battle of Churubusco, August 20, 1847; (Bvt. First Lieut., August 20, 1847 for Gallant and Meritorious conduct in the Battles of Contreras and Churubusco) Chapultepec Seeptember 13, 1847;

197

(Bvt. Captain, September 13, 1847, for Gallant and Meritorious conduct in the Battle of Chapultepec) Mexico, September 13–14, 1847; as Adjutant, Mounted Rifles, November 1, 1847 to May 1, 1850; in garrison at Jefferson Barracks, Mo., 1848; on Recruiting Service, 1848–1849; on frontier duty at Fort Leavenworth (Camp Sumner), Kan., 1849; March to Oregon City, 1849–1850; Acting Assistant Adjutant-General, Department of Oregon, October 3, 1849 to May 8, 1850; and at Fort Vancouver, Wash., 1850; on Recruiting Service 1851; (First Lieut., Mounted Rifles, June 30, 1851) in garrison at Jefferson Barrcks, Mo., 1851–1852; Scouting, 1852; Fort Merrill, Tex., 1852–1853; Edingburg, Tex., 1853; and Fort Merrill, Tex., 1853–1854; on Recruiting service, 1854–1856; on frontier duty at Fort Union, N. M., 1856–1857; Gila Expedition, 1857, being engaged against Magolan Indians in a skirmish at the Canon de los Muertos, N. M., May 24, 1857; Fort Defiance, N. M., 1857–1858; Navajo Expedition, 1858, being engaged in a skirmish near Laguna Negra, N. M., September 25, 1858; Fort Defiance, N. M., 1858; Scouting, 1858; Fort Craig, N. M., 1858–1859; Scouting, 1859; Fort Craig, N. M., 1859–1860; and at Albuquerque, N. M., 1860–1861 as Depot Commissary;

(Captain, Mounted Rifles, October 13, 1860) and as Chief of the Commissariat, Department of New Mexico, May 23 to August 1861.

Served during the Rebellion of the Seceding States, 1861–1866: (Brigadier-General, U. S. Volunteers, September 28, 1861) in command of Cavalry at Annapolis, Md., December 24, 1861 to March 28, 1862, and of the Post, February 7, to March 28, 1862; in command of the Cavalry of 5th Army Corps, in Operations in Shenandoah Valley, March 28 to July 29, 1862, being engaged in the Combat of Winchester, June 26, 1862; and Retreat to the Potomac, June 26, 1862; in the Northern Virginia Campaign, August 1 to September 2, 1862 being engaged in the Combat of Graveton, August 28, 1862; (Bvt. Major, August 30, 1862 for Gallant and Meritorious Service at the Battle of Manassas, Va.,) Battle of Manassas, August 29–30, 1862 where he was wounded; and Battle of Chantilly, September 1, 1862; in the Maryland Campaign, in command of Division (Army of Potomac), September, 6–14 being engaged in the Battle of South Mountain, September 14, 1862 where he was severely wounded; (Bvt. Lieutenant-Colonel, September 14, 1862 for Gallant and Meritorious Services at the Battle of South Mountain, Va.) on sick leave absence, disabled by wound,

September 15, 1862, to February 18, 1863; on Court Martial duty, February 18 to July 28, 1863; in command of Draft Rendezvous at Philadelphia, Pa., July 28 to October 31, 1863; (Major, 4th Cavalry, October 27, 1863) in command of Cavalry Depot at St. Louis, Mo., November 9, 1863 to February 29, 1864; in command of District of Florida Department of the South, March 28, to April 20, 1864, being in command of the forces operating on John's Island, S. C., July 1–10, 1864, including the Action of July 9, 1864; of District of Florida, August 4 to November 10, 1864; of Northern District, Department of the South, November 18–27, 1864; of Coast Division, Department of the South, November 29, 1864 to February 26, 1865, being in command at the Attack at Honey Hill, S. C., November 30, 1864; and Action of Tullafinny River, S. C., December 7, 1864; Afterwards under General Sherman's orders, co-operated with him while moving up the coast, participating in several Skirmishes, and of District of Charleston, Department of South Carolina, February 26 to August 26, 1865; (Bvt. Colonel, March 13, 1865 for Gallant and Meritorious Services During the Rebellion; Bvt. Brigadier-General U. S. Army, March 13, 1865 for Gallant and Meritorious Services in the Field During the Rebellion; Bvt. Major-General, U. S. Volunteers, March 13, 1865 for Gallant and Meritorious Service During the Rebellion) at New York City, awaiting orders, August 26, 1865 to April 6, 1866; mustered out of Volunteer Service, January 15, 1866.

Served: in command of regiment, Department of Texas, May 9, 1866 to January 1868; as acting Assistant Inspector-General of the District of Texas, January 10 to May 1868; as Superintendent of Mounted Recruiting Service at Carlisle, Pa., May 16, 1870; in command of Fort Concho, Tex., June 9, to July 3, 1870; as Member of Board for the purchase of Cavalry Horses, August 28 to October, 1870; in command of a battalion of regiment at Fort Concho, Tex., to Janurary 6, 1873; on duty at headquarters of the Department of Texas, January 15, to September 8, 1873; (Lieut. Colonel, 5th Cavalry, January 15, 1873; (Transferred to 4th Cavalry, April 10, 1873) in command of regiment and Fort Clark, Tex., March 21 to June 12, 1875; on frontier duty at Fort Sill, I. T., March 21 to June 12, 1875; in command of regiment, June 12 to July 21, 1875; on leave of absence, July 27, 1875 to January 8, 1876; on duty in New York City to April 17, 1876; as Member of Board on Army Supplies, April 17, to June 8, 1876; and in command of Fort Sill, I. T., August

2, 1876 to January 30, 1877; of Fort Ellicott, Tex., July 19, 1877 to March 9, 1879; Fort Sill, I. T., to March 28, 1880; and Fort Elliott, Tex., to July 26, 1881; (Colonel, 2d Cavalry, June 26, 1881) 1881; on leave of absence, to December 9, 1881; in command of Fort Custer, Mon., to February 24, 1884; and Fort Walla Walla, Wash, Territory to December 3, 1885.

John Porter Hatch retired from active service, January 9, 1886, he being 64 years of age.

Arizona Album

Ninety-three years ago in the Old Pueblo

TUCSON, ARIZONA TERRITORY, JANUARY 30, 1880

Don't disturb our Indians

Our New Mexico exchanges inform us that Gen. Hatch, commanding the Department of New Mexico, is now organizing a vigorous campaign against the renegade Indians, and that by the earnest solicitation of the General, the War Department has granted him authority to follow any of these renegades upon reservations and fight them wherever found.

We most heartily endorse the proposed campaign, and hope it may meet the greatest success, but if the fighting on reservations is to apply to San Carlos we enter an iron-clad protest right here, before any mischief is done. Such measures may be necessary and even desirable in New Mexico, but would certainly prove suicidal to the present favorable condition of Indian affairs in Arizona.

The San Carlos reservation is the home of the great Apache family in Arizona, and at no time within the past five years have the disturbing elements there been able to get beyond the control of the Indian police force.

Hundreds of the tribe have been arrested and confined, and two of the more desperate characters killed by them. They are still willing and able to arrest all local offenders, as well as any atrocious renegades who may seek an asylum at San Carlos.

The Indians of Arizona are, we may say, entirely at peace, and this peace must not be disturbed should a few renegades from New Mexico attempt to take refuge among them.

200

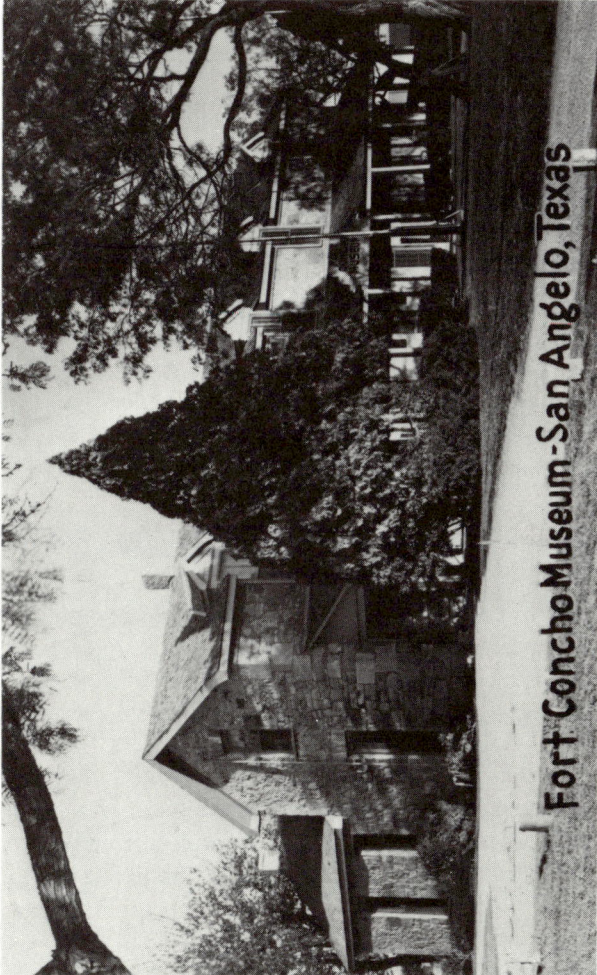

Fort Concho Museum - San Angelo, Texas

201

Personal History

John Porter Hatch was born on January 9, 1822 at Oswego, New York, the descendent of a Kentish family which came to the American colonies in 1634. Major Moses Porter was aide de camp on the staff of General Benedict Arnold at the Battle of Saratoga. His parents were Moses Porter and Hannah Reed Hatch. His mother was a sister to Mrs. Matthew (Linda) McNair, Mrs. Peter D. (Sally) Hugunin, and Mrs. Theophilus S. (Harriet) Morgan, prominent Oswego families. The Hatch family once occupied a house on what is now the site of the Pontiac Hotel building.

At the age of 18, he entered the United States Military Academy from which he graduated in 1845. Lieutenant Hatch kept close touch with his Oswego friends while he was in the midst of the fighting in Mexico. To his father he sent home newspapers and other mementos of the war, which his father took pleasure in exhibiting at the newspaper offices. Finally on April 3, 1847, he sent home a first copy of the American Eagle, issued that day at Vera Cruz. It contained an account of the bombardment of that city and its castle. It also contained the articles of capitulation imposed upon the Mexicans by the United States forces.

On October 27, 1848 the Mayor submitted the following communication:

Oswego, October 20, 1848.

To the Mayor and Common Council
of the City of Oswego:

Gentlemen:

While in the City of Mexico I learned that my native village had become a flourishing city. The American Governor, on my applying, granted me permission to take from the National Palace the accompanying chair. Should it be considered a fit seat for the Mayor of our city, please give it a place in your Council Room.

Your obedient servant
J. P. Hatch, U. S. A.

On motion of Alderman Mollison,

Resolved that the chair, presented by Lieut. Hatch be accepted, and placed in the hall of the Common Council for the purposes designated, and that the Mayor be requested to tender to Lieut. Hatch the thanks of the Council therefore.

The chair (locally referred to as the "chair of the Montezumas") is made of Spanish mohogany with red plush upholstery, and bears a silver plate telling of the gift. After much usuage the chair had been reupholstered several times and the springs readjusted.

Lieutenant Hatch came to Oswego early in 1848 on a long furlough at the end of the war. He spent the winter with his parents here. During that time he inserted an advertisement in the local papers stating that he would be leaving in May for the Pacific Coast for a new line of duty and offering to take along with him any Oswego young man who might be interested in going. He offered to discuss the matter with any who were interested. Actually he left Oswego in March, considerably earlier then he expected to leave. Officially he was listed as being on recruiting service in 1848–1849.

The regard and esteem which Oswego citizens felt towards Brigadier General John P. Hatch was manifested January 26, 1863 in a most unmistakable manner. The announcement that a presentation would be made to him sufficed to fill Doolittle Hall to overflowing. Every inch of standing room was occupied by the earnest friends of the General. The splendid Band of the 16th Infantry was present, and discoursed some of their excellent music. The appearance of the wounded General upon the platform leaning on his crutches, was the signal for a spontaneous outburst of applause that told how much the citizens appreciated that officer's gallant services to the flag of his country.

Mayor Daniel G. Fort made a short but exceedingly happy speech expressing his gratification at being present to discharge the pleasing duty of honoring the brave, and glancing briefly at the progress of the war.

The special service of silver, consisting of a massive silver pitcher, four goblets and a tray, each bearing an appropriate inscription, were placed on the table in plain view of the audience, and were much admired by all.

The Mayor introduced Judge David P. Brewster, who made the presentation of the silver service to the general in behalf of the friends of General Hatch. The judge also presented to the General a policy of insurance on his life for $5,000.

Among the several remarks the Judge said that it had been the ambition of him whom they saw to do honor to do his duty, and eulogy could not add to it or detraction take from it. He had in his possession a letter written by the General twenty-two years (1841) ago in which he solemnly consecrated himself to his country and promised that he would not disgrace his profession he had chosen. This testimonial, this proud array of friends, and the wounds he had received showed how well the soldier had kept his faith.

General Hatch was loudly applauded and he spoke substantially as follows:

My friends and fellow townsmen: A soldier of the Republic, the approbation of my fellow citizens is prized next to that of my Maker. The many acts of kindness extended to me whilst stretched on a sick bed had already shown me that I possessed your sympathy and esteem. Today the very flattering remarks of my friend, Judge Brewster, and the large numbers assembled here to greet me, make me feel that you overvalue the service I have been able to render my country. I have endeavored to do my duty. I will (inspirited by the recollection of this day) continue to do so, hoping by future acts to merit the praise bestowed upon me. The knowledge that the dear ones at my fire-side, in the event of my death are by your kind consideration, placed beyond want, removes from my mind a load that bears on too many of the brave men this day periling their lives for their country. This beautiful testimonial I receive with pride; it will be the inheritance of my son, should God spare him after my course is run. What richer bequest to a son, than the proof that his father possessed the respect and esteem of his fellow citizen.

Soldiers are generally but poor speechmakers and I am no exception to the rule, but I cannot close without a word for a body of brave men lately under my command. In the latter part of my service, I came in command of one of the best brigades in the Army. I have lately heard it called the "Iron Brigade" and well it merits the name. In this Iron Brigade there is no better regiment than your own gallant Twenty-fourth. It is an honor to the State, and to the county, and you may well be proud of having furnished the country such a band of heroes. When this rebellion is finally crushed, the thousands of patriotic men who have left their homes and their businesses for the country's service will again return to you. Receive them with honor, for you they struggle with hunger, with desease. On the field of battle they sustain the honor of our flag, knowing that individual acts of bravery, which would in any officer of rank make a page of history, are in the private soldiers unnoticed and unknown. They are gallant men; do them the honor their gallantry deserves.

General Hatch prized very greatly the silver service presented to him. Each piece was engraved "Presented to General John P. Hatch January 1863 by the Citizens of Oswego, N. Y." Today the silver service reposes in a glass case at the Smithsonian Institute in Washington, D. C. In 1948 when the City of Oswego was celebrating its centennial, the set was on display in the Oswego County Historical Society's Museum.

The 24th Regiment was raised in Oswego in April 1861, and days after a call for its enlistments went out Captain John D. O'Brien as the first officer in New York State to be commissioned under Lincoln's first call for volunteers led its first company to Elmira, then a mobilization point. O'Brien's company was the first to reach this rendezvous where so mnay other regiments were to assemble. The regiment moved from Elmira to Washington where it remained until after the Battle of Bull Run. As they marched from Washington the morning after the rout of Union soldiers at Bull Run after victory had seemed within their grasp, the regiment met the fleeing Union army returning to Washington. At the cross roads the regiment was ordered to go on picket duty at this point so that it became the only organized force between Washington and the victorious Confederates. They remained on this duty for three weeks without having been supplied with tents, blankets or other supplies.

After they were relieved they were brigaded with the 14th New York Regiment (Zouaves) and the 22nd and 30th New York Volunteers. Later they joined the Second United States Sharp Shooters. That fall they moved to Upton Hill where they constructed Fort Upton and went into Quarters for the winter. In the spring of 1862, the brigade marched on McClellan's orders through Bristoe Station, Catlett's Station towards Fredericksburg. Reaching Falmouth they were in contact with the Confederates whom they drove across the Rappahannock. While they were in camp there, General Hatch succeeded General Augur as their commander.

Following his retirement the General lived an uneventful life at his home in New York City, until his death at the age of seventy-nine. The funeral was held at St. Andrew's Church in Washington, D. C. The interment was at Arlington, among those he loved and those who loved him. Full military honors were given to General Hatch. His widow, a son and daughter survived him.

Family History

Moses Porter Hatch, the father of John, was born on August 7, 1796. He had a store and dwelling combined and also a distillery in the village of Mexico, New York, before he came to Oswego. For many years he was one of the most active and prominent business men of the city. In 1827 he bid and obtained the contract to build the pier for the Oswego Harbor. He was occupied in this work until 1829; and in 1852 and years afterward did the repair and maintenance of the pier although he was not a civil engineer. He was an extensive operator of real estate being an early landlord of the Welland Hotel and in 1835 purchased the Oswego Hotel. He was engaged in the milling industry and was listed in the city directory as a forwarder. He was also a member of the Board of Trade.

Mr. Hatch took part in various other activities, some being: 1822, Vestryman of Christ Episcopal Church; 1837, first chief of the Fire Department; 1834, 1835, 1837, Trustee of the Village; 1851, City Clerk; 1851, Democratic member of the State Assembly (resigned); 1851, State Senator; 1849, Trustee of Riverside Cemetery; 1852, one of the incorporators of the Oswego Orphan Asylum.

In 1869 Mr. Hatch sold his home to Sylvester Doolittle who built the Doolittle House on the site and in 1912 was replaced by the Pontiac Hotel. Mr. Hatch passed away on January 4, 1871 in Chicago, Illinois. His wife, Hannah D., whom he married in 1820, also died in Chicago on February 25, 1878. On the Hatch lot in Riverside Cemetery, Oswego, New York, besides Mr. and Mrs. Hatch, there lies Harriet Hatch, (died 1848) and Elizah M. Hatch (died on March 13, 1898 at the age of 73).

G. N. Barnard, Painesville, Ohio

GEORGE N. BARNARD
Civil War Photographer

George N. Barnard, the Connecticut-born photographer took up the profession in 1842, three years after Daguerre disclosed the process. One of the earliest references to the photographer's presence in Oswego was in 1847 when an enthusiastic admirer remarked "Mr. Barnard, at his rooms in the Palladium Building (northwest corner of West First and Cayuga Streets), is taking some of the finest pictures, we have ever seen. They seem to be fully equal to Plumbe's (prominent New York City photographer). Mr. Barnard is one of our most meritorious citizens, and we hope those wanting anything in his line will give him a call." Again in 1848 reference is made to "Mr. Barnard who has taken up a permanent residence in this city (Oswego) executes Daguerreotype liknesses at his office in the Woodruff Block (northwest corner of West First and Cayuga Streets), with life-like truth and fidelity."

G. N. BARNARD,

PORTRAIT AND LANDSCAPE

PHOTOGRAPHER

No. 263 King Street, Charleston, S. C.

STEREOSCOPIC VIEWS OF

Charleston, Fort Sumter, Old Goose Creek Church,
Ingleside, Drayton Hall, Magnolia Gardens,
painted and plain, and other points of
interest in this vicinity.

WHOLESALE AND RETAIL.

In 1851 George N. Barnard "respectively informs his friends and the public generally, that he had removed to his new rooms, over E. P. Burt's store (137 West First Street, the former Coe's laundry). He has perfected a powerful skylight, yet so mellow that he has enabled to take the likenesses of children and all other, in a few seconds, with perfect ease to the sitter; retaining a natural expression."

In 1853 Mr. Barnard's studio was located on the third floor of the City Bank, 147 West First Street (southeast corner of West First and Cayuga Streets) and he resided at 105 East Fourth Street. This bank building was demolished in 1962. He advertised himself as a daguerrean who took pictures in every style in all weather; he, also had a large assortment of gold and plated lockets, plates, cases, frames, chemicals etc., constantly on hand, wholesale and retail. "We took occasion to visit him in his new quarters and were highly pleased with all his arrangements" wrote a reporter. An elaborate account of the premises included a description of the Reception, Operating Room, Toilet Room, and other apartments for the convenience of the patrons and the sales of wares, chemicals, etc. There was no doubt that the facilities for operating were excelled this side of New York, and of Mr. Barnard's reputation and his abilty to please as an artist was established.

It was from these quarters that he took his cumbersome camera to the foot of West Cayuga Street where one photo was taken directly east. The other photo was taken near West Oneida Street, looking northeast. Mr. Barnard advertised from July 12 to August 1, 1853, that "pictures of the late fire taken while burning" could be obtained. These pictures are copied from large pictures, and are faithful representations of the different stages of the fire as it appeared on on the (July) 5th. Also views of the ruins as they now appear."

THE LIBERIAN SHIP "AZOR."—(Photographed by G. N. Barnard, Charleston, South Carolina.)

Harpers Weekly April 20, 1878

The fire destroyed an area extending from the river to East Sixth Street and from East Bridge Street to Fort Ontario grounds, sparing only a few buildings.

In 1854 Mr. Barnard formed a partnership under the name of Barnard & Nichols, practicing their art from 7 o'clock A. M. to 6 P. M. at their rooms over the City Bank. A card informed the public that Mr. Barnard has recovered from his sickness and has just returned from New York with a large variety of goods. He is listed in the Syracuse directories of 1854, 1855, and 1857, the first two years at 4 Franklin Building, now c. 128 East Genesee Street. There was no 1856 directory. In 1854 the firm of Barnard & Nichols is given, but no photographer Nichols is listed as an individual, 1853–1857. Isaih Taber and B. F. Howland took over the location in 1857. Mr. Barnard's listing, if there was one, was not located in the 1855 census. Barnard's ambrotype gallery was at 6 South Salina (n. 8 Wieting Block) in 1857. He does not appear in the 1859 book. H. Lazier advertised at the Wieting Block address in 1858. J. H. French lists G. N. Barnard as one of three artists who assisted on his State Map and Gazetteer. (Title verso, 1859) He subsequently was employed by Matthew B. Brady in his New York studio. The first week of February, 1861, Mr. Brady sent for two of his best photographers, G. N. Barnard being one, to come from New York to Washington to help him with preparations to cover Lincoln's inauguration.

George N. Barnard was among the first persons to photograph scenes of the Civil War battles and campaigns. Brady, a studio portrait photgrapher, had myopia as early as 1851 and was unable to do studio work by the mid–1850's; therefore, Brady depended upon field photographers to take the many Civil War pictures for which he was later credited. A large number of photographs heretofore credited to Brady have proved to be photographs by Barnard.

According to Manuel Kean, Philadelphia pictorial archivist, ''It has been an article of faith with many historians that any photograph showing a Civil War scene is a Brady. Yet whenever it has been possible to check out a so-called Brady, it has been established that it was made by someone else. In my opinion the greatest of the Civil War photographers was George N. Barnard.... His work is noteworthy for the fact that he was concerned with the terrain over which wars are fought. In Barnard's photographs people are secondary and, when present, are subdued to the composition.''

210

Looking North East from the present site of the Pontiac Hotel

Looking east from the foot of West Cayuga Street.
East Cayuga Street is to the left of Ames Grain Elevator.

211

Mr. Barnard came to Oswego for a brief stay in 1862. A notice in a local newspaper stated that "having secured the services, for a limited period, that celebrated artist, George N. Barnard (Formerly of this, and late from Brady's Gallery, Washington)....will find Mr. Barnard at Gray's Gallery at the east end of the Iron Bridge (southwest corner of East First and Bridge Streets), where he will be pleased to see his old customers and former acquaintances and friends."

After his short visit to Oswego, he was appointed as the United Sates Army's official photographer on Sherman's "March to the Sea" and the later campaign in the Carolinas. In 1866 he published an album of views taken in Tennessee, Georgia, and the Carolinas in 1864 and 1865 that sold then for $100 a copy and is "now so excessively rare that few collectors or institutions have copies."

Mr. Barnard is listed in the 1864 directory as "engineer, depart. govt. photographer," no business address, home 228 Townsend (Syracuse). This home address is continued in 1866, 1867 and 1868. He is "photograpger" the first two years, "artist" the third and that was the last listing there. In 1867, his only daughter, Miss Mary Grace Barnard (born November 19, 1849) is shown as a boarder at 228 Townsend. On September 22, 1867 she was married by Rev. S. J. May to Edgar O. Gilbert.

From Syracuse he went to Charleston, South Carolina before moving to Chicago. In 1871 he was burned out in the Great Chicago Fire but returned the following day to document the fire's destruction with photographs. In 1883 he helped George Eastman introduce dry-plates which eliminated the cumbersome wet-plate process and revolutionized photography. His last known studio was in Painsville, Ohio, between 1884 and 1886. Barnard died during a bad snow storm at his son-in-law's farm in the Town of Onondaga, just south of Syracuse, on February 4, 1902.

Literataure

MORGAN ROBERTSON AND HIS SEA STORIES

Today he is regarded as one of the finest writers of sea stories in English.

Morgan Andrew Robertson (Sept. 30, 1861—Mar. 24, 1915) was born in Oswego, New York, the son of Andrew (1817—Mar. 16, 1897) and Ruth Amelia (Glassford) Robertson. His father was born in Arguilshire, Scotland. At the age of 27 he crossed the sea and found his way to Oswego. There he became a seaman on the Great Lakes and eventually a well-known captain. He commanded the schooners *Tilton, Kingsford, Fornana, Lucy J. Latham, Jamaica,* and *Albion.* After retirement he commanded the steam Yacht *Aida* (built by the Goble Ship Yard in 1885 for James MacFarlane). Two months after the death of the mother, Morgan's sister Mabel, aged 6 years and 10 months, died of diptheria. Both, mother and daughter, were buried from their residence at 95 East Seventh Street— renumbered 103 today. Mrs. Robertson's sister, Verona (d. May 1, 1914, aged 73) married Moses Prouse Neal (d. Dec. 22, 1900, aged 73), a tailor, merchant and mayor of Oswego. Her sister, Margaret (d. Feb. 9, 1923) married Captain Morgan Miles Wheeler (May 10, 1835—Mar. 26, 1877), a prominent self-made man, the owner of several tugs and a large number of vessels in Oswego. There was another sister, Mrs. Alzina Curtiss, and a brother James. Captain Andrew Robertson was twice married. To his first wife were born two sons, Morgan and William, and a daughter, Alice, Mrs. William Sheldon. In 1876 he married Anna Lent (d. Jul. 15, 1927), and by her had one daughter, Clara.

"Gathering No Moss," published in the *Saturday Evening Post,* March 28, 1914, is the title Morgan Robertson gave to the story of his own life. Full of ups and downs and roundabouts, his life ranged from sailing the great Lakes, circumnavigating the globe, cowpunching in Texas, learning the goldsmith's art, diamond-setting, and clock repairing, through the disheartening and valiant struggle to earn a living, hand-to-mouth, in New York City, through threatened blindness and nervous breakdown. Always on the move, never completely bogged down, forever dabbling and experimenting—small wonder that he thought of himself as a rolling stone. As for moss, what had he accumulated? Certainly little money, few possessions, no establishment, but friends, yes, many of them, maybe even a few enemies for good measure, and a rich treasure of experience.

His books made friends for him. Those stories of the sea, so vigorous, so salty with humor, so direct in action, so skilled in seamanship, found favor with those who enjoyed a well spun yarn, whether they went down to sea in ships or stayed ashore.

Charles Lee Lewis, instructor at Annapolis Naval Academy, writing about Morgan Robertson in the *Dictionary of American Biography* (vol. XVI, p. 27) thus catalogs his stories:

> His stories deal with sailing ships, steam vessels and the long steel men-of-war. They treat of mutiny and bloody fights, shipwreck and rescue, brutality, shangaiing, courage and wild daring, telepathy, hypnotism, dual personality, and extraordinary inventions.

Booth Tarkington, in *McClures Magazine* (October, 1915, p. 90), wrote: "His stories are bully, his sea foamy, and his men have hair on their chests."

Joseph Conrad (Josef Korzeniowski) wrote to Robertson: "Indeed, my dear Sir, you are a first rate seaman—one can see that with half an eye."

Included among his friends and admirers were such writing notables as Irwin S. Cobb and William Dean Howells. Shortly before his death, Robertson was listed in *Who's Who In America* and, after his death, he became the subject of a book, *Morgan Robertson, The Man*, a collection of panegyics from the pens of some of the leading writers of the times.

Little is known of his early years. It is certain that he had attended Public School No. 6. He probably attended Oswego High School but is not listed as a graduate. (St. Paul's Church now occupies the site of the former School No. 6 and the Salvation Army building occupies the former high school site opposite West Park). He learned to sail on lake-going vessels under the tutelage of his father, whom he later called, in the dedication of one of his books, the "ablest seaman" he had ever known. Although the boy made frequent trips on the lakes during summer vacations he could take his trick at the wheel "when the weather wasn't too heavy," the elder Robertson insisted that the youth take up a career ashore.

It is surmised that he found it difficult to live with his step-mother, and like the hero of his novel, *Master of Men*, Robertson ran away to sea at the age of sixteen. A Captain Davis, and like the hero of his novel, *Master of Men*, sailing a clipper ship out of Boston in the China trade, offered him passage as a cabin-boy. He accepted gladly and sailed away into China trade. It was several years before he came back. He developed a dislike for Captain Davis who he found not like the free and easy skippers of the lakes. That he knew and who made much of him because he was Captain Andy's boy. Robertson also sailed on the *Ringleader*, with Captain William E. "Billy" Bray. The ship was built in Chelsea, Massachusetts, in 1868. A clipper of the same name was built at Medford, Massachusetts in 1853. In this school of hard knocks he developed from an "underbilt little runt" into a powerful bucko first mate able to trash any man aboard ship. One of his contemporaries described him as "strong as a bull, with a 46-inch chest." He described himself as "short of stature" with "every earmark of the man before the mast." He had a deep, booming voice and an abrupt manner of speech that often irritated editors during the years he was writing. His loud voice and his strength no doubt served him well at sea for these qualities, along with a total lack of mercy, he ascribed to all of the mates who appeared in his many tales of the sea.

Robertson never agreed with the then-prevalent doctrine of American deep-water seafaring, which he described as holding "that sailors, like mules, could only be governed by fear." Yet he apparently was very good with his fists and did what was expected of him in order to advance his career. It is not known how he felt about the well-known adage among sailors, "sailors work like mules and spend their money like jackasses."

Starting in 1877 as a cabin boy, he attained the rank of first mate before leaving the sea in 1886. According to Irvin S. Cobb, Robertson's decision to give up the sea was prompted by a sudden realization of the horror of his own brutal treatment of foremast hand. In his 1941 autobiographical work *Exit Laughing*, Cobb recounts a story he says Robertson told him about how he was sickened by the sought of a bleeding seaman whom he had beaten and thrown down a hatch for a minor infraction. Robertson went ashore that night, Cobb says, and never set foot on a ship again except as a passenger.

In the earlier years, his success with his stories was a surprise to his friends in Oswego. He was better remembered there as a sailor than as a writer. He usually wore the square-cut mariner's reefer jacket. From five dollar gold pieces he fashioned buttons for his coat and appeared one autumn in Oswego all a-glitter to the astonishment, especially, the young ladies. As the winter of his stay lengthened, the buttons gradually disappeared from the jacket, returned, it was surmised, to circulation by the owner.

One winter, between voyages, he settled down to learn the jeweler's business with a Mr. Barnes, who had a jewelry store at 210 West First Street. He made his home with his uncle, Mr. Moses P. Neal at 53 East Fifth Street. Wishing to express his appreciation for that hospitality, he insisted on installing cathedral chimes, a complete set of them, in the clock that stood on the shelf in the Neal sitting room. So loud and so long were the hour changes rung by the resonant chimes that the exasperated uncle vented his wrath: "I always thought he was a fool, and now he had made himself a monument for it with that clock." Everyone who knew him seemed to cherish a good story about him, as a sailor, as an original, as a master hand and unique.

An obituary does not always give a true picture of a man, but the tribute that appeared in the Oswego *Palladium*, March 25, 1915, the day following Robertson's death, is so sincere, from the nickname of his boyhood, "Morg", to the last picturesque detail of his cabin in a studio, that it was known it was written by a friend. Reports such as the one that Robertson was employed by Tiffany's in New York City as a diamond-setter are incorrect. Major John W. Vess, Jr., U. S. A. Retired, a biographer of Robertson, was unable to substantiate this assertion. He also found to be incorrect the story that Robertson studied jewelry at Cooper Union.

His obituary stated:

While afloat Mr. Robertson became adept as a worker in gold. He made handsome watch chains with anchors and snatchblocks, through which ran the finest of gold wrought chains. When he decided to quit sailing, he went to New York City where he studied the jewelry trade and opened a small shop, specializing in diamond-setting. He soon became an expert in this field, but his earnings were never spectacular. He continued in the vocation until 1894, when his sight failed.

On May 27, 1894, he married Alice M. Doyle, daughter of William and Anna (Rose) Doyle of New York City, whom he later described as a "frail little woman." Although she outlived her husband by a good many years, Mrs. Robertson was frequently ill and Robertson found himself doing household chores, in an autobiographical article entitled "Gathering No Moss." He says: "I knew how to cook—thanks to my training as a sailor—and we had enough groceries on hand for several meals; but the clothes had to be washed. It is impossible for my wife to do this and there was not enough money on hand to have it done; so I undertook the job."

Robertson took up writing in 1896 when failing eyesight forced him to give up his diamond-setting business. He began writing in the hope of making money; with no business he was financially embarrassed. His obituary told how he began his writing. "In 1896 while he was in New York, a friend handed him one of Rudyard Kipling's sea stories and told him to read it. He did and that night he began and finished a short story, writing on a washtub." Capitalizing on his sea experiences, he wrote "The Destruction of the Unfit," an 8,000 word story. He submitted it to a newspaper syndicate, where it was refused because of its length. It was then sent to a magazine and after a long delay was accepted for $25. During the year that followed, Robertson wrote and sold about twenty short stories of the sea." He earned about a $1,000. He wrote more than 200 stories in leading American magazines and English periodicals.

Although Robertson knew his subject, and soon mastered the art of expressing himself, he was never a business man. His most successful years were between 1898 and 1905, but even then he was never free from financial worries. When he made money he spent it, although he said later that he was never a spendthrift. As he explained it, living the life of a writer was simply more expensive than following the daily walks of a sailor or a diamond-setter. As his name began to appear more frequently in the better magazines, he felt obliged to cultivate the acquaintance of other writers. Being sociable did not create a drinking problem for him; he had the seaman's love for sociability and a drop of rum.

He felt completely out of place at formal dinners. Robertson described one of his formal dinners in his *Post* article by asking the question, "did you ever see a sailor in a dress suit and a high hat?" One dinner of interest to Oswegonians was held on Saturday evening January 25, 1902, at the Arena in New York City. The *Oswego Daily Times* reported that former mayor John D. Higgins, then of New York, would be the Chairman of the Committee on Arrangements. This dinner, it was expected, would be the first of many that would be arranged annually. The paper followed this announcement by reporting the activity on Monday January 27, 1902. "Half a hundred loyal sons of Oswego gathered on Saturday night at the Arena, 41 West 31st St., New York, enjoyed a sumptuous dinner, sounded the praises of the city of their birth or adoption and founded the Oswego Society in the City of New York, with Ex-mayor John D. Higgins as its head." Among those in attendance were the famous painters James G. Tyler and J. Francis Murphy, and equally famous author Morgan Robertson. Speakers included Frank B. McLean, former assistant engineer of Oswego; Charles Tremain, the shade cloth manufacturer; Abraham Meyer and Lawrence Churchill, lawyers; Dr. F. X. Pidgeon, John Daley of the police department, Claude P. Boyle and Percy Owen. "When one speaker referred to the old home city as 'God's Own Country' there was prolonged applause, the term seeming to strike a tender chord in every heart." Included was a list of fifty-two native Oswegonians and attendance would increase when all those who claim Oswego as their home join the society."

Continuing the tribute in Robertson's obituary, the friend wrote: 'His first book was A Tale Of A Halo! It was a good seller and then a suggestion was made to him that he specialize in sea stories. He did and while he never proved a Clark Russell, he wrote many interesting stories, of which the following were some of his best 'Where Angels Fear To Tread', published first in *Atlantic Monthly*; 'Salvage' in the *Century*; 'The Brain Of The Battleship', 'The Wigwag Message', 'Between The Millstones', 'The Battle of the Monsters', all in *Saturday Evening Post*; 'The Trade Wind', *Colliers*; 'From The Royal Yard Down', *Ainslee's*; 'Needs Must When The Devil Drives' and 'When Greek Meets Greek', *McClures*; 'Primordial', *Harper's*.

"The Wreck Of The Titan" written in 1898 before the sinking of the steamer "Titanic" in 1912 was regarded after the accident as almost a prophecy; telling how such an accident was possible by collision with an iceberg, and it was reprinted in many magazine editions of Sunday newspapers.

Yet success as a writer did not bring the complete financial security he sought. He continued to produce stories and they continued to sell, but he never reached the pinnacle of $5,000 in a single year tht he apparently had set for himself. Then, after a few years, he found it more and more difficult to write, and more and more difficult to sell what he had written.

Seeking new material, he turned to the occult, studying subjects of reincarnation, hypnotism, dual personality, and mental telepathy. As an uneducated man, he had always found writing a difficult task, and he often sat at his typewriter for hours waiting for the right word to come. Then, suddenly, in a burst of inspiration, he would begin writing and produce a near masterpiece. Because of this, he toyed with the idea that his works were produced by some descarnate soul, a spirit with literary ability, who commanded his body and brain on special occasions.

Plagued by financial worries until he was on the verge of nervous breakdown, and drinking more than was good for him, Robertson began to fear that he was losing his mind. For some reason, he had long suspected that he harbored within himself latent insanity that needed only extra mental strain to bring it to the surface. Urged by his wife and friends to go into the hospital for a rest, he became a volunteer mental patient at Bellevue Hospital. There the doctors soon found him to be entirely sane and discharged him with a certificate of sanity.

Major Vess in his biography of Robertson relates the following incident:

> Robertson's first act upon release from the hospital was to head for the nearest bar to test his will power. He ordered a drink of good whiskey, and as soon as it was served, poured it into the cuspidor.
>
> "Where'd you come from?" the shocked bartender asked.
>
> "The psychopathic ward," Robertson replied.
>
> "How'd you get out?"
>
> "The gate."
>
> "Well," the bartender observed, as he moved the whiskey bottle carefully out of Robertson's reach and wiped the bar, "You can always go back."
>
> Robertson responded by whipping out his certificate of sanity, as he was to do on many occasion, much to the delight of his friends and to the confusion of people who did not

know him. He also capitalized on his experiences at Bellevue by producing a magazine article, "My Skirmish With Madness," which he sold to the *National Sunday Magazine.*

In another instance, he was ready for the man who called him (as some were occasionally tempted to call him) crazy. "Crazy am I" "What'll you bet that I can't prove I am sane and not crazy?" With the wager made, Morgan would triumphantly produce his legal discharge from Bellevue Hospital as the document in evidence and laughingly gather up the stakes.

Besides his being a sailor, a diamond-setter and an author, Robertson was an inventor. While doing research on the subject of submarines, which he featured in several of his short stories, he became intrigued by the need that existed for the invention of a practical periscope. He resolved to solve this problem, and, in the course of subsequent experiments, he made thorough study of optics. Using his diamond-cutting skills, he even ground his own lenses when he found he could not buy them in shapes he needed. Robertson was successful in designing a much improved periscope and apparently for two years was on the payroll of the Holland Torpedo Boat Company.

Robertson's studio in New York was fitted like a ship's cabin, with all the comforts of sleeping room, dining room, kitchen, bathroom, library and den. On one side of a draped couch he had a cushioned window seat, under a porthole. His bathtub could be covered and used as a table. In one corner was a gas range on which he could make coffee and other light repasts when immersed in his work. The room was papered with illustrations from his stories.

Thus the friend described the author's studio in his obituary.

Robertson renewed his efforts to produce stories that would sell. But he found it almost impossible to write. He felt himself a sponge that had been squeezed dry.

In early 1914, penniless and facing eviction from the Harlem apartment where he and his wife lived, Robertson swallowed his pride and used his financial problems as a theme of the autobiographical article he sold the *Saturday Evening Post* which had published nineteen of his short stories over the years. He insisted, however, that the story appear without a by-line. If Robertson's only goal in writing the article was earning immediate cash, he was soon surprised. Even though there was no by-line, the author of the article was promptly recognized. His many friends were shocked to learn that he and his wife were completely destitute.

After the appearance of the *Post* article a number of Robertson's friends, sparked by Irvin S. Cobb and Bozeman Bulger, baseball editor of the *New York Evening World* rallied to his aid. A collection was taken to provide for the immediate needs of Robertson and his wife, and subsequently his friends made arrangements for the publication of new collections of his short stories as well as the re-publication of many of his previous works in a uniform edition.

The published volumes of Robertson's stories include: *A Tale Of A Halo* (1894); *Spun Yarn* (1898); *Futility* (1898); *Where Angels Fear To Tread* (1899); *Masters Of Men* (1901); *Sinful Peck* (1903); *Down To The Sea* (1905); *Land Ho!* (1905); and "Chivalry" a play (1913). In 1914 the author gathered his tales for a uniform, complete edition which comprised eight volumes.

The Oswego *Daily Times*, October 1, 1914, under the heading "Oswego Writer Is Recognized," wrote of Robertson's plight. The article stated:

> Morgan Robertson, once of Oswego, and now of New York, where for the past few years he has been making a hard go of a literary life, is to receive a reward for the contribution which he has made to the literature of the country in his sea stories, known wherever sailors and the lovers of the sea congregate. Metropolitan and McClure's, two of the best known monthly magazines in the country, backed by a big publishing house, have taken up Mr. Robertson's battle and will fight for his recognition.

Last March Oswegonians read with interest an autobiography of an anonymous writer of short stories, tales of the sea, and his troubles, published in a weekly magazine. It was at once set down as the life story of Morgan Robertson, born in this city, but for many years a resident of New York. Apparently the same story was read and aprreciated by others for it was through this autograph that publishers of the two monthlies above mentioned got together and decided to bring out a deluxe edition of the best tales of Mr. Robertson. They are announcing now the opportunity to secure a set of books with their magazines, but more interesting than that, they promise to pay the author a generous royalty.

The article was generous in its tributes to Mr. Robertson, and among other things said:

Morgan Robertson's stories will live after him, but he has been a poor business man. Famous he is, but fame is a poor substtute for beefsteak. Will the American public allow the tragic end of O. Henry to be repeated? Will they allow another of their great writers of short stories to die in want, without reward or recognition? That is what the Metropolitan and McClure's propose to find out. If this genius of the sea cannot get now, while he and his family are in need, the reward and the recognition which are his right, it will not be from lack of proper aid.

An edition of Robertson's works (selected from what he has written by the author himself as his best stories) is being published. Upon every book sold we shall pay him a generous royalty.

In every one of his long stories there is an affectionate reference to his old home town. In his *Masters Of Men*, he best known tale of the Spanish American war, the description of the city, the home of the hero, could not be taken anything else but Oswego, and it is claimed by those who know the boyhood of the author that some of the incidents chronicled in the book actually occurred to him.

So ends the article.

A few words about his stories would not be amiss.

Masters Of Men is dedicated, "To my wife, a good woman." It is the story of Dick Halpin, a red-haired and freckled orphan lad, who joins the navy, a few years before the Spanish-American war. The boy goes through the rigorous training on shipboard, rising step by step to be signal man. By reason of Dick's gallant service in action at the blockade of Santiago, he wins a commission. Bronson, Halpin's sponsor and himself in the service, gives the keynote of of the story: "It's a tough life, amd makes a machine out of a fellow." A hilarious section of the story tells how young Halpin brings home a dozen shipmates to help him pay back a grudge against a group of hateful schoolmates. As the fight mounts to a climax, the citizens bring out the fire department to drown the fracas. *Masters Of Men* was made into a movie. It was played in Oswego at the Orpheum theater. [The theater was located on West Bridge Street between

222

Second and Third Streets.] Mr. Charles P. Gilmore was the manager.

Sinful Peck, the second full length tale, is built around a practical joke played as a result of an election bet when Bryan ran for President. Peck, the loser, must ship out for a year as a sailor, or forfeit $10,000 to Seldom Helward. A group of old shipmates, now successful men of Cleveland, Ohio, go to New York to give "Sinful" a fitting send-off. At the dinner given the night before "Sinful" is to sail, he drugs the other guests and has them shangaied to his ship. The adventures that follow the gamut of stirring mutiny, pirates, storms, rescues, hairbreath escapes, and fights aplenty.

"THE PIRACY WAS COMPLETE."

223

Sinful Peck and his friends first appeared in the short story, "Where Angels Fear To Tread," one of Robertson's early tales which is especially interesting to Oswegonians because a lively group of lake or "fresh water" sailors, all from Oswego, sign up with a square rigged merchant ship, the *Almena*, which of course, was outward bound, round the Horn of Gallos. They are all "well-fed, well-paid, self-respecting citizens" who sign up using their nicknames. These nicknames are authentic. The late John S. Parsons of Oswego knew the real names of the men who answered to them on the lake front. Here they are as Morgan Robertson fitted fictitious last names to the nicknames: Tosser Galvin, Senator Sands, Turkey Twain, Big Pig Monahan, Gunner Meagher, Moccassey Bill, Yampaw Gallagher, Ghost O'Brien, Sinful Peck, Sorry Welch, Poopdeck Cahill, Seldom Helward, Yorker Jimson, Shiner O'Toole, General Lannigan. The humorous point of the story is that sailors on the Great Lakes are better men than salt water sailors. They are used to better treatment. Their awakening to the realities of seafaring is startling. These Oswego men "would rather fight than eat." There is a fort at Oswego (the story dates back to the early 1880's), and whenever a company of soldiers becomes unmanageable, the War Department transfers them to Oswego—and they are well-behaved, well-licked soldiers when they leave. "An Oswego sailor loves a row." How these Oswego sailors get the upper hand and escape, even from the police in New York harbor, makes lively reading.

One of the figures Robertson invented is the lovable old Finnegan, on the battleship *Argyll*. In the stories the kindly rascal is like Mulvaney, the soldier in Kipling's stories. He appears in *The Brain of the Battleship* and several other tales.

Another group of stories deals with a pirate ship, Captain Swarth and Angel Todd, the first mate.

One of the physicians in Oswego, it was reported, thought the finest story Robertson wrote is *The Battle of the Monsters* because of its imaginative and original representation. It tells of the struggle in the blood-stream of germs—the germs of hydrophobia and cholera—and how they are conquered by the leucocytes. Robertson dramatized Metchnikoff's theory, based on microscopic examination of blood, of fighting leucocytes.

To another reader—a business man—there is the greatest thrill in "The Closing of the Circuit," included in the volume *Down to the*

Sea. This is the story of a boy, born blind, brought up in ignorance because of his lack of sight. How he runs away to sea and regains his sight by shock is the action. The thrill lies in the vivid realism of the scene where the boy gradually becomes aware of the miracles of vision.

Morgan Robertson's obituary stated that the author was found dead in his hotel room in Atlantic City as a result of heart trouble. "Mr. Robertson came here a few days ago suffereing from a nervous collapse. He spent most of his time on the beach and on the boardwalk. The change of air was apparently having a good effect upon him. He went to his room shortly before noon to lie down and asked that bellboy call him in time for luncheon. A rap at his door at one o'clock failed to bring a response. The boy opened the door and found him leaning lifeless across his bureau."

Another source gave a different version of his passing. When Robertson confessed that all his life he had longed for a fur coat and a gold-headed cane, Cobb and Bulger managed to obtain these for him, second hand and somewhat battered. Not long afterwards Robertson was found dead in a shabby hotel in Atlantic City, seated before a window that overlooked the sea and with his fur coat about his shoulders and cane across his knees.

"His fame, though short-lived, was not ill-founded."

H. C. Bunner

HENRY CUYLER BUNNER

"...He practically founded a new
genre in the United States, the anectodal tale."

Henry Cuyler Bunner (Aug. 31, 1855—May 11, 1896) editor
of the famous comic weekly, *Puck*, poet, and master of the art of the
short story, was of the third generation of his family to live in
Oswego. The mother was of New England stock, a sister of Henry
T. Tuckerman; the father also belonged to an old New England
family. Let us trace the background of the Bunner family.

Rudolph Bunner (Aug 17, 1779—Jul. 16, 1837) was born in
Savannah, Wayne County, New York. He was graduated from
Columbia College at New York City in 1798; studied law; was
admitted to the bar and practiced in Newburgh, Orange County,
from 1819 to 1822; and moved to Oswego in October 1822. He
married Elizabeth Church, the daughter of John B. Church, reputed
to have been one of the wealthiest men in America during the
Revolutionary War period. She was the niece of Alexander
Hamilton and of Catherine Cockran, and mother-in-law of John
Duer. (Catherine Cockran was the daughter of General Philip
Schuyler and sister of Mrs. Alexander Hamilton). Mr. Bunner came
to Oswego to administer an extensive part of Alexander Hamilton's
original Oswego holdings which he inherited. He did not practice
law while in Oswego but engaged in manufacturing and served as a
director of Oswego Cloth & Carpet manufacturing Company, and
was one of the first directors of the Oswego Canal Company. He
was an eloquent political speaker and was elected to the 20th
Congress (March 4, 1827—March 3, 1829). He first lived in a
house located on the southeast corner of West Second and Cayuga
Streets. In 1825 he built a spacious stone mansion on 15 Bronson
Street. At that time his land extended to the lake bank. This house
is noteworthy because it is the only Oswego mansion which has
been the residence of three representatives in Congress (William
Duer, 1847; Dewitt Littlejohn, 1863). Unfortunately the mansion,
occupied by the Delta Kappa Kappa Fraternity, was destroyed by
fire on January 9, 1983.

Henry's father, Rudolph II, (there was also a Rudolph III) was
an editor of the Oswego *Palladium* during 1852 and 1853. The

Oswego directories listed his residence as 71 West Seneca Street as a bookkeeper and real estate agent. Several years later the houses of the city were re-numbered redesignating 71 to 92.

John C. Bunner, Henry's uncle, was the editor of the Oswego *Patriot*; he was an ardent "patriot." When the Canadian "patriots" were all dispersed, transported or hung, the Oswego *Patriot* was also suspended. In 1840 he became assistant editor of the Buffalo *Republican* and in 1841, its editor serving until that newspaper changed ownership January 1, 1842. John C. Bunner removed to California in the late 1840's drawn there by the "gold rush." He served in the Union Army from that state in the Civil War, and after the war returned to that state where he continued to reside. He left several children.

Sometime in the 1860's Rudolph Bunner moved his family to New York City. They did not return to Oswego, henceforth Henry lived near or in the great city. Oswego honored the Bunner family by naming a street after it.

A digression at this point would be of interest to Oswegonians as it relates to the origin of some street names in the Eighth Ward. They were named after Rudolph Bunner, the Congressman; Alexander Hamilton, Secretary of Treasury during Washington's administration; Catherine Cockran (d. Aug. 26, 1857), daughter of General Philip Schuyler and sister of Mrs. Hamilton; John B. Church; and Judge Laurence, a judge of the United States Court of New York and United States Senator from New York, 1796–1800.

The three men, Hamilton, Church, Lawrence, bought a tract of land first known as the Roosevelt and later as the Scriba Purchase. (Roosevelt and Scriba Streets are also in the Eighth Ward). When Alexander Hamilton was killed in his duel with Aaron Burr, his sudden death made it expedient for his friends to become subscribers to a fund to hold all his real estate, that it might be protected from forced sale, and thus secure themselves and Mrs. Hamilton from serious loss. [Alexander Hamilton's will can be found at the Oswego County Clerk's Office.]

Lots Nos. 1 and 2 of the Hamilton Gore, which lay south of Fort Ontario, extended south to the city line. In 1825 "the Hamilton Tract" as Lots Nos. 1 and 2 came to be known, was surveyed by Jacob Lamb and divided into thirty-two subdivisions, which were divided among the heirs of the original proprietors. In 1838 the subdivisions were further divided into building lots by S.

228

A. Beers. A document made in 1825 and on file in County Clerk's Office is the report of the commissioners defining the boundaries and ownership of the various parcels. Thus the streets received their names.

Henry C. Bunner became the editor of *Puck* within a year of its founding in 1877 and ran it until his death. He wrote mainly for its columns. *Puck* was a profusion of prose, verse, jokes, paradies, lyrics of all sorts, brief stories, character-sketches, and editorials. Bunner's editorials were directed to the intelligence of his readers; they were effective because they were always simple, sincere, straight-forward, and because they were never aggressive, domineering, or abusive. Moreover, the character of his writing was to some extent determined by the nature of *Puck*, which demanded material not merely humorous but brief. He was above all a writer of short stories, tailored to fit the pages of a magazine determined not to be boring. To him his work as a journalist was as important as his work as a man of letters and he gave his newspaper articles the polish which characterized his more ambitious and less ephemeral efforts. Although he never weakened in his allegiance to *Puck*, Bunner contributed poems and stories to other magazines.

How did Bunner's friends see him? Witty, brilliant, and versatile, he often wrote, according to his good friend, Brander Matthews, half the good things in an issue. He was tireless as a worker, contributing regularly to the leading magazines—sometimes his delightful verses, sometimes his entertaining, deft stories. Mr. Jenson (Gerard Jensen: *The Life and Letters of Henry Cuyler Bunner*, Duke University Press, 1940) quotes that some of his best friends had to say about him. A description of his personal appearance is given by Henry Gallup Paine in *The Bookman*, June, 1912: "Of medium height and slight frame, a smooth upper lip and close cropped sidewhiskers, he looked, when his face was in a response, more like a clergyman than the editor of a comic weekly—but he bubbled with humor." Among the tributes paid to him, his friend and associate in letters, Brander Matthews, has written, "A cheery helpfulness was the keynote of his character. He was honest and open in his opinion, witty in conversation, considerate, a good listener, of wide erudition in literature, possessing an excellent memory, especially in poetry." Jensen sums up his character thus: "Bunner was a gentleman, a scholar, a good man, and a good American and his fame rests equally on what he wrote and what he was."

For the amusement and the fun he provided for his friends, a couple signs are noted here. A sign posted in his house, copied by a visitor and printed in *The Book-Buyer*, July, 1896, read:

> This is the Home of Harmony and Quiet.
> It loves no personal and Club riot.
> Come! and be WELCOME!! - but let this remind you.
> You've prayed to leave your Grievances behind you.

The following lines were posted in the bath room:

> No one in this household oughter
> Leave these faucets running water;
> And no one, I am certain would
> Who was entirely kind and good.

Henry C. Bunner died May 11, 1896, in Nutley, New Jersey. It was a short life, untimely ended, remembering that it was constant overwork, and a driving energy that sapped his strength beyond recovery. These years were filled to the brim with eager living, creative writing, and the give and take of newspaper work. He had a wide circle of friends, both personal and professional. Eleven years before he died, he married Miss Alice Learned, sister of his friend, Walter Learned. He was most happily married. Oswegonians are proud to recall that he began life here.

Comments on Bunner's literature are taken from a paper by Dr. Lida S. Penfield, former Director of the English Department of the Oswego State Normal School.

Henry C. Bunner's first volume of verse, *Airs from Arcady*, is a delightful introduction to his way of thought. The poem, "My Shakspere," recalled Bunner's life in Oswego. Mr. Bunner writes of himself as a small boy when he read "Shakspere" in his grandmother's garden that surrounded the second home on Bronson Street. The verses reveal his pleasant memory of life in Oswego. The poet received a new richly bound copy of the *Works of William Shakespere*. He contrasts the fresh elegance, with the worn shabiness of the volume from which he first came to know the plays of the great Elizabethan dramatist. The poem is included here for readers who would find it difficult to find a copy since many of his works are out of print.

MY SHAKSPERE

With beveled binding, with uncut edge,
With broad white margin and gilded top.
Fit for my library's choicest ledge.
Fresh from the bindery, smelling of shop,
In tinted cloth, with a strange design -
Buskin and scroll-work and mask and crown,
And an arabesque legend tumbling down -
The Works of Shakespere were never so fine.
Fresh from the shop! I turn the page -
Its "ample margin is wide and fair,
Its type is chosen with daintiest care;
There's a New French "Elzevir" strutting there
That would shame its prototypic age.
Fresh from the shop! O Shakspere mine,
I've half a notion you're much too fine!

There's an ancient volume that I recall,
In foxy leather much chafed and worn;
Its back is broken by many a fall,
The stitches are loose and the leaves are torn;
And gone is the bastard title, next
To the title-page scribbled with owner's name,
That in straggling old-style type proclaims
That the work is from the corrected text
Left by the late George Steevens, Esquire.

The broad sky burns like a great blue fire,
And the Lake shines blue as shimmering steel,
And it cuts the horizen like a blade;
And behind the poplar's a strip of shade -
The great tall Lombardy on the lawn,
And, lying there in the grass, I feel
The wind that blows from the Canada shore,
And in cool sweet puffs comes stealing o'er,
Fresh as any October dawn.
I lie on my breast in the grass, my feet
Lifted boy-fashion, and swinging free,
The old brown Shakspere in front of me,

And big are my eyes, and my heart's abeat:
And my whole soul's is lost - in what? - who knows?
Perdita's charms or Perdita's woes -
Perdita fairy-like, fair and sweet.
Is any one jealous, I wonder, now,
Of my love for Perdita? For I vow
I loved her well. And who can say
That life would be quite the same life to-day -
That love would mean so much, if she
Had not taught me its A B C?

The grandmother, thin and bent and old,
But her hair still dark and her eyes still bright,
Totters around among the flowers -
Old-fashioned flowers of pink and white;
And turns with a trowel the dark rich mold
That feels the bloom of her heart's delight.
Ah me! for her and for me the hours
Go by, and for her the smell of earth -
And for me the breeze and a far love's birth,
And the sun and the sky and all the things
That a boy's heart hopes and a poet sings.
Fresh from the shop! O Shakspere mine,
It wasn't the binding made you divine!
I knew you first in a foxy brown,
In the old, old home, where I laid it down,
In the idle summer afternoons,
With you alone in the odorous grass,
And set your thoughts to the wind's low tunes,
And saw your children rise up and pass -
And dreamed and dreamed of the things to be,
Known only, I think, to you and me.
I've hardly a heart for you dressed so fine -
Fresh from the shop, O Shakspere Mine!

There is no doubt that Oswego is the locale for the story "Round Up." The city of Trega has the appearance of Oswego in the 19th century. The heroine Rhodora Boyd. Rhodora Pennington came to Trega as the guest of her uncle, the Commandant of the Fort (Ontario)—for Trega was a garrison town. She was beautiful and she was an accomplished, delightful, impartial flirt. There was much social gaiety in her honor. Claude Bragdon, in his autobiography, *More Lives Than One*, noted that there was a distinction among the upper class of society in Oswego. The Sloans were on a higher level than the Kingsfords, and all vied for invitations to the officer's social functions held at the fort. The story continues:

The Shakespeare Club and the Lake Picnic,—which had hitherto divided the year between them, were submerged in the flood of social entertainments—Trega's square stone houses were lit up night after night, and broad moss-grown gardens about were made trim and presentable, and Chinese lanterns turned them into a paradise for young lovers.

It was a great year for Trega! The city had been dead, commercially, ever since the New York Central Railroad had opened up the great West; but the unprecedented flow of champagne and Appollinaris actually started a little business boom, based on the inferable wealth of Trega, and two or three of Trega's remaining firms went into bankruptcy because of the boom. And Rhodora Pennington did it all.

As a word of explanation for those unacquainted with the history of Oswego, it was claimed that Oswego's decline in the latter half of the 19th century was due to the railroad's by-passing Oswego. Actually the decline was due to the failure of Congress to renew the Reciprocity Agreement with Canada, with the milling industry moving westward closer to the grain supply, and the abolition of tolls on the Erie Canal.

Nevertheless, the story counted nine engagements at the end of the year.

The only union of the nine came as a surprise to the community was the engagement of Rhodora to Charley Boyd. The beauty of the season had picked up the one crooked stick in the town—a dissolute, ne'er-do-well hanger-on of Trega's best society, who would never have seen a dinner card if he

233

had not been a genius at amateur theatricals, an artist on the banjo, and a half-bred Adonis.

Rhodora's Adonis deserted her. Rhodora nursed her bed-ridden mother until she died, supporting them both by teaching music and French at the Trega Semminary, down by the Falls. So at last Rhodora Boyd died. The conclusion of the story is in dialog, a reminder that Bunner also wrote plays. Each of the eight men who had been refused by Rhodora in the year of her triumph, found himself summoned to be a pall-bearer at her funeral. Without exception the eight wives were indignant and the men embarrassed by "The Round Up."

"Squire Five-Fathom" is easily recognized as a story about experiences in Oswego. Mr. Jensen says that Henry's brother, Rudolph III, who helped Jensen while he was writing his book about Henry, told him:

"There was a family legend that my grandfather cut down some trees on a point and the land was washed away in consequence." This is practically the only tragic story among the many. A serious undercurrent is often an element, but disaster is not usually a part of his plots.

"That was the first time Squire Five-Fathom spoke to me."

The story of the Squire was first written for a magazine then later found in a collection named from the first story in the book *Zadoc Pine and Other Stories*. There are names of Oswego in the story. (Gerrit Smith owned valuable harbor property on the east side of the river). There is the city a father and son have come to found on Lake Ontario, "that shall rival Rochester and Oswego in commerce." There is a fine mansion built upon a bluff overlooking the Lake, afterwards lost to the man who built it. There is a great expectation of the protecting value of a new extensive breakwater. When the breakwater is completed, the son now elderly and poverty stricken, again has hopes that his settlement will grow and prosper, but soon a terrible storm out of the northwest sweeps away the breakwater and completely erases the settlement. The distracted old man rushes into the whelming breakers and is drowned. The whole narrative has a tantalizing legendary flavor, and is recounted as the memory of a small boy who saw and made friends with the old man when he was living in a log hut that survived earlier washouts on the land his father had bought with much bright hope of riches, before his losses and death.

Bunner was, too, an expert parodist, particularly in his multiple parodies of "Home, Sweet Home, With Variations Being Suggestions of the Various Styles in Which an Old Theme Might Have Treated by Certain Metrical Composers."

Of the six divisions, the first is, "The original theme, as John Howard Payne wrote it." The second, "As Algernon Charles Swinburne might have wrapped it up in variations"; the third is in dialect, "As Mr. Francis Bret Harte might have woven it into a touching tale of a western gentleman in a red shirt." The fourth is a double parody dealing with an Englishman of Bunner's day and a Roman of the time of the Emperor Augustus; "As Autin Bobson might have translated it from Horace, if it had ever occurred to Horace to write it." Moreover, for good measure, the skit is cast in the French form of the Rondeau! Part five turns with equal ease, to the eighteenth century; "As it might have been constructed in 1744. Oliver Goldsmith, at 19, writing the first stanza, and Alexander Pope, at 52, the second." The sixth, last, and longest, pokes genial fun at the "good grey poet of Camden Town", "As Walt Whitman might have written all around it." This engaging play of wit and fancy swings to the very best of the rhythm, and the flavor of the style of each of the subjects of the parody, showing how thoroughly well Bunner knew his poets.

In the volume of ten short stories called *Made in France: French Tales Retold with a United States Twist* (1893) another type of clever adaptation is exhibited. These tales were transmuted rather than translated into American idiom and folkways. Included was one story by Bunner himself hidden away among the rest and undetected by contemporary critics. Henry Bunner admired the skilful art of Guy de Maupassant, the French writer of short stories, and believed that in translation much of the life and flavor of the originals were lost through the difference in idiom, usually ignored by the translator. Bunner undertook to render into American idiom some of Maupassant stories, with delightful success. There is "Tony" the simple, big, fat good-natured glutton of a French innkeeper in a small country town. After a stroke has made him bedfast, his sharp money-grasping wife, utilizing the heat of his heavy body, lays beside him a clutch of eggs to hatch; the interest of the whole town centers in the experiment. When the chicks finally emerge from the shells there is great rejoicing. A friend, who has just called to congratulate Tony, replies to the query of a neighbor as to how Tony is, "He's as well as can be expected." If the story calls for country half-witted stupidity, Bunner, in "A Pint's a Pound" uses characters and dialect from the settlements back from the Hudson River. He shows ingenuity in finding an American setting that would make French character and speech natural; as in "Father Dominick's Convert", the scene is a village in Lower Canada, near Quebec.

The most famous of his books is *Short Sixes: Stories to Be Read While The Candle Burns* (1891). The title takes its name from the trade name for short candles that used to be sold six to the pound. Every one of these compact, agreeably ironic vignettes moves with lively precision to a surprise ending. "The Tenor" is an 1890 version of an adored matinee idol. Today he would be a movie star. The denouement is a big splash. "The Two Churches of 'Quawket" deals amusingly with two rival churches in a village of New England. "The Love Letters of Smith" takes us to the top floor of the kind of old-time shabby boarding house New York used to have on some of the cross streets. Bunner here brings romance to two shy, lonely people.

"Zenobia's Infidelity" has been made into a movie. It is the hilarious account of the embarassing devotion of a greatful elephant

236

to the country doctor, who has healed her burns. The strategy the doctor used to free himself from Zenobia's unwelcome attentions, how he reacts like a boomerang, and Zenobia's downfall are extremely comic. "The Nice People" begins in a summer hotel, and ends in a shower of rice, but the story could not be told without spoiling it for the reader. "Hector" is a huge mastiff sent to a family of women utterly ignorant of dogs and their ways. The ladies learn several things, especially when Hector has puppies.

He published *More Short Sixes* (1894). The best of his poems appeared in *Airs From Arcady And Elsewhere* (1894), later in a collected edition of his poems (1896). He wrote a few long stories. "The Midge," one of his long stories, is set in the old French quarter of the city. The story is about a man who found himself with the responsibility of caring for an orphaned French child, left friendless in this country. Their efforts at housekeeping, the problems of education and training of a young girl, as well as the studies of the people who are concerned with the action are freshly imagined and convincingly wrought.

It is hoped that some of Henry Bunner's works would be reprinted for the enjoyment of his excellent literature.

Alvin Bronson
Attributed to T. A. Wentworth

Art

THOMAS HANFORD WENTWORTH

Oswego's First Artist

Mantle Fielding in his *Dictionary of American Painters, Sculptors And Engravers* wrote:

WENTWORTH—portrait painter in oils and miniature; also made profile portraits in pencil. He was working about 1815 in Utica, New York.

Thomas Hanford Wentworth was a descendent of Elder William Wentworth, signer of the *Exeter (New Hampshire) Agreement* in 1639, and of Thomas Hanford, the first minister at Norwalk, Connecticut, in 1654. Through his grandmother he was a descendent of Francis Cooke, a signer of the *Mayflower Compact* in 1620. Mr. Wentworth married Hannah H. Smith June 5, 1806.

Beyond a few sparse facts little is known about Thomas H. Wentworth (1781-1849). He was born in Norwalk, Connecticut, on March 15, 1781. During the Revolutionary War period Mr. Wentworth's mother possessed loyalist sympathies. She had a brother in the British service while her husband embraced the Patriot cause. The mother took her son, accompanied by her brother, fled to St. Johns, New Brunswick, in the "Great Migration" of 1783. Young Thomas was brought up and educated to business in a commercial house in St. Johns. He went to England after coming of age and later returned to America in the early part of 1800.

In the spring of 1806, a Utica business man, on his way to Canada, he stopped at Oswego and remained a few days awaiting a schooner that would take him across to Canada. On viewing the location of the place, its river, with its spring flow of water, its harbor and with the broad Ontario before it and the green grass growing on its banks, its commerce passing through from Albany to Canada and the West, presented, in a bright spring morning a panorama of beauty which met his romantic ideas of a business life. Pleased with the prospect it gave for a young man to enter upon a commercial business and "growing up with the place" he, before leaving for Canada entered into an agreement with Archibald

Fairfield who owned Lots 5 and 6 (Block 12) and wharf property thereon, for leasing or purchasing the same (the terms being stipulated) on his return from Canada under forfeiture of either part of $100. He decided to purchase and did so, in that year and commenced business of "transportation and forwarding." He was known for his acquired knowledge of commercial transactions, his fine penmanship and his accuracy as an accountant. His early association with business man and gentlemen of other localities made his house a reception for such, passing on their way to Canada and the West, and thus many pleasant interviews were had and enjoyed, which seemed like an "oasis in the desert," he being unused to the customs and habits of those who had taken up the "pioneer life."

After purchasing of Fairfield, he found the property much encumbered, which involved him in many difficulties, and embarrassed him in his business enterprise which after passing through the "embargo" times, was obliged to abandon. As an aside it is noted that there was an insurrection and rebellion by the residents of Oswego against the enforcement of these laws of the United States during the spring and summer of 1808. Riots and other disorders occurred along the waterfront and the harbor and the situation became so serious that it was necessary to call armed troops into service to preserve order, protect property and uphold the laws of the country. For some years after the repeal of the Embargo Act, Joel Burt, the customs collector, was involved in suits alleging interference with domestic trade. For instance, Thomas H. Wentworth was subpoened on June 2, 1810, to appear at the Court House at Onondaga to testify what he knew in a cause to be tried between George Kibbs, plaintiff, and Joel Burt, defendant. In 1812, Jacob T. and Thomas Walden, New York City merchants, purchased Wentworth's property (West Seneca Street between West First Street and the river) at a sheriff's sale for $170. Beginning about 1815, Joseph Walden began to develop the land as the primary commercial district of the growing village and eventually resold it in smaller lots.

The Artist

Mr. Wentworth was by nature a man of genius and had a fine taste for drawings, which made him a skillful artist, well-known for his penciling and miniature, portrait and landscape painting. Later his artistic talent led to his devoting himself to the art of painting in which he attained success as it is noted in one of the County's histories:

> Though bred to mercantile pursuits he was artist of much ability and in after years was in great demand as a portrait painter. He was the first devotee of the fine arts in Oswego, and should the lovers of those arts ever dedicate a gallery in their honor, his portrait would be entitled to especial prominence.

Although little is known about the activities after leaving Oswego, the presence of his works in Utica, Auburn, other sections in New York State, in New England, and Canada, he must have left Oswego before 1815 to place all his endeavor in the artistic field, but he returned from time to time. Evidence of this was found in the local newspaper when he gave notice of his "intentions to employ himself from this time on (1823) until spring in the Village of Oswego at fancy painting, etc." It has been said that he brought the first camera and made the first daguerrotype in this part of the State. The writer has not been able to sustain the claim.

In an article, Antiques Magazine of May 1930 says that Mr. Wentworth was extensively occupied in Connecticut during the 1820's. A number of his pencil miniatures are in the possession of older families of Hartford: One of Miss Lewis (5-1/2 by 3-1/2 inches) signed and dated in 1821, in the collection of the Litchfield Historical Society. The Society also has a portrait of Miss Deming (4 by 3 inches) and Lucretia Deming (4 by 3 inches). These three portraits were of young ladies who attended the Litchfield Female Academy where he taught for a time. The Mattatuck Museum in Waterbury, Connecticut, has four more pencil drawings on paper in its collection. They are: portrait of Mr. Thomas Johnson and his wife, Mrs. Hannah Davis Johnson, (6-1/4 by 8-3/4 inches); portrait of Mr. Wells (4-1/2 by 3-3/4 inches); portrait of Hannah Johnson Wells (5-1/4 by 4 inches).

241

The unknown portraits reproduced (page 423, figure 4 and 5) are the property of Mr. and Mrs. Robert C. Earle, South Salem, New York. They are but a fair specimen of the artist's works. However, the present samples give a sufficient idea of Wentworth's abilities as a portrait miniaturist. These unknown portraits by T. H. Wentworth are "technically amateurish, but, in the case of the woman's profile, no doubt painfully true to life."

The Antiques Magazine of January 1937 reproduced a remarkable group of signed drawings from the collection of Marshall G. Hill of Afton, New York. Says the editor about the portraits:

All the persons represented in this group are members of the Pease family of Auburn, New York. Dates inscribed on three of the drawings indicate that the entire series was produced during the period of approximately two years, from 1824 to 1826. Evidently the artist began with the third generation of the Pease family, the two little girls, whose profiles he numbered 3225 and 3226. Some weeks or months elapsed before he was called to immortalize the lineaments of the parents, Mr. and Mrs. Erastus Pease, both of whom he posed in three-fourths view. It is difficult to account for the sudden improvement in the artist's powers revealed by those two accurately drawn, delicately executed, and singularly convincing portrayals. The heads of the two little girls are poor in proprtions and limited techniques. Those of the parents, on the contrary, are handled with an admirable assurance of touch that approaches brilliance. Perhaps Grandfather and Grandmother Pease appealed less vividly to the artist than did their son and his wife, perhaps their portraits have been impaired by rubbing. Nevertheless, the likeness of the old man, toothless, wrinkled, slightly in need of a shave, yet still shrewd of eye, must be recognized as far above the ordinary. If, as we may reasonably surmise from the numbering on certain of his drawings, Wentworth had executed well over 3,000 portraits by September 1824, his services as a limner must have been greatly in demand. Hence it is probable that many more of his works survive than has been called to public attention.

The drawings reproduced in the magazine are: Fig. 1, Persis Cordelia Pease (1824) by T. H. Wentworth. Drawn in soft pencil. Size of paper approximately 4-11/16 by 3-11/16 inches. Fig. 2, Harriet Marie Pease. All portraits in this group are of the same dimensions. Fig. 3, Persis Pease. Fig. 4, Erastus Pease (1824). Fig. 5, Mrs. James Pease (1826). Fig. 6, James Pease (1826).

In the June 1937 Antiques Magazine the well-known connoisseur and historian of art, Harry McNeil Bland, stated that Wentworth painted excellent large portraits in oil as well as miniatures on ivory. He also worked in aquatint and published a set of lithographs of Niagara Falls. He mentioned that Alfred Brooks Merriam (of New York City), grandson of Wentworth, owned a number of the artist's more important works, among them a self portrait.

The July 1937 Antiques Magazine reproduced the lithographs of Niagara Falls from the collection of Mrs. Richard H. Hobbie of Oswego, New York. Fig. 2, is a view of Niagara Falls from the American side; from an undated lithograph by T. H. Wentworth; size of picture 6-3/8 by 4-1/4. Fig. 3, is a General View of Niagara Falls (1821); from a drawing by T. H. Wentworth, probably engraved by the artist; size of the picture 6-3/8 by 4-1/4 inches. In additon Mrs. Hobbie three copperplate engravings in mixed techniques, which, though signed by T. H. Wentworth Del., probably exemplify the artist's handling of the burin. Two carry a caption of the effect that they were entered according to Act of Congress, June 4, 1821, by T. H. Wentworth. The other is doubtless of the same date.

Mrs. Richard H. Hobbie, formerly of 117 West Fifth Street, Oswego, New York owned a signed pencil drawing of her great-grandfather, Eleazer Perry by T. H. Wentworth. As payment for the picture, he received from Eleazer, a barrel of cider applesauce.

The Oswego County Historical Society has in its possession a set of 3 lithographs (plus 2 duplicates) of the Niagara Falls by T. H. Wentworth. One is a view of the Great or British Falls of Niagara as seen from Goat Island; note, Goat Island divides the two Falls of Niagara which "at Niagara" are distinguished by the American and by British Falls; from an undated lithograph by T. H. Wentworth, Del., size of picture 6-3/8 by 4-3/8 inches. Another is a view of the River Rapids and Falls as seen from a Position above the Falls upon the high Grounds or Upper Bank of the Canada Side. Entered

View of the Falls of Niagara from the Canadian Side

according to Act of Congress the 4th day of June 1821 by Thomas H. Wentworth of the State of New York. Size of picture 6-3/8 by 4-1/4 inches. The third in the set is a View of the Falls of Niagara as seen on the Canada side; from a position near the Table Rock, T. H. Wentworth, Del. The caption is the same as above pertaining to Act of Congress. Size of picture 6-3/8 by 4-1/2 inches. It may be of interest or value to note that the artist actually worked on the lithographs in 1818 when he said, "I go tomorrow to the falls where I shall remain a considerable time as I am going to undertake a painting of the Falls of Niagara on a large scale."

Also in the Society's collection, attributed to the artist, is an oil portrait of Alvin Bronson (1783–1881) when he was a young man. It is an oil on panel black wood, size 32-1/4 by 27 inches. The subject was born in Waterbury, Connecticut, May 19, 1783, the second son of Josiah and Tabitta Bronson and a grandson of Lieutenant Josiah Bronson. On his death at the advanced age of ninety-eight years, a memorial resolution (April 5, 1881) was passed by the Common Council which stated in part:

His experience was marked by keen perception, adherence to principle, firmness of principle, firmness of purpose and integrity of character. He also held offices of honor and trust;

244

having been elected to the office of state Senator, first president of the village of Oswego, first president of the board of trade, president of Oswego Bank, the first in Oswego, and president of the Northwestern Insurance company.

The Board of Trade resolution called attention to his chiefest characteristics, namely, "Integrity, benevolence, strong intellectuality, unbending purpose, serenity of temper."

Note should be taken of an item in a local newspaper of the artist's early work: "We have been shown a drawing of Oswego as it appeared in 1807 when the city comprised but fifteen families."

In the search for sources of information in locating extant works of the artist, the Smithsonian Institution listed Yale University as possessing an oil painting. It is an oil portrait of Thomas Minor (1777–1841) by T. H. Wentworth; size is 30 by 25 inches. The New York Historical Society has a pencil drawing on paper, 5 by 3-1/4 inches, ca. 1820, of Charles Hawley, signed lower left: T. H. Wentworth, del. Inscribed at the top by the subject's daughter, Elizabeth King Hawley de Groot: My Father, Charles Hawley. When presented to the Society the drawing was in an envelope bearing the inscription by his daughter, Elizabeth King Hawley, which reads: "Portrait sketch of Charles Hawley in his youth—made by one of his friends." The reference to the subject's friendship with Wentworth accounts for Hawley's interest in painting and the fact that he himself produced a pencil drawing and watercolor now owned by the Society.

The subject was the son of Captain Cyrus Hawley and Mary (Curtis) Hawley. In 1821 he married Mary Stiles Holley. They became the parents of eight children including the artist, Elizabeth King Hawley. Hawley was a prominent lawyer of Fairfield County, Connecticut, and a member of the state legislature as well as lieutenant governor of Connecticut from 1838 to 1842. He was an amateur artist.

245

The Wentworth Dwelling

As an aside and of interest to Oswegonians, the Wentworth dwelling had the distinction of being the oldest house in Oswego. It was built in 1808–1809 at (then 326) now 420 West First Street, at the corner of Murray Street. The Wentworths lived in the family home as late as 1878. It was purchased by the Kingsford Starch Company in 1907. A part of the house was raised and a section was bought by Joseph McGowan. It was moved across the street a short distance of Sayer's Grocery store and next to the McGowan brewery. It has since been demolished.

Older residents of the city recalled the house as a rambling structure with a porch which extended full length of the front. During the British attack on the village in the War of 1812, Wentworths, was looted by the British Marines. Edwin Waterbury, of the *Palladium-Times* (Feb. 7, 1937) wrote:

According to a diary record, Mr. Wentworth had invited Colonel Mitchell, defending the fort, to dinner on the second day (May 6, 1814) of the attack, after the Americans had successively resisted the first day, but the second day saw the British ashore and the American troops fleeing up the river. A detachment of Royal Marines in pursuit tarried long enough, however, at the Wentworth house to eat 20 roast ducks which were to have graced the Wentworth board and to pocket the family silver. This respite is said to have allowed Colonel Mitchell and his men time to escape.

246

CHARLES HENRY GRANT

OSWEGO ARTIST

Charles Henry Grant is one of several Oswego artists who had gained national renown. He is represented in Fielding's *Dictionary of American Painting* as follows:

Marine painter. Born in Oswego, New York, 1866. Studied at National Academy of Design, New York, San Francisco Art Institute. Exhibited in leading cities; also San Francisco Exposition, 1915. Principal works: 'Will the Anchors Hold?', 'Ship of the Starboard Bow', 'Nearing Post', 'At the Mercy of Neptune', 'Under Sealed Orders', 'The Arrival of the Atlantic Battleship-Fleet at the Golden Gate -1908'. Address: The Bohemian Club, San Francisco, Calif.

Grant's artistic ability must have been well appreciated because he was commissioned to paint the Pacific Fleet.

Little is known of his youth. Grant lived at 181 East Fourth Street. He attended Oswego High School but there is no record of his graduation from that institution. One of his classmates was Claude F. Bragdon who lived at 160 East Fourth Street. Claude kept an illustrated diary. One entry, Saturday, November 26, 1881, had this comment: "I ... also went to Charlie Grant's and saw the model of his new Yacht. She is a daisy." Two years later an advertisement in the local paper, dated May 8, 1883, gave notice that Charles Grant was opening a studio in the Arcade Block (north side of East Bridge Street between First Street and the river). C. F. Bragdon graduated from Oswego High School in 1884 at the head of his class and was a self-educated architect of considerable fame.

Daniel A. Williams knew Grant personally. What is known of the artist is largely taken from Mr. Williams' reminiscences.

Grant had a studio in the attic of his home, and there he gave lessons in painting. He also made crayon portraits. Mr. Williams was informed that at one time Grant was located in the Grant Block (West Bridge Street between First and Water Streets), Oswego. An item in the local press called attention to his having opened a studio in the Guimaraes Building on West

First Street (south of the Grant Block). A few years later he was doing his painting in the same city, on West Bridge Street, between First and Second Streets. Mr. Williams remembers him as a very charming man. He did not seem to discourage the calls of some of his fellows from the nearby offices, although he must have known that there were no prospective clients among them.

It seems that M. F. H. DeHass, a celebrated marine painter, was spending a summer at Hamilton, New York. He learned that Charles Grant was a promising artist, and offered to give him free lessons for a while. If he were to take advantage of this tempting opportunity, Grant would have to receive financial assistance. At the time Grant was a member of the old 38th Separate Company of the New York National Guard. A friend of his who was also a member of that Company, offered to pay for the trip. The offer was accepted. The incident was related to Mr. Williams somewhat in this fashion:

"Charlie always said: 'I am going to pay you back.' "

"That's alright Charlie," came the friend's reply, "when you get in shape to do it and can spare the money I would be glad to have you do it, because it would show your appreciation."

"I'll be glad to make a painting for you now," concluded Grant.

The benefactor realizing that very likely he would get a more desirable picture if he could delay the work until the artist had gained thorough experience, maneuvered matters so that the time of repayment was postponed until 1899 when the American Yacht *Columbia* was to defend the America's Cup. Then the long sparring ended, and it was arranged that Grant should go to New York and make a picture of the race for the friend who had backed him. A painting was made of the winning yacht *Columbia* running before the wind, with spinnaker set. Later, this gentleman said, he presented the painting to the Oswego Yacht Club.

Grant removed from Oswego shortly after the turn of the century. He died in California sometime during the 1930's.

When Mr. Williams was in San Francisco in the autumn of 1941, he learned at the very pretentious Bohemian Club that Mr. Shirrell Graves, of Graves Gallery, 1335 Sutter Street, in that city

249

would know about him. When called, Mrs. Graves was in charge. The story she told was sad. Apparently Mr. Grant had been in poor health and straightened circumstances for too long a while before his death. Fortunately, he had been befriended by Mr. Graves and his wife. Upon Mr. Williams' arrival, the lower gallery was practically entirely devoted to a special exhibition and sale of Grant's pictures. Most of them did not seem to be representative of a man who had become so celebrated as an artist. Mrs. Graves appeared to be much disappointed that there were so few buyers. It was hoped that there would be sufficient financial returns from the sale of the paintings to repay those devoted friends for their long-continued kindness.

One of Grant's paintings, depicting the Evacuation of the British from Fort Ontario, hangs in the City Hall, Oswego. A large canvass, one of his best known, "At the Mercy of Neptune", was familiar to Oswegonians as for many years it was owned by Judge L. C. Rowe family of Oswego. Dr. Joseph M. Riley of Oswego, also owns a Grant painting.

Evacuation of Fort Ontario by the British in 1796

250

JAMES G. TYLER
Marine Artist

James G. Tyler (Feb. 15, 1855—Jan. 29, 1831) was born in Oswego, New York, the son of Rodolphus D. S. and Mary J. Hubbell Tyler, one of the first chiefs of police. J. G. Tyler was a direct descendent of the colonial governor, William Bradford, of the Mayflower company.

The youth was a frequenter of the water front, drydocks and ship yards and haunts of sailors and shipping men. His uncle, Capt. Joel Tyler, was a prominent lake captain. As a boy he displayed an aptitude for drawing and naturally drawing of schooners. From pencil and crude crayon sketches he drifted into water color.

A current story at that time was told how Morgan M. Wheeler, who at one time was the owner of a considerable fleet of vessels, gave Tyler his modest start as an artist. The boy, 15 years old, was down on the docks sketching a boat. Mr. Wheeler saw him and called him over. Young Tyler said he loved to draw boats, so Mr. Wheeler took him uptown and bought for him pencils, crayons, and other items that must have delighted and encouraged the talented young lad. Tyler got his first commission from Captain Wheeler, who asked him to paint a picture of each of his vessels. Tyler was paid $1 a piece by Wheeler. It took Tyler four days to paint the first one, but within three months he was turning out three or four a day. From other vessel owners he received $2 for a two-masted schooner, $3 for a three-master, $1 for a sloop and 50 cents for a canal boat. By January 1871, Tyler had saved $300. With this he went to New York City to become an understudy.

The Tug *Morse*

Courtesy of the Oswego County Historical Society

251

Mr. Tyler studied with A. Cary Smith, a marine artist and later a naval architect, in New York in 1871, and as a result of his application this was said of him: "The artist has been chiefly successful for the reason that, unlike some other marine painters, he has made of himself a sailor, and a few Yachtmen and even professional seamen are better versed in the science of navigation and a technical knowledge of the handling of sailing craft." Later he went to Chicago, but lost everything he had in the great fire. He returned to New York City and painted pictures of tugboats, receiving $5 to $15 apiece for them. Eventually, he developed his skills and his best canvasses brought up to $350 each. His painting of the Mayflower was sold for $1,200 and hung for many years at the Washington Hotel.

Tyler returned to Oswego. He was listed in the City Directory, 1877-1878, "Tyler, James G., Painter, 8 Oswego City Savings Bank Bldg. rooms, do." Many of his pictures are owned in Oswego County. Later he located in New York City where his maritime paintings found ready sale. It was said that "a representative collection of American paintings should have in it an example of Tyler." He exhibited first at the National Academy in 1880. At the beginning of the century his work was hailed by critics for its faithfulness to his subject, and its conscientiousness of execution. He became Americas best known marine artist, so well known that more than 100 pictures were faked signed by his name and sold. Other of his work was pirated for commercial purposes, on calendars and the like. He brought and recovered on several civil actions in courts in New York City.

His ships and yachts were familiar sights in New York City galleries, and they were often on sale at the important auction rooms. His reputation was enhanced by paintings of every international yacht race for the American Cup from 1875 On. Large colored prints were made of some of his important pictures. Sketches could be found in *Harpers, Century, Truth,* and other periodicals. Tyler's large picture of the Pilgrim ship "Mayflower" was prominently hung in the Mayflower Hotel, Washington, D. C. The artist sent a picture to Oswego to Mayor Daniel Conway. It hung in the Mayor's office and then placed in the City Library where it is at present.

Mr. Tyler's best known works included "The Abandoning of the Jeannette," painted for James Gordon Bennett, the elder, "The

Mayflower," "St. Paul's Shipwreck," "The Constitution," "The Half Moon," "The New World," "Norman's Woe," "Towing in The Prize," "Under Steerage," "The Fortunes of War," "The Mad Atlantic," "First American Shipwreck," and "Flying Dutchman." His paintings are in the Corcoran Gallery and the National Museum in Washington, D. C., the Huntington (L. I.) Museum, the Omaha Museum, the Hartford Museum and the Tokyo Museum.

An important art critic's assessment of Tyler's ability is an article by Jno Gilmore Speed entitled, "James Gale Tyler, A Painter of Marine Subjects" in *The Monthly Illustrator*, New York, 1894:

When an artist has enthusiasms, and the courage of them, he is likely to get a good deal of happiness out of his art, 'whatever woe betide'. When these enthusiasms, and the following of them, lead to success, the artist thus possessed and thus guided is to be envied among men. This reflection has been suggested by the work and the personality of James G. Tyler, the well-known marine painter, for both the man and his pictures are alive with enthusiasms which will not be denied but, on the contrary, are apt to become contagious. He paints just the way he thinks he ought to paint, without reference to what critics may say and other artists think, and he speaks out his mind with a manly freedom which seems to count silence as cowardly. One of his friends, commenting on this characteristic in reproving tones, said 'Jim talks too much!' Fortunately for those who come within this circle, Mr. Tyler does not agree with this friend, and therefore his acquaintances are not denied the pleasure and the profit of the thoughts of a mind untrammeled. Such enthusiams can only be accompanied with great sincerity. In Mr. Tyler's case we have not only courageous enthusiasms and frank sincerity, but genius as well, and therefore, both the man and his work are potent with charm.

So much of the space allotted to this article is wisely given up in reproduction of Mr. Tyler's pictures and the sketches that it is not possible for me to enter into any discussion of the merits of his work. Through these reproductions, however, his pictures speak with an eloquence that no writer could command. Therefore, I shall be content to say a few words about the man himself and his career as an artist.

The Alanson Sumner
James G. Tyler

T. S. Mott
James G. Tyler

Mr. Tyler began painting in 1870, when he was fifteen years old. He was then living in native Oswego. He gained some little local fame before he had been at work a year, when a member of the National Academy visited the town he was taken to see the youthful celebrity. The Academician, though a man of genuine well-earned fame, is not a handsome man in the eyes of strangers, nor does he clothe himself with any degree of smartness. His fame had not yet reached young Tyler's studio, and the man himself did not look in the least as the boy artist thought an Academician should look. The elder somewhat shabby man looked at the lad's canvass through his glasses and said kindly: 'Your boat moves, but your clouds should move with it.' The young man thought that there was a deal of sense in the comment but at the time he was suspicious that a joke was being played upon him, and that a casual tramp had been pressed into service to play the part of the visiting Academician. At this day, some twenty years later, Mr. Tyler is not sure that the shabby gentleman who called on him in Oswego is not the ablest of all American landscape painters. The writer is tolerably sure that he is. At all events he has many admirers. The next year Mr. Tyler painted about three months in the studio of A. Cary Smith, then well known as a marine painter, though at present he has the pictorial art to be a designer of yachts. This is the only instruction Mr. Tyler has ever had save that which he has given himself. And to himself he has been a hard and exacting master, for never yet has he produced a work that was to himself entirely satisfactory. Recognizing, however, that what he did was as good as he at that time had power to make it, he has given his works to the world with a clear conscience. Mr. Tyler, like Mr. Albert Ryder, for whom, by the way, he has a very warm admiration, paints from the imagination, and his imagination should be spelled with a big I. He, therefore, escapes the commonplace, and in this achieves no mean distinction. It must not be understood by this that Mr. Tyler is a painter of the uncanny. It is true that an exhibition at the Academy a few years ago he had a picture of the 'Flying Dutchman', and Mr. Ryder, by the way, treated the same subject for the same exhibition. But even in putting on canvass was a beautiful subject as this, Mr. Tyler was equal to the occasion, and came near to satisfying the very

255

severst critics who were gifted with an imagination. It was most interesting at this exhibition to contrast the conceptions of Ryder and Tyler and their methods of treatment. The opinion of the connoisseurs was about equally divided, and the critics as well. This was without doubt Ryder's masterpiece, and Tyler had said with characteristic frankness that he greatly preferred it to his own. Tyler's was a study in gray, the phantom ship half revealed in a bank of fog; Ryder's phantom ship was seen in a blaze of glorious color.

Both were poetical; both were satifying.

Mr. Tyler's masterpiece, according to his own judgment, is a painting recently finished and called 'The Dawn of the New World'. This picture is a result of much hard work and study. It is an effort to represent the little fleet of Columbus just as land is discovered. Mr. Tyler made this picture before the Columbian caravels had been built and he needed to find the models in the old records. He succeeded most admirably, and in this picture there seems to be a happy combination of the real and the ideal. Without this combination probably no picture is quite worth while to be made. It would be a pity for such a picture as this to be buried in some private collection, and it is to be hoped that the movement to secure it for the Capitol at Washington will be successfully pushed. There is room in that great pile for may pictures, but there are unfortunately not many now there worthy of national ownership.

Mr Tyler is an impressionist, and sacrifices nothing whatever to the finicky detail upon which many artists waste all their time and power. Painting from within himself, instead of copying merely that which he sees, it is only natural that he should frequently produce results incomprehensible to those who have had no head above their eyes. But this lack of appreciation, manifested now and again by hanging committees, bothers Mr. Tyler not in the least, for he feels that it is his mission in life to paint his own pictures in his own way; to please himself and satify his own sense of beauty and what Carlyle called the 'eternal varities', without reference to a few nobodies who have elbowed themselves into places and authority for the sake of the cheap fame which passes almost as soon as it has come. When Mr. Tyler sees his own picture

Oswego Harbor & Lighthouse by James G. Tyler

rejected, and the half finished offerings of his pupil hanging upon the line, he merely laughs and sells his own canvass for five hundred dollars or so. He has his money, and his sustaining enthusiasms remain with him always. These enthusiasms would go far towards making Mr. Tyler happy with his lot, even though he would have to do without very much of the money. Not that he despises money - not at all. Even though gifted with an imagination that soars and soars in newer atmospheres and sails and sails on undiscovered seas, he is too human to despise money, though he confesses freely that he has hated to have to make many of the pot-boilers to which he has signed his name. Fortunately for him and his art the pot-boiler era has been passed.

One of James Tyler's paintings.
This one is hanging in the Oswego City Library.

JOHN FRANCIS MURPHY
Landscape Artist

The writer confesses to being exposed to a college level course in "Appreciation of American Art". It should be understood that this far from being even an amateur expert. Therefore the writer must rely on opinions of art critics by including items and articles in assessing the quality, or the lack thereof, of native Oswego artists unknown to the present generation. With these disclaimers let us rediscover an artist's name not very familiar in the city of his birth, Oswego, but who gained great national renown.

Much of the information about the Oswego painter is gathered from an excellent paper written by a prominent Oswegonian, Daniel A. Williams. He personally knew the Oswego artists or interviewed persons who were acquainted with them. Mr. Williams based his manuscript on an impressive list of sources.

J(ohn) Francis Murphy (May 11, 1853—Jan. 30, 1921) was born in Oswego, the son of a sailor. His father's name was also John. At one time the family lived in "the Flats", a notorious section of the city north of West Seneca Street and west from the river. Later the family made their home on West Seneca Street, near Eight.

J. Francis was at one time a printer's devil. Early in life he left Oswego for Chicago where he was employed as a sign painter about 1870. Although he was reasonably efficient, he was noticeably lazy and in consequence was discharged. In 1875 he moved to New York City. The comparatively few studios were centered about the old Tenth Street studio building. Largely self-taught, in 1876 he first exhibited at the National Academy of Design in New York. There he struggled, or perhaps better expressed, fought on and earned his way to an enviable position as a landscape artist. His paintings had a poetic atmospheric feeling, and were much in demand.

Murphy was a lover of nature as few painters have been. He loved not only the pictoral aspect but, with a true nature lover's sincerity, the ways of the trees, of birds, and of the little animals that found him a friend in his home among the Catskill hills at Arkville. Painting in his studio, he carried there with the visions that only one who sees and knows who has gone directly to the sources of inspiration.

259

His approach to nature was intuitive. He was not learned or scientifically schooled, but there was a natural affinity between himself and the animate world. Squirrels were easily tamed and would come to him unafraid. In the winter at his studio in the "Chelsea" he supplied the finishing touches to his paintings.

Murphy relied on a certain texture by the gradual scraping of hard pigment which necessitated the material being prepared many months before the final painting. It came in a sense to be personal mannerism, stated with a vigorous and free brush work, the paint lost something of its initial vigor but gained in that atmospheric and tonal quality so characteristic of Murphy's art. His pictures were in consequence started well in advance without a definite or final idea.

It was well said of him by a fellow painter that he took infinite pains and was never afraid of his work. To an artist who was much bothered over the rendering of foliage in a landscape in which he took much pride Murphy advised: "Make a number of drawings from nature with a sharp pencil." This was his own practice, and no one can look at his trees simplified and softened as they may be with the mist of spring or the haze of autumn without a consciousness of the fact that beneath the sensitive handling exists a positive knowledge of their anatomy and real aspects.

Perhaps to cite what critics have said about Murphy is much better than the vague interpretations of a neophyte. With that in mind the following are extracts or condensations about him.

Charles W. Caffin, *Story of American Painting*, (1907), p. 342, illustration "The Road To The Old Farm", by J. Francis Murphy:

Impelled perhaps by popular demand for his 'character-istic' work, this artist has confined his observation to a limited phase of nature. The present example with its stretch of meadow, sprinkling of delicate tree forms and distant hillside enveloped in a smoky haze of atmosphere, well represents him. Within this restricted range of expression, he is a master.

Alan Burroughs, "John Francis Murphy," *The Arts*, March, 1921:

Although neither a great nor an inspiring American painter, the late J. Francis Murphy has surely built himself a position in the art world that is the envy of many an artist of greater individuality.

Born in Oswego in 1853, he taught himself to paint, using his native countryside for subject matter. From 1885 on he won medals in many important exhibitions with his quiet landscapes.

Murphy was a sincere painter somewhat in the tradition of Wyant and Inness, though he consciously followed no master. His landscapes show a calm unconcern for the complexities of nature. They are the stronger for being so simple. He toned his canvass with matter-of-fact treatment of the traditional 'poetic atmosphere' and was unaware of any of the various problems of color relationship which are troubling modern artists. In another painter this homely accepatnce of the traditional treatment of landscape, both in its light and in its composition, might be a weakness, but in Murphy it takes on the straightforwardness of his own character. Undoubtly the popularity of Corot's later work, emphasized a mood similar to Murphy's, gives additional reason for success which Murphy had during the last years of his life. This success, however, was earned through sound technique acquired by many years of steady work.

James B. Carrington, and other contributors, in *An Appreciation of John Francis Murphy*, 1853–1921, Salmagundi Club, 47 Fifth Avenue, New York City, November 12 to November 26th, 1921, inclusive has this to say:

There could be no more fitting place for an exhibition of the work of John Francis Murphy than the gallery of the Salmagundi Club that he loved so well and with which he had been associated for so many years.

Coming to New York in 1875 he soon found in this club friendly associates, and in 1878 he himself became one of its active members. He was an exhibitor at its member shows, especially of notable sketches in black and white, and his work was early recognized as that of a thorough artist and a patient and very sincere student of natural forms. From the first, his homely simplicity and his fine capacity for friendship were manifest and with these qualities went an always generous appreciation of the work of others. His early days in art followed no primrose path but the narrow ways of discouragement and very limited means, and he knew well the hardships that have beset the beginnings of so many great names in art. Murphy was not the sort to pose as the neglected genius, however. He met hard conditions with a determination to find himself in his work, and no one worked with more earnestness to lay a foundation of real accomplishment. It is impossible for anyone to study his early drawings without realizing that in them he was laying the foundation of the very real knowledge of nature that later was to give his paintings the element of intrinsic truth based on a complete and smpathetic understanding. Like Inness and Wyant, he was self-taught, and like them he has left behind him a sense of great loss and great achievement. How fine it was that Murphy's fame should have met him more than half way; that honor in his own country was not denied him while he lived; that he should have had the satisfaction of seeing his pictures sold to famous collectors at prices that would have seemed a princely fortune to him in his early days. In the maturity of his life and art he came into his own, and the pictures of no American painter have been more widely sought or more highly valued, not alone for the mere money they represent, but for their beauty, their lovely coloring, their poetic and serene revelation of the moods of nature he loved so well, in the early spring and fall.

Murphy liked to paint in the spring, and in the fall when the old brown earth and the silhoutted trees stood out and the colors of the autumn were golden.

His lovely transcripts of those particular seasons were expressions of man's own sensitive response to the season's moods. They revealed Murphy's heart, his ever fine poetic responses to the quieter aspects of nature that he loved to paint and upon which his reputation was established. How few have ever enveloped a landscape with a finer truth of atmosphere, painted lovelier or more expressive skies or brought to view a more convincing feeling of the particular scene and time.

He was never the facile worker and as the years went went on he painted fewer pictures, ever striving with all the means in his power and with an increasing command of his medium and his own special technique to say the things he felt, to decalre in his beautiful pattern of pigment the thing that was in his soul.

He first exhibited at the National Academy in 1876, the year after his coming to New York, and in 1885 he won the Second Hallgarten Prize for a characteristic picture called

"Tints of a Vanished Past". Two years later he received the Webb prize. In 1885 he was made an Associate of the National Academy and two years later a National Academician.

Murphy was never led away from his own sincerity and purpose by the vagaries of the Impressionists or by any of the Modernists that have proved so destructive to many of the young men of today. He knew the thing he loved and painted it with the inspiration and regard for truth that belong with rare exceptions only to men of great talent and individuality combined with great simplicity of character.

Murphy's popularity and keen competition for his late pictures that might have excused a certain degree of pose and bumptiousness, made no difference in him. He was as ready to greet an old friend whose ways had gone hard, to say a kind and encouraging word to the young painter, in the days of his great success, as he was when he wondered where he could sell a few sketches to pay his studio rent.

His influence on American art was a wholesome one, and in his achievement in the lovely things that he cared most to paint he has given great pleasure to thousands and made thousands realize that with him as with Inness, Wyant, Martin and Homer, the American landscape came into its own as the best in the world.

Murphy sent forth kindling sense of the magic in the woods and skies and he carried that magic with such feeling into his work that we owe him a heavy debt.

That he lived to be recognized as a leader in American landscape, to find both the satisfaction and the ease of mind that come with an adequate financial return for all his labor was something that every one who knew him rejoiced in.

His was the fine gift of seeing nature and of making her beauty known to others through his own sympathetic vision, and his was even the greater gift of generous appreciation of the work of others, of inspiring affection and love in those whose privilege it was to call him a friend.

He has taken a place, and a notable one, among our old masters in the category that includes Inness, Wyant, Martin and Homer, and and his message will go on as theirs goes on, the message of inspiration and truth. His pictures, the treasured possessions of thousands who have them, will be even more appreciated with the passing of years.

Murphy was ever jealous of his own reputation and sincerity and was never content with any work that did not represent his best evdeavor. His was indeed an artistic conscience that never yielded to the too-eager demands of the moment. The world could wait while he was doing the one thing that he loved best to do in his own way in his own time. His record stands on solid accomplishment. It grew slowly with the years, and late in life he could look back when at the height of his fame and talk and smile over early hardships with the old spirit of youth and the seriousness that comes from having passed through the trials that test men's souls and prove them.

Eliot Candee Clark, *J. Francis Murphy*, (Privately printed, 1926).

To his friends he was simply Murphy; to his intimates, including his wife (Adah Clifford Murphy), he was "Murph"—a term of affection. He combined a simple, unaffected, easy-going nature with a shrewd and calculating comprehension. He was not intellectual. He ran around the corner from what might be termed culture. Though he seemed lethargic, indolent, almost lazy, informal, plain and outspoken, his artistic expression was, nevertheless, highly sophisticated. He was fond of calling his associates by their first names; his greeting was always intimate and hearty, but his conversation was not either spirited or comprehensive. In expressive language, he had an uncommon vocabulary not found in the dictionary and, when animated, a keen Irish wit. Murphy disliked anything that made him self-conscious. He did not care for polished manners and dispensed entirely with form, Murphy's physiognomy was distinct, not for any picturesque or striking peculiarity but rather because his head was particularly well formed. It is difficult to associate this plain, simple and rather coarse nature with the delicate and highly sensitive artist; yet no artist was more truly one than Murphy.

Apart from his art, Murphy's life was singularly devoid of any great interests. For nearly forty years of his life he spent the greater part of the year at Arkville, his summer home in the Catskill Mountains, but in his work we have hardly a suggestion of his enviroment.

Murphy's artistic career embraced three periods. The first is associated with the so-called Hudson River school; the second shows the influence of the French school of 1830 and its American exponents, Inness and Wyant, while the final period belongs to the mature and ultimate style of the master. Each change marks a decided sacrifice but also brings him nearer to himself.

From the scenic landscape to the chioroscure of autumnal sunsets, he gradually develops a simple theme of earth and sky, of air and expanse,—the serenity and beauty of nature's unaffected harmony. From the conventional attributes of the picturesque he seeks more and more the humble unadorned simplicity of the fields and the ever-changing hues of heaven.

Reflection on Murphy's work reveals the skilled picture maker finally discovered that in landscape man sees but the reflection of himself.

So spoke the people who knew him.

In 1885 Murphy was awarded the Second Hallgarten Prize, and in 1910 the Inness Gold Medal by the National Academy of Design. In 1902 he received the Carnegie Prize from the Society of American Artists. Others were: 1894, Evans Prize, American Water Color Society; 1899, Gold Medal Pennsylvania Academy, Philadelphia; 1887, Webb Prize, Society of American Artists; 1894, Evans Prize, American Water Color Society; 1901, Silver Medal, Pan American Exposition; 1902, Gold Medal, Charleston Exposition; 1904, Silver Medal, St. Louis Exposition; 1911, Evans Prize, Salmagundi Club and 1915, Silver Medal, Pan-Pacific Exposition, San Francisco.

Murphy was a member of the National Academy of Design, Society of American Artists, New York Water Color Club, American Water Color Society, Salmagundi Club, Lotus Club, and the Century Club of New York.

In the American Artist Series, the Murphy book was printed in 1926. Volumes honoring George Inness, Homer, Martin, Alexander Wyant, Ralph Blakelock, Winslow Homer, Albert Pinkham Ryder, John Twachtman had already appeared in that order.

John Francis Murphy died in New York City, January 30, 1921. His funeral was held in the National Academy of Design in New York City, Murphy being the first and, to date, the only artist to have his memory so honored by having his funeral held at this academy.

265

Third Battalion, N. G. N. Y., in Camp at Beach Oswego

Selleck's Shoe Store brochure

266

The Spanish War

"They also serve who stand and wait."

F. D. Roosevelt

Using as a source the Bureau of Census, Statistical Abstract, 1975, Allan L. Damon in an article in the American Heritage magazine (June 1976) gleaned some interesting figures in regard to the Spanish-American War. Approximately $33 million in current federal budget will go to about 1,200 veterans and 27,000 surviving dependents from the Spanish-American War of 1898. Postwar pensions cost now total an estimated $5.6 million.

There are several reasons for this story on the Spanish-American War. First, the writer was an enlisted man in World War II. He left with a contingent for a camp on Long Island with no fan-fare. Experiences in the United States Army were not unlike those of Company D, Third New York Volunteers. Company D of Oswego was inducted into federal service on October 15, 1940, and were ordered to Fort McClellan, Alabama. When Company D marched the following Monday to board the train for departure, it was led by the Naval Militia Color Guard, High School Band, College Band and Pathfinder Corps. The College was dismissed to see the send-off in honor of Captain Ziel. The Naval Militia followed shortly. On October 20, 1940, every male over 18 years of age was required to register for the draft.

After reading John D. Billings, *Hardtack and Coffee, or the Unwritten Story of Army Life* (Civil War), the writer was induced to delve into the local newspapers of the year 1898. Here the local press fully described the experiences of Oswego's soldiers in camp. Furthermore there were several veterans of the Spanish War who the writer was acquainted with or knew of several more.

Another reason for delving into the war was to discover the effects of the press on the people. The people were patriotic and emotional to a high degree. The newspapers detailed every facet of the excitement.

267

Causes of the War

The war, as is well known, grew out of the general irritation caused in this country as a result of the struggle of the Cubans to free themselves from the control of the Spanish Government, and the efforts made by that government to suppress all tendency to revolt. American public opinion was overwhelmingly on the side of the islanders to independence. The yellow press led by William Randolph Hearst's New York *Journal* and Joseph Pulitzer's New York *World* filled the front pages with exaggerated and sometimes untrue stories of Spanish atrocities.

But something happened that could not be met by diplomacy led to war. On the night of February 15, 1898, the United States battleship *Maine*, commanded by Charles Dwight Sigsbee, a native of Albany, anchored at Havana, was destroyed by a terrible explosion that killed 260 of her crew. Investigators tried to ascertain the cause of the wreck but their opinions varied. To this day the cause of the disaster is unknown.

But the yellow press had no doubts. "Remember the Maine" became the slogan of the day. Popular sympathy for the Cubans and indignation against Spain mounted.

Congress Acts

President McKinley placed the issue with Congress; and on April 18th, a joint resolution was agreed upon, the full text of which was as follows:

WHEREAS, The abhorrent conditions which have existed for more than three years in the Island of Cuba, so near to our own borders, have shocked the moral sense of the people of the United States, have been a disgrace to Christian civilization, culminating, as they have, in the destruction of a United States battleship, with two hundred and sixty-six of its officers and crew, while on a friendly visit in the harbor of Havana, and cannot longer be endured, as has been set forth by the President of the United States in his Message to Congress of April 11, 1898, upon which the action of Congress was invited; therefore,

Resolved, By the Senate and House of Representatives of the United States of America in Congress assembled:

First—That the people of the Island of Cuba, and of right ought to be, free and independent.

Second—That it is the duty of the United States to demand, and the Government of the States does hereby demand, that the Government of Spain at once reliquish its authority and government in the Island of Cuba, and withdraw its land and naval forces from Cuba and Cuban waters.

Third—That the President of the United States be, and he hereby is, directed and empowered to use the entire land and naval forces of the United States, and to call into actual service of the United States the militia of the several states, to such extent as may be necessary to carry these resolutions into effect.

Fourth—That the United States hereby disclaim any disposition or intention to exercise sovereignty, jurisdiction or control over said Island except for the pacification thereof; and asserts its determination when it is accomplished to leave the government and control of the Island to its people.

The adoption of this resolution was looked upon at home and abroad as a practical declaration of war, and preparations which had been rapidly pushed forward since the destruction of the "Maine" began to be rushed at high speed. For the sake of avoiding complications that might arise in connection with the blockade, etc., President McKinley recommended and Congress passed, on April 24th, a bill as follows:

First—That war be, and the same hereby is, declared to exist, and that war existed since the 21st day of April, A. D., 1898, including said day, between the United States of America and the Kingdom of Spain.

Second—That the President of the United States be, and he hereby is directed and empowered to use the entire land and naval forces of the United States, and to call into the actual service of the United States the militia of the several States, to such an extent as may be necessary to carry this act into effect.

So a "splendid little war" in the words of Secretary of State John Hay, began. On April 23, the President called upon the States to mobilize their militia, to the number of 125,000, and authorized

269

the expansion of the regular army to 61,919, a little later calling for 75,000 additional volunteers.

States' Quick Response

The national government and the States had, indeed, carried their preparation well forward during the last days of peace. On March 25, the Adjutant-General of New York State (C. Whitney Tillinghast) telegraphed to brigade commanders of State troops: "Hold your officers within call. Allow none to absent himself from these headquarters." On April 18, local commanders were asked to ascertain how many soldiers of the National Guard would volunteer for active service with the United States Army. Response was quick from all units. New York State troops, it would seem, were in a more efficient state of preparation than the militia of many other States. In less than a week after the President called for State troops, the National Guard regiments of New York began to gather on Hempstead Plains, near Garden City, Long Island, the rendezvous becoming known as Camp Black.

The 48th Separate Company

Oswego's "Old Forty-eight" came into existence on July 19, 1838. Its history was presented in an excellent paper before the Oswego County Historical Society by John M. Sullivan, Jr., on January 18, 1967. In the Spanish War Oswego's 48th Separate Company became Company D, 1st Battalion, 3rd Regiment, Infantry, National Guard, State of New York.

Following their induction into Federal Service, the 3rd Regiment, New York Volunteers, was assigned to Camp Black. On May 24th they were ordered to Camp Alger, Virginia (just outside Washington). They were stationed there during the summer where they suffered greatly from sickness. The situation became so serious that the regiment was sent to Camp Meade, Pennsylvania, a healthier place, on August 17. Following the cessation of hostilities (August 12) the units departed for their respective home stations, receiving demonstrations of welcome in the cities through which they passed. Though the men of the 3rd Regiment never got to Cuba the hardships they suffered in the service of their country were not forgotten by the people.

Oswego Newspaper Reports

Tuesday April 26—Three thousand people crowded in to the State Armory (East Firts Street, built in 1870, now occupied by the Cylcotherm firm) Tuesday evening and cheered the ninety-four officers and men of the Forty-eight Separate Company, who stepped paces to the front signifying their willingness to go wherever the President of the United States may direct to defend the country and uphold the flag, while three thousand more people, who were unable to get inside, crowded in a solid mass in front of the building and took up the cheering, making their voices heard for several blocks away. The scene was one never before witnessed and it will remain forever impressed upon the memory of all who were present.

Tuesday afternoon when the order was received telling Captain Albert M. Hall to assemble his company and ascertain who would go to the front, he issued an order calling upon his men to report in uniform at 7:30 o'clock in the evening. Long before that hour the parents, relatives, friends and sweethearts of the members of the company commenced to arrive. The spacious floor of the Armory and the large gallery were filled to overflowing. Still the crowd continued to increase, and the asphalt pavement in front of the building was black with a surging mass of humanity straining and crowding to reach the inside, but all good-natured. At eight o'clock Captain Hall and his own officers came down the gallery stairs from the headquarters and the command was given for the company, which stood under the gallery, to march out on the floor.

The Forty-eight Separate Company band, in full uniform, struck up a lively quickstep and the word "march" was all that was heard and then, as the first set of fours reached the center of the floor, the audience broke out in one grand cheer. Hats were thrown in the air, men stood on the chairs and climbed on each others' backs to get a glimpse of the soldier boys, while the women— mothers, sisters and sweethearts—waved their handkerchiefs and lifted their voices in the deafening uproar. It was fifteen minutes before the cheering quieted down and even after that it could be heard from the outside. Captain Hall put the company through a short dress parade and review, Mayor John D. Higgins acting as reviewing officer. With each evolution the crowd broke out into cheers which it was impossible to stop.

Captain Hall brought his command up in company front facing the gallery, and raising his hand for absolute silence, addressed his company as follows: Officers and members of the Forty-eight Separate Company:

I have been a National Guardsman fifteen years. I have been your Captain for eight years. During this time we have received many calls to duty. No demand has ever been made upon this company in vain. During all these years we have never once been assembled under circumstances and conditions the like of which calls us here tonight. Your country's flag has been assailed by a foreign foe; your Chief Executive, the President of the United States, has asked you to come and help defend it. The conditions under which he asks you to come are these: You are expected to enter the Federal service for a period of two years unless sooner discharged. You are to be ready to go wherever he may direct, perhaps to the coast defenses, perhaps to Cuba, perhaps to Spain; no man can tell. Now I am going to ask the officers and men of this company who feel that they can enter their country's service under these conditions to step to the front. I want to have it thoroughly understood that no man need go who feels that he has home ties that he can not break. Men who have families, or mothers dependent upon them are privileged to remain at home if they see fit, though the people of Oswego, through the Mayor who reviewed the company a moment ago, gives me assurance that the families of those left behind who may need assistance will be cared for while you are away. I also have the assurance of superior authority that if this company volunteers its services it will be accepted as a company under its own officers. I am going to ask the officers first. Those who are willing to go with me into the service of the United States, under the conditions I have named will step four paces to the front.

First Lieutenant DeSolvo H. Tifft and Second Lieutenant Fred L. Pattberg and Michael O'Donnell stepped forward. The right of the company began to move and the left joined the movement. When the four paces had been made it was found that all had volunteered excepting ten, and no disgrace or ban was place upon them, for they were all men either with families or aged parents depending upon them for support.

It was impossible to do anything further in the line of drilling; the company was dismissed, the men allowed to go to their homes to remain until called upon to go to the front.

The next day the places of the ten members who refused to enlist had been filled by persons who had their applications on file for several days. Captain Hall was at the Armory awaiting orders for his company to move.

Saturday April 30—The order giving the hour when the company should board the train and be carried to their first destination was received by Captain Hall and read as follows:

Dated Albany
April 30th, 1898

Commanding Officers Forty-Eight Separate Company:

General Headquarters, State of New York, Adjutant-General's Office, Albany, Special Order No. 70: The organization named herein will embark at their home stations for the camp at Hempstead Plains, Long Island, as indicated below. Companies to consist of one Captain, one First Lieutenant, one Second Lieutenant and eight-one enlisted men. All properly armed, uniformed and equipped, musicians being of the enlisted men the only one not armed with rifles. All tents and buzziecut stoves and cooking outfits; also regimental, company, desk, medicine chests, ammunition at the rate of forty rounds per man and arm chests will be taken with the command . The surplus ammunition will be properly packed and left in charge of the armorer. Receipts in duplicate will be given at station to agent for the actual transportation received. Shortage in officers and enlisted men or of property including leggins will be reported direct to the Adjutant-General at the time of departure. The senior officers on the train will be in charge of the troops. On arriving at camp commanding officers will report to Major-General C. F. Roe, commanding camp at Hempstead Plains, Long Island, for assignment duty. On train No. 1, N. Y. C. & H. Railroad, the First and Eight Separate Companies will leave Rochester at 7 P. M. May 1st, the Thirty-fourth Separate Company will leave Geneva at 7:30 P. M. and take the train at Lyons at 8 P. M. May 1st. The Forty-eight Separate Company will leave Oswego at 7 P. M. and take the train at Syracuse at 9:20 P. M.

May 1st. By order of the Commander-in Chief.

C. Whitney Tillinghast
Second Adjutant-General

It was this order that had been patiently waited for several days, and although all the important matters had been attended to there still remained several minor matters needed attention. Callers were many and influential citizens volunteered any aid that might be in their power. The men were allowed to go to their homes and spend a last night with their loved ones, but had explicit orders to assemble at the Armory at nine o'clock Sunday morning for the final inspection.

The Sunday Syracuse *Herald*, April 30th, had a special article entitled "Patriotic Oswego" describing the arrangements for the grand sendoff. Also Mayor Higgins will call a mass meeting for the purpose of providing for those dependent on the departing militia men. The order of the parade and the corrected roster of the company was printed.

May 1—The Last Day—Bright and early the Sabbath dawned, clouds which had threatened rain during the early morning rolled away. As early as seven o'clock brave young men in the uniform of the National Guard of this State could be seen moving rapidly through the streets bearing bundles under their arms, all bound for the State Armory. Their bundles contained the last gifts of loved ones and were to be placed carefully away in the already crowded knapsacks, to be used in camp or on the field.

Arriving at the Armory Captain Hall found the greater portion of his company present and gave all who wished permission to attend church. Nearly every one of the boys took advantage of the offer. In every Catholic and Protestant church prayers were offered for the Forty-eight Separate Company and blessing invoked on their mission.

Patriotic sentiments were expressed from two Catholic pulpits. At St. Paul's the Rev. J. L. Lindsman, assistant pastor, spoke of the duty which Catholics owe their country in time of war. He said that Catholics were patriotic, but were not anxious for war merely for the sake of fighting. It becomes necessary, he said, at times to fight in order that a lasting peace might be attained. In conclusion he likened the present conflict with the struggle which every man must wage against the spirits of darkness in order to find peace and joy eternal.

Father Fournier at St. Mary's spoke at high mass regarding the departure of the Forty-eight Separate Company. He bestowed high words of commendation the citizen soldiery, paying a high compliment to the officers and men for their generosity and charity of the past. In conclusion, he requested that the prayers of the congregation be offered for their safe return.

An impressive service was held at Grace Chapel in honor of the five boys of the Sunday school who left with the Forty-eight. The following were members not only of the Sunday school but also of the church: John Henry, William Clark, George Kinsett, William Fender and Neal Wheeler. They were presented with a nice pocket Testament. Several resolutions were adopted. The Rev. David Wills gave a short address. At the close a farewell reception was held. Special prayers for the church and the company were given both morning and evening.

As Captain Hall was leaving his home Sunday morning he was handed the following letter:

Oswego, N. Y., April 30th, 1898

Captain Hall and the Forty-eight Separate Company:

My Dear and Honored Brothers—You respond to the call of your country, permit me to give you a most sincere God speed.

Yours is a brave response. You go out in the interest of humanity, to proclaim liberty to the downtrodden; no grander cause for war ever stirred the soldier's heart.

I am glad our citizens are arranging to give you so noble an escort as you start for your great work. It will be Sabbath well spent bestowing honor to where honor is due.

May the God of love be with you and keep souls from evil; save you from every enemy and give you victory.

I assure you that in the church of which I have the honor to be pastor continual remembrance and prayer shall be made for you and yours.

Very sincerly,
J. Calvin Meade.

A touching letter received from Father Auger and published in the *Palladium* affected Captain Hall the same as did the epistle from Minister Meade. Tears, which he could not force back, came to his eyes and he could not help but send a prayer thanking the noble hearted persons who have shown their sympathy and patriotism in that never forgotten hour. Father Augur's letter:

Captain A. M. Hall,

Commanding Officer of Forty-eight Separate Company:

Dear Sir: In answer to the summons of duty, to the call of patriotism, you shall leave ere long you happy homes; my best wishes and most fervent prayers will accompany you and those courageous men who form the Forty-eight.

In my church every Sunday public prayers shall be offered to so solicit the protection of heaven on you and your brave soldiers. May the God of armies guide you through the dangers and difficulties you may encounter: May you, under His providential guidance and care, return to your dear homes as strong and vigorous as you leave them, bearing also the palms of victory. The ties of affection that will be severed will cause many a sacrifice, but my earnest supplications are that that those dear ones be granted the courage and resignations requisite in such trying moments.

Kindly assure all married members of your company that I will gladly contribute my share toward the support of their respective families. I remain with the greatest esteem and consideration, your devoted servant,

Rev. J. J. Augur

Rector of St. Louis church.

Oswego, N. Y., April 30th, 1898.

The Inspection

It was ten o'clock when the company's musician sounded "assembly" and the men fell into line for the final inspection before they should start to the front. Guards had been stationed at the entrance to the Armory and the public kept on the outside. Among those who occupied seats in the gallery were about a dozen ladies, wives of men, and Colonel John T. Mott, and his nephew, Lieutenant Philip R. Ward, of the Seventh Artillery, U. S. A. The men lined up, reaching nearly the entire length of the Armory, a sturdier, a better looking lot of young men never walked on the floor of any armory. Captain Hall had taken great pains in selecting only the best material among the hundred who wanted to volunteer to fill the vacancies caused by the order reducing his men from 107 to eighty-four. Married men having families to support who wanted to stay at home, were allowed to do so, and many young men who were anxious to go with the company but who were not considered of sufficient strength to withstand the fatigue and hardships certain to be encountered, were weeded out and left behind. Every man was in fatigue uniform with his knapsack and haversack strapped to his back. The inspection did not take a very great while. The knapsacks were unslung and opened. Each man was found to have provided himself with all necessary articles called for: one change of underclothing, one extra pair of socks, three handkerchiefs, two towels, one cake of soap, comb and clothes brush, knife, fork, and spoon, four provision bags, one meat can, one tin cup, one pair extra shoes, flannel bandage. Besides the articles necessary nearly every member had provided himself with extra things for their comfort. One man had his knapsack half full of dime novels, stirring stories of the Cuban war, with which to pass the hours in camp.

The flannel bandages were given by the Women's Relief Corps of the G. A. R. and are considered most essential of the many things taken. They are to be worn about the waist and are a preventative for fever. They were distributed by First Sergeant McDonald. Commissary Sergeant Tifft distributed the cross-guns to be worn on the fatigue hats and which were donated to the company. It was found that there were sixteen of these cross-guns missing and among those who failed to get one was Captain Hall. As he was passing down the line one of the privates noticed the front of his hat and quickly abstracting his own pinned on the coat of the Captain. It was a little thing, but it showed the feeling of the men for the officer who was to command them.

The Roll Call

After the inspection the roll was called and the men answered to their names. The corrected roster of the company was as follows:

Captain—Albert M. Hall.

First Lieutenant—DeSolvo Tifft.

Second Lieutenant—F. L. Pattberg.

ENLISTED MEN:

First Sergeant—John McDonald.

Sergeants—Grant G. Vickery, William Dunn, F. J. Hirshhols, John Monaghan, Frank Gill.

Corporals—William Monaghan, Frank Bough, Frank Harvey, George Schafer, Clyde R. Harris, B. A. Harris, Thomas Walters, George Decker, George Kinsett, William Hennessey, Herbert Williams, James Mullen.

Privates—J. J. Clancy, John A. Decker, Frank Dake, Patrick Donovan, John W. Dessmore, Joseph W. Edland, William Fender, Thomas Gaffney, John Gregory, William Gilbert, Andrew Anderson, Peter Aumond, R. Althouse, Edward S. Bishop, Willis E. Burns, Jr., Alexander Beiss, Torrey A. Ball, Martin G. Cahill, George Cronk, William Clark, Francis D. Culkin, Edwin I. Hatch, Charles Hunt, Thomas J. Somers, Joseph Peters, George W. Morley, William Maloney, James O'Neil, Arthur Owens, Elmer Olmstead, Arthur Owen, William Parr, Charles Perry, Edward Peavy, John B. Perry, H. B. Place, William B. Purdy, Frank Return, Edward C. Reid, Button L. Rider, Elac Rickey, Burt Simmons, William Taylor, Jesse D. Taylor, Walter Vickery, Walter Van Pelt, Robert Walsh, John C. Henry, John E. Imlay, William Imlay, William Kinney, Louis King, Joseph La Porte, William Murtha, Edward Murphy, William McCann, H. P. Marshall, George Neal Wheeler, Frank J. Yeager, Thomas D. Gill, and Edward Slurff.

Articles of War

After the roll call, the men were marched to the company's quarters where Captain Hall read the articles of war. The reading was in private, but the cheering of the men could be plainly heard. Captain Hall also made an address to the men explaining that they were to go into camp at Hempstead, Long Island, there to await orders and that they were now members of the Regular Army of the United States and no longer National Guardsmen of the State of New York, having entered the service of the Government at nine o'clock yesterday morning. He also said that General Hoffman would be their regimental commander with the rank of Colonel and the men cheered. Almost every one of these knew General Hoffman and were willing and anxious to serve under such a leader. The men were then returned to the floor and discharged to go home to dinner.

The Afternoon

About two o'clock the friends and relatives of the soldier boys commenced to assemble in front of the Armory. The general public was kept out of the building, only friends of the officers being admitted. Many prominent citizens called, among them Mayor Higgins. Captain Hall took the occasion to thank the Mayor for the many favors he had shown himself and men and the Mayor returned the greeting, wishing Captain Hall and his men all kinds of luck and prosperity. As the afternoon wore away the crowd continued to increase in number; there were about three thousand people present.

About four o'clock Miss Amelia Oliphant, of 75 West Mohawk Street, called at the Armory with a large box. When the word was first received that the Forty-eight would be called Miss Oliphant told Captain Hall that she would do something for the "boys". The something proved to be most useful gift of the many received. The box, when opened, was filled with small cloth bags, the name of each man being neatly printed on each. They contained everything that a man away from home would need as could be seen by the following list: one Gospel of St. John, one corn cob pipe, one package of tobacco, one package of chewing gum, one roll of bandages, one roll of string, one pencil, linen thread, pin cushion, darning cotton, patent buttons, court plaster, scissors, white and black thread, shoe strings, buttons, safety pins, cigarette paper, thimble, comb, bottle of magnetic balm, package of writing paper and envelopes. There was also a package for Major Bulger for the hospital corps.

Among other presents sent to the company were four hundred ten cent cigars from Colonel John T. Mott for the enlisted men, a knife, fork and spoon kit from Thomas Moore, seven caddies of plug tobacco and forty-five pounds of fine cut tobacco from F. L. Smith and other friends and a case of wine for the officers from Michael Gill.

At five o'clock the baggage was put aboard the baggage car that had been run in front of the Armory. The three days' ration of the men were placed aboard the car. They consisted of one day's cooked rations and two day's regular ration as follows: Cooked— forty-seven pounds boiled ham, sixty-three pounds canned beef, ninety-five pounds of soft bread, thirty-two pounds crackers, thirty-two pounds canned beans, forty-two pounds cheese, two gallons vinegar, five pounds candles, one-half pound pepper, ten pounds salt, thirty dozen boiled eggs. Two day' regular rations—one hundred and eighty-nine pounds soft bread, sixty-three pounds crackers, forty-two pounds onions, 189 pounds potatoes, eight and one-half pounds rice, eighteen and three-quarter pounds beans, twenty-seven pounds coffee, forty-two pounds sugar, eight-four pounds cheese, three gallons vinegar, ten and one-half pounds candles, twenty-six pounds soap, twenty-five pounds salt, one pound pepper, 294 pounds of fresh beef or mutton, to be purchased at camp.

The company also has the following extras, purchased out of the company fund: ten quarts pickles, twenty-four cans mustard, twenty-four cans condensed milk, three gallons syrup, five boiled hams, twenty gallons coffee.

The Departure

At six o'clock every member of the company was in the Armory ready to move. Outside fully five thousand people were congregated and every minute added hundreds to the number. The different organizations, who had volunteered to act as an escort to the company from the Armory to the depot, commenced to arrive. At 6:50 sharp Marshal Vowinkel gave the order to move and the parade started in the following order:

FIRST DIVISION

Oswego Fire Department
Chief R. G. Blackburn, Commanding.

SECOND DIVISION

Grand Marshal Vowinkel
Chief of Staff, Alonzo Cooper
Aids—A. A. Wellington, R. L. Moore, Benjamin Baker, Dr. J. T. Dwyer, F. W. Loomis, Major A. R. Penfield, John S. Harris, Charles Dain, Thomas McKay, H. L. Lavere
Platoon of Police.
Kingsford Band.
Canton Oswego, I. O. F.
Knights of Pythias.
B. P. O. of Elks.
Knights of Columbus.
C. M. B. A., Branch 115.

THIRD DIVISION

A. O. H. Drum Corps.
National Guard Cadets.
P. O. S. of A.
Old Citizens Corps.
Foresters.
Liederkrans.
Old Volunteers.
Post O'Brien.
Post Stacey

FOURTH DIVISION

48th Separate Company Band
48th Separate Company.

The parade moved down east First Street to Bridge, to West First to the station. The entire march was a grand ovation to the Forty-eight Separate Company. Never before did the people turn out in such vast numbers, and when it commenced to rain there was no scurrying for shelter, but every person stood their place and cheered as they never cheered before. Both sides of the street all along the line of march was one solid bank of humanity, and it was all that those in charge could do to keep the passage open wide enough for the parade to pass through. The organizations presented a handsome appearance, each being fully represented, but the eyes of the people were on the soldier boys who were leaving their homes, possibly never to return. Every available place where a sight of the company could be secured was occupied, the windows of the blocks were filled. And how the boys did march. Every head was erect and they looked every inch the soldiers they were. When the lower bridge was reached the boom from a cannon was heard. It came from the yacht "Katie Gray" anchored in the middle of the river decked in holiday attire. As fast as the cannon could be loaded it was fired. The continued cheering and the blowing of steam whistles made it impossible for an order to be heard and when the corner of West Bridge and First Streets was reached and Captain Hall wanted to take his company up in platoons he could not make his voice heard and the boys were forced to march in column of fours. At the City Hall there was a short rest while the escort arranged themselves on either side of the street to allow the company to pass through. Here the people pressed forward and took occasion to say goodbye. When Grand Marshal Vowinkel had the escort arranged the order was given for the company to move forward. The cheers were deafening, but no organization sent its voice louder than did the two posts of the Grand Army of the Republic. These old heroes who had faced the terrors and hardships of war swung their hats aloft and yelled like good fellows. They had been through the same experience themselves and knew the struggle that was being made.

Three coaches and a baggage car attached to locomative No. 478 was standing on the track of the R. W. & O. Railroad ready to move when the company arrived. The men marched aboard the train. Guards were stationed at each door so that none could leave, while two policemen stood on the platform of each car to keep the crowd from boarding the train. Oswego had something like 25,000 inhabitants and it seemed as if every man, woman and child was around the train.

Captain Hall boarded the train and gave the signal for departure. A song, the "Soldiers Farewell", sung by the Pierce quartet, could be heard. When the train moved out slowly so as not to injure anyone, that great mass of people gave a mighty cheer.

Just before the time to leave Dr. William J. Bulger received a telegram stating that his commission as surgeon of the Provisional regiment, with the rank of major, was ready for him at Albany. Doctor Bulger had full charge of all sickness in the regiment. His pay was $2,500 a year. Other salaries were as follows: Colonel, $3,500; Captain, $1,800; First Lieutenant, $1,500; Second Lieutenant, $1,400; Chaplain, $1,500.

The Trip

The trip to Syracuse was an interesting one, the company received ovations at every stopping place. The station at Fulton was packed. The G. A. R. and the Sons of Veterans made arrangements to meet them at Broadway. The G. A. R. fired a salute and the cheering was deafening. At Phoenix it appeared as if the entire town was out to greet them. There was a band, fireworks, etc. As their train pulled into the Syracuse station they were greeted with the cry:
Remember the Maine
And to hell with Spain.
The station was one mass of moving humanity. Colored lights illumined the street as far as the eye could reach and the sky was ablaze almost, with bursting rockets, Roman candles, etc. The company left Syracuse shortly after 10 P. M. When they arrived in New York, large crowds surrounded the armories and cheered enthusiastically when the Guardsmen commenced their march; they being the first out of town troops to reach the city on their way to Hempstead Plains. A communique from Westbury, New York, dated May 2, stated: "we arrived in camp on Hempstead Plains this morning. We were assigned right of line in Third Provisional Regiment. All well."

Military Relief Fund

Generosity was always a characteristic of the American people and Oswegonians were not lacking in that spirit. The families of the members of the Forty-eight Separate Company were to be provided for during the time they were away to the war, be their time of enlistments thirty days or two years. Mayor Higgins issued a call, Monday May 2, in regard to raising a relief fund to be expended in the care of families of members of the local military company. Tuesday evening a citizens' meeting was held in the Common Council chambers at the City Hall. A resolution was adopted empowering Mayor Higgins to name a committee of eight, one from each ward, to collect and distribute the fund. From the estimates secured it was thought it would cost from seventy-five to one hundred dollars a week to do the work. The committee was to be appointed immediately, or as soon as they could be selected, until that was done, the Mayor was empowered to use the funds already in his hands.

The next meeting was called to order by Mayor Higgins and George T. Clark acted as secretary. The chair announced that pursuant to the resolution passed by the meeting Tuesday evening, he had appointed George T. Clark, L. C. Rowe, E. H. Farrell and H. A. Wilcox the committee to formulate a plan for the raising and distributing of money. He said the committee was ready to report and Mr. Clark read the following:

Report of committee by resolution of meeting of citizens, held in the Common Council Chambers, May 3rd, 1898, to propose a plan for raising and distributing funds to provide for the families of volunteers for military service in the war with Spain:

Your committee report that, so far as they have been able to learn, the approximate sum which will probably be needed for the present, to care for the families of volunteers in the Spanish war, who have been left or practically without support, is from seventy-five to one hundred dollars a week. It may be necessary to add to this estimated sum as time shall furnish additional information of the needs to be met, or as the war with Spain is prolonged. To provide for raising distributing this money we recommend that a committee be

284

appointed of one citizen from each ward, which committee shall discharge the duty of collecting and disbursing contributions to the fund, this committee to have power of substitution in case of vacancy in any membership. For the reason that such committee would be charged with the responsibility of raising, distributing and accounting for the funds contributed, we are of the opinion that it should be left to that committee to decide what measures will be best to accomplish the object in view.

In view of the fact, however, that the resolution under which we were appointed seems to involve some recommendations from us, we would suggest:

First—That the committee should cause a notice to be published in the daily papers making for voluntary contributions from the public, in any amount, monthly or weekly payments preferred, in order that every one may have an opportunity to contribute something.

Second—That the co-operation of all clubs, societies or corporations who are disposed to raise funds for the purpose by entertainments or otherwise be welcomed, with the recommendation that the approval of the General Committee of the methods by which it is proposed to raise the funds be first obtained.

Third—That the committee should, if necessary, provide for the soliciting of funds from citizens by personal application.

Fourth—That the committee provide for the return of any funds which may not be needed according to method that shall be fair to all contributors, or otherwise to dispose of same as duly authorized by them.

Oswego, N. Y., May 6th, 1898.

(Signed) E. H. Farrell
George T. Clark
H. A. Wilcox
J. D. Higgins
L. C. Rowe

The report was adopted unanimously. Mr. Rowe moved that the Mayor be empowered to appoint a committee of eight, as recommended in the resolution, and that the committee have power to select the treasurer. The General Committee of Eight, appointed by Mayor Higgins, Saturday, organized and agreed on a plan of work.

The mothers, wives and sisters of the members of the Forty-eight Separate Company met on Friday, May 6, at the State Armory to take steps for supplying such necessities and comforts for the men in the field. The organization of the National Guard Relief was affected. Mrs. A. M. Hall was elected President; Mrs. Frank Gill, Vice-President; Miss Lulu Parkhurst, Secretary; Mrs. L. G. Palmer, Treasurer. Several G. A. R. ladies expressed their willingness to help the association in any way.

The boys by no means have forgotten the ladies of the Women's Relief Corps, Post O'Brien, G. A. R. and Miss Oliphant. In a letter to the Editor of the *Palladium*, dated May 2, said, among other things, "Please don't forget; put a letter in the papers and tell the ladies of Oswego how grateful we are for their kindness." Another letter, prepared by a committee, dated May 3, to Miss Oliphant expressed "their extreme gratitude for the 'comfort bags' presented them on Sunday last." The committee added "that the bags have been at once a source of jealousy and admiration to the other companies of the Third Provisional Regiment."

Fund-raising activities were reported in the press such as outright donations by individuals and organizations. For instance, a check for $67.00 was donated by the pupils and teachers of the State Normal and Training School; the Masonic order, $75.00; Branch No. 136 C. M. B. A., St. John's initial contribution $10.00; from the Police Pension Fund, $100.00. Aid was promised from church funds and from various organizations. Notices were published for an ice cream social, basketball game, steroptican lecture, etc. The Relief Committee met for the first time on May 9th and concluded its labors on December 6. There were 149 individual and organzation contributors; sixteen families and individuals were given relief. After turning over a balance to the Oswego Hospital, the committee's work was finished.

N. Y. O. & W. R. Railroad Company informed local officials that all officers and employees who enlisted in the Army of the United States or the National Guard would not lose their positions, but the same would be retained for them until their return. The Standard Oil Company also had assured all employees that their positions would be ready for them. Other corporations were considering taking similar action. Officials and employees of the city were also assured of their pay and postions upon their return from service.

The One Hundred Forty-eight

Captain Hall's last official act before he left the Armory, May 1, was to file the appointment of Charles Tifft and William Parkhurst as Armorers. The appointments were subject to the approval of Lieutenant Michael O'Donnell. Thirty-six members of the Forty-eight Separate Company were left behind when the company went away to Camp Black. They were the nucleus for the new One hundred Forty-eight Separate Campany. Call for recruits were issued and sufficient number of enlistments made possible a new company.

Lieutenant O'Donnell received from Brigadier-General Peter C. Doyle of Buffalo, Commanding the Fourth Brigade, N. G. N. Y., Special Order No. 40, directing him to prepare the new militia company. At the State Armory, Monday night June 6, Major Frank E. Wood, of Buffalo, mustered in the One Hundred Forty-eight Company of Oswego. After the men were sworn in the election of officers occurred.

Lieutenant Michael O'Donnell, who had been a member of the Regular Army for the past thirty-three years, was unanimously elected Captain; Michael Walsh, First Lieutenant; and Montcalm D. Brown, Second Lieutenant. The muster roll of the company contained the names of fifty officers and men as follows:

Abbey, Walter J.; Barbeau, Samuel; Brown, Montcalm D.; Brown, Luther O.; Brown, Ward Lester; Cates, Frank J.; Clark, Abraham C.; Coleman, C. Adelbert; Craley, Louis E.; Decker, John; Derry, Thomas W.; Doran, William A.; France, Robert; Frisbee, John; Gaffney, Thomas; Guilds, Albert R.; Henry, John; Holland, Ira; Hunter, Francis T.; Ketcham, Ira W.; King, Edward A.; Kinney, William; Kirk, Joseph W.; Lagoe, John; Metcalf, Wilson A.; Mosier, Frank; Murray, Charles; Nettle, Charles B.; Newstead, George; O'Donnell, Michael; Pelky, Harry; Pelo, John E.; Pero, Cal William; Place, Harry; Plank, Fred W.; Preamo, George; Wuel, Alexander;

287

Sketches from the *Palladium* of May 9, 1898

Rowlee, Eugene; Smith, Judson; Smith, Lucian F.; Stever, George; Tifft, Charles A.; Tifft Milo A.; Traua, Ernest G.; Van Pelt, Walter; Vickery, Thomas; Walsh, Michael; West, George; Wood, Frank.

Nine recruits to replace those who failed their physical tests were ordered as early as May 12. It was announced on June 6, at Camp Alger, Virginia, that Company D strength was to be increased to 106; this necessitated 25 more recruits. Sergeant William J. Dunn, of Company D, Third Regiment, was sent to Oswego for the purpose of obtaining twenty-five recruits for Company D from the One Hundred Forty-eight Separate Company. The Sergeant left Oswego on June 22, with his twenty-five recruits.

Camp Life

From their arrival at Camp Black on May 2, and until their departure for Camp Alger, and to Camp Meade, there were daily despatches (special) to both local papers. Details of camp life, gossip, rumors, and other ways of passing time were reported in great detail.

There were two newspapers in Oswego; the Oswego *Palladium* (Demorcrat) and the Oswego *Times* (Republican). Captain Albert M. Hall was the editor of the *Palladium*. The *Palladium's* war correspondent was Francis D. Culkin. He was a law student of George N. Burt and enlisted in the Forty-eight Separate Company on April 22, 1898. Mr. Culkin was formerly connected with the reportorial staff of the Rochester *Herald*. He was employed to send special despatches, and the paper boasted that Mr. Culkin "is a most entertaining writer to furnish this paper with the latest gossip from the camp of Forty-eight." Mr. Culkin's articles were signed "c."

Clarence S. Martin, of the *Palladium's* local staff enlisted May 13, 1898, to join Captain Hall's Company. "He was moved by purely patriotic motives." (He was sent to report the progress of recruitment and came a recruit). The previous year Mr. Martin was employed as a reporter by the *Times*. After being mustered out of service he removed to Cortland as a reporter. His aricles were signed c.m.s.

Oswego Boys at Cooking Quarters—Camp Black

New York Globe, May 12, 1898

The *Times* articles were mostly unsigned but several were identified on the signature "Recruit." DeSolvo Tifft was a foreman in the job room.

Although there was a common similarity in both papers, the *Palladium* articles were more detailed and informative, and therefore, generally used.

To detail the daily occurrences at Camp Black, Camp Alger and Camp Meade would be wearisome to the reader. Suffice to say that sickness among the soldiers increased and became progressively worse during the summer. Forty cases of malaria were reported by July 1st and by July 28th typhoid fever was quite general, affecting each regiment; hospitals were crowded to the limit. Finally the troops of the Second Corps left Camp Alger on August 18.

Middletown was situated on picturesque Susquehanna River, some fifteen miles south of Harrisburg. There was excellent drainage and an abundance of water could be piped from the Pennsylvania capital. Then, the altitude was high and mosquitos would not be as warlike as at Camp Alger.

Hostilities between the United States and Spain ceased on August 12. The war was over and the men were ready to depart for home. The first authentic news received that the regiment was to be mustered out came on Saturday September 3, through a private telegram sent to Chaplain Brainard from Congressman Sereno E. Payne, which said that all arrangements had been made whereby the Third New York would leave for home within the next fifteen days. The men took the news quietly. There was no cheering or demonstration of any kind, the men being overjoyed that they were to be relieved from the monotony and many disagreeable features of camp life that they went to their tents and there talked the good news over. Ten days later Company D was in Oswego.

New York Globe, May 12, 1898

Preparations For The Reception

A special Reception Committee was appointed by Mayor Higgins to make arrangements to Receive Company D, Third New York Volunteers, upon their arrival in the city on Tuesday evening September 13. C. J. Vowinkel was elected Grand Marshal. Invitations had been extended to all various civic societies of the city. Grand Marshal Vowinkel announced the following formation of the parade:

FIRST DIVISION
Oswego Fire Department
Chief R. G. Blackburn
Assistant Chief John Nacey
Platoon of Police
Grand Marshal C. J. Vowinkel
Captain A. E. Seliger, Chief of Staff

STAFF

L. Wiegand, Jr.
Rollo G. Jermyn
A. H. Ames
S. C. Conde

H. S. Lavere
George Kohoe
Harry Sayward
George Trageser

SECOND DIVISION
Doctor J. T. Dwyer
Aids: Fred Loomis, John F. Dain, Jr.,
John H. McCarthy, Fred Schuler
Kingsford Band
148th Separate Company
Canton Oswego, I. O. O. F.
Knights of Pythias
B. P. O of Elks
Branches 76, 115, 136, and 140 C. M. B. A.

THIRD DIVISION
Colonel John S. Harris, Commanding
Aids: Benjamin Baker, William Desens,

Thomas L. McKay
Oswego Letter Carriers
Minetto Band
National Guard Cadets
Oswego German Liederkranz
Knights of Maccabees
Young Men's Lutheran Society
Foresters
Street Railway Motormen Conductors

FOURTH DIVISION

Major A. R. Penfield, Commanding
Aids: Alonzo Cooper, James M. Himes,
C. C. Mattoon, Robert L. Moore
A. O. H. Drum Corps
Citizens' Corps
Old Volunteer Firemen
Post Stacy, G. A. R.
Post O'Brien, G. A. R.

FIFTH DIVISION

Major A. M. Hall, Commanding
Forty-eight Separate Band
Company D, Third New York Volunteers
Captain D. H. Tifft
The Knights of Columbus. Y.M.C.U. and P. O. S. of A. will be
represented in the other organizations which turned out.

LINE OF MARCH

From West First and Utica to Oneida, to Third, to Cayuga, to
First, to Bridge, across lower bridge to East First, to Armory.

The City Hall bell will ring one hour before the arrival of the
company.

A feature of the demonstration will be the reception to be
given to the returning heroes by the children of the schools. No
triumphal army of a Roman Caesar was more royally acclaimed
than will be Oswego's representatives of Uncle Sam's Volunteer
Army. Flowers will be strewn in their pathway and through solid
lines of wild enthusiastic people will they march through the

thoroughfares the recipients of a grateful people's homage. At the corner of East First and Bridge Streets a number of girls arrayed in white and bearing flowers will meet Company D and, preceding them through solid human square, formed by the participating organizations lined up on either side of the street, will throw blossoms beneath their feet all the way to the Armory. The school children were dismissed early that morning to give them an opportunity to gather a supply of flowers. Flags and bunting will form the decorations and every business house and residence along the line of the march should be decorated.

The Trip Home

The troops left Camp Meade on September 12. After an all night ride, they reached Elmira where Colonel Hoffman reviewed the entire regiment. Colonel John T. Mott acted as host to the men at Syracuse, and sent as many as could be allowed to go to the Mansion House, where an appetizing meal had been prepared at the Colonel's expense. Among others who met the company at Syracuse were City Clerk Wheeler, George N. Burt, Trainmaster J. G. Halleron, W. J. Dempsey and the members of the Reception Committee, John F. Dain, W. H. Selleck, O. S. Osterhout, Louis Wiegand and B. R. Ketcheson. Again the troops paraded in Syracuse then boarded the special train for Oswego at 6:40. At Phoenix the entire population turned out and as the train pulled in, the crowd shouted to accompaniment of cannon. Major Hall was compelled to make a speech. It was very brief and in it the Major said that the regiment lost eighteen men by death and had left two hundred men behind in the hospital. He was cheered. The following members of the Reception Committee: Chief R. G. Blackburn, the Hon. C. N. Bulger, J. B. Alexander, Fred M. Bishop, George S. Benz, John K. Lynch, Lawrence Clancy, A. Salladin, Jr., Frank N. Breed, of Phoenix, and others met the troops in the city of Fulton. At Fulton there was a great turnout. Greek fire was burned and the troops were received with unbounded enthusiasm. Major Hall said, when seen by a *Palladium* reporter, that there were seventy-two men all told, including himself and the other officers. The number swelled at Fulton by the addition of the following men home on furlough: Corporal Kinsett and Morley, Private Fitch, Marshall, Mullen, Ketchum, Vickery, Donovan and Foote. Private Grimm, Ninth United States Infantry, met the train at Fulton. A stop of but three minutes was made there and the train proceeded on its way. At the West end of the railroad bridge at Oswego the train slacked up, owing to the tremendous crowd and only crawled into the station.

A Royal Welcome

A demonstration which in magnitude and enthusiasm surpassed anything of its kind in Oswego's history was given by a loyal, loving people to the self-sacrificing young men who represented the city in Uncle Sam's Volunteer Army. Oswego had a plethora of celebrations but none that could be compared for a moment with that of the night of September. "it beats all I have seen," said Major Hall, as he stepped to review his soldiers, "Oswego has certainly outdone herself."

The blare of trumpets and the rattle of drums announced the arrival of the returned volunteers. Instantly there was a rush for the train and the corps of policemen were powerless to stay the human torrent. The soldiers had their heavy knapsacks strapped to their backs and their guns in hand prepared for the command. As soon as a space could be cleared they formed in line with Captain Tifft and Lieutenant Pattberg at their head. Major Hall, mounted his horse, forced a passage through the throng and received a grand welcome. About twenty minutes after the train reached the city Grand Marshal Vowinkel gave the command to start the parade.

Eventually they reached the armory. In a moment the Armory was packed and the company experienced considerable difficulty in passing through. At length the balcony was reached and then Captain Tifft led his men into company parlors, where packs were unslung and rifles laid down.

Captain Tifft directed First Sergeant Vickery to read the roll call. All present responded and each man checked off. About twenty were left behind at the hospitals and others of the command who lived in Syracuse and elsewhere had left the train before arriving here. The roll call finished, Captain Tifft directed Sergeant Vickery to read orders issued at Camp Meade by the Acting Adjutant. The order was

295

to the effect that the members were given furloughs, the reading of the order taking place of the written furlough usually issued.

All members were required to report on the thirtieth day from the time of the reading of the order at eight o'clock in the morning in full uniform, to be mustered out. It was agreed that the packs and other Government property should be left at the Armory under guard and the men to return the next day and obtain their personal belongings. Captain Tifft made a few remarks to his men and said that he desired to have all the liberty consistent with their positions. He hoped that they would conduct themselves as true soldiers and impressed upon them the necessity of reporting at the expiration of the thirty days' furlough.

Mayor Higgins mounted a table and said:

Officers and men of Company D, Third New York Volunteers, there is no time now, when you are hungry and tired, to say anything but that Oswego welcomes you back to her midst. We are proud of Company D as we would have been had you been at Manila or Santiago. You stood ready to obey orders and are entitled to the appreciation of the city of Oswego. So I say again, 'welcome!' Three cheers for Company D.

Major Hall mounted the table. After the cheering was stopped with difficulty, he said:

I want to thank the Mayor for the officers and enlisted men of Company D for your welcome. We went out many months ago ready to obey orders, and though we did not get near the front, whether at Manila or some other point, yet we made our full sacrifice. I wish to say that I have brought back every man I took away, save those in the hospital. Not one has died. And I have the statement of the surgeons that all the sick will receive proper care and will return to this city. I thank you for your reception.

The men were then invited to the parlors, which were beautifully decorated with flowers, flags and bunting and where a bountiful repast was served by the Women's Relief Corps.

296

"All Present and Accounted For."

The list of the men who came home was as follows:

Major Hall, Captain Tifft, Lieutenant Pattberg, First Sergeant Vickery, Quartermaster-Sergeant Gill, Sergeants John and William Monaghan, Corporals B. A. Harris, Hennessey, Keeler, Decker, Walters, Harvey, Shaefer, C. R. Harris, Rickey, Bough, Privates Clark, Purdy, Comstock, Edland, Maloney, Althouse, Owens, Vincent, Martin, Keefe, Parr, Woods, William Taylor, Baehr, Slattery, Murtha, Harlow, Rider, Aumond, Brown, Gill, Slurff, Godon, Culkin, Hart, Fred LaPorte, Yeager, Cronk, Adriance, Fender, Cahill, Henry Wise, Bishop, Walsh, Duffy Desmore, Joseph LaPorte, Dewey, John Wise, Olmstead, Snyder, Roland Clark, Wheeler, Welling, Gilbert, Mitchell, Return, Wagoner, Anderson, Artificer Somers, Musician Hatch.

The following men were on sick leave:

Sergeant Hirshholz, Corporals Morley, Kinsett, Privates Thomas D. Gill, Henry Gill, Marshall, Pease, Mullen, Murphy, Donovan, Vickery, Ketchum and Stoutenger.

Daniel Henderson, John McBride and Albert King, who left here to join the Regimental band, also came home with the company.

The following men were in hospital:

First Division, Dunn Loring, Virginia, Sergeant Dunn.

Fort Meyer Hospital: Privates Beiss, Ball, Clifford.

Saint Mary's, Philadelphia: Joseph Drumm.

University Hospital, Philadelphia: Corporal Williams, Clifford Perry, Arthur Owen.

Medical-Surgical Hospital, Philadelphia: Privates Brunot, Peavey, Ketcham, Jesse Taylor.

Sloggs Hospital, Philadelphia: John Imlay, Harry Pelkey.

General Hospital, Philadelphia: Charles Hunt, James O'Neil.

Red Cross Hospital, Camp Meade: Privates Joseph Anderson, Simmons, Louis King.

After several dissapointments, Company D, 3rd New York Volunteers, was finally mustered out on December 1, 1898. Dr. Henry C. Baum, United States Volunteers, of Syracuse, and Colonel

297

E. E. Hardin, 2nd New York, Captain E. R. Hills, United States Army, Major T. C. Goodman, Lieutenant George W. Gatchell, A. W. Dale, United States Army, Richard Hook, Jr., and Dr. A. F. Brugman arrived the previous night to work out the details. Captain Hills and Lieutenant were the mustering out officers; Major Goodman, the paymaster. The others acted in the capacity of clerks, except Drs. Brugman and Baum, who made the examinations as to the physical condition of a few members of the company.

At 12 o'clock assembly was sounded and Company D formed on the main floor of the Armory. The muster roll was called by Captain E. R. Hills, only Private Thomas Gill did not respond because of illness (died 12/98). Private Rider reported this day for the first time since he was taken sick. Captain Tifft called from the muster roll the name of the soldier, who stepped forward, saluted Major Goodman and received his wages. They received on the average about $108. Some men were dissapointed upon receiving their discharges, for in some instances objections for re-enlistment in the service were inscribed, because of physical unfitness.

At two o'clock that afternoon Company D, 3rd Regiment, New York Volunteers ceased to exist. The 148th Separate Company, it was thought, would be mustered out in the near future, and the old 48th Separate Company would continue to flourish. Those members of that Company who were transferred to the 148th Separate Company were again transferred this time back to the original Company. The others of the 148th were mustered out of service. Those of the 48th whose time of service in the National Guard had expired were discharged, if they wished it.

Uniforms discarded—the volunteer soldiers dropped out of sight quickly.

Albert M. Hall

Albert M. Hall was a native of Oswego, New York, where he was born in 1861. After completing his education in the Oswego public schools, he owned and operated a small printing office in Oswego. When the *Morning Express* was founded about 1880 he became a reporter on that newspaper and continued with it until the *Oswego Daily Times* purchased that newspaper and consolidated it with the

Times. Mr. Hall then became associated with John R. Walkup in establishing the Oswego *Morning Post*, which was published for a short time with George C. Bragdon as editor-in-chief. When the *Post* was suspended Mr. Hall joined the staff of the Oswego *Palladium* as a reporter. In 1883 he resigned to go to Syracuse where he became city and state editor of the *Herald*. In 1885 Mr. Hall returned to Oswego and rejoined the *Palladium* staff as city editor. He soon became its editorial writer, a position that he thereafter continued to fill during his long connection with the newspaper.

Mr. Hall early became identified with the Oswego National Guard Company. He enlisted as a private, and rose through all the ranks until he became captain of the company. He was called into active service with the Oswego National Guard Company in 1898 in connection with the Spanish-American War from which he returned with the rank and title of Major by which he was invariably thereafter identified. He was elected mayor of Oswego in 1899 and served in 1900–1901. He remained with the *Palladium* until 1903 when he resigned to go to Geneva, New York, to become the editor of the *Review* which was just then being established in that city. It proved to be short-lived and after a few months, Major Hall removed to Elmira, New York, where he became the editor of the *Elmira Advertiser* a morning newspaper, then owned by J. Sloat Fassett, one-time Republican candidate for governor of New York and later a member of the House of Representatives at Washington. After leaving Elmira in December, 1908, Major Hall removed to Maryland where in 1913 in collaboration with his son-in-law, David Dean, he founded the *Sykesville Herald* which he edited for eight years. He also conducted for a time the *Westminster Enterprise*. In 1921 he removed to Florida where he founded the *Apopka Chief* which under the influence of his powerful editorials and special articles became recognized as the one of the leading weeklies of the South. In 1935 he sold his paper and its plant and retired finally from newspaper work. He died at the Bay Inies, Hospital for veterans on May 19, 1937.

N. Y. State Armory—Oswego

THE FLAG

Cheers for the sailors that fought on the wave for it,
Cheers for the soldiers that always were brave for it,
Tears for the men that went down to the grave for it.
Here comes the Flag.

Arthur Macy (1842-1904)

The Massacar at Samar

When an Army, Navy, Marine Corps veterans appeared at Military Gatherings, the order was given, "Stand, Gentlemen, He Served at Samar."

Introduction

On April 16, 1898, the Ninth Infantry received an order to proceed to Tampa, Florida. The Ninth left Tampa June 14, 1898, for Cuba. The regiment received orders early in September to return to its former station, Madison Barracks, arriving there on September 11. The authorized organization and strength of the regiment, under the provisions of the Act Congress, approved, April 26, 1898, and General Orders No. 27, Adjutant General's Office, Series 1898, had become one Colonel, 2 Majors, 12 Captains, 14 First Lieutenants, 12 Second Lieutenants, and three battalions of 4 companies each—authorized enlisted strength of each company, 106, authorized total of regiment, 42 officers, 1,277 enlisted men. The number actually arrived at Madison Barracks after the Cuban campaign was 18 officers, 363 enlisted men. Eighteen officers and 279 other enlisted men were absent on detached service, with leave, or sick. About 600 men were required to fill the vacancies, and as time disclosed, over 300 more were necessary to take the place of men who were too debilitated by the Cuban campaign to again participate in tropical service. One company, Company C, was sent to Fort Ontario at Oswego to regarrison that post, which had been abandoned for several years. The company took station there on December 19, 1898, leaving on March 17, 1899, when the company joined the regiment for Manila, Philippine Islands. From a table of enlistments prepared from regimental records, Fort Ontario was credited with 17 enlistments from Oswego. As far as it can be ascertained, they are: George F. Allen, William Archambeau, Sylvester Burke, Roland T. Clark, Guy C. Dennis, Joseph Godon, Nathaniel Meade, Charles Meeker, James J. O'Neil, Owen F. O'Neil, Peter Pelkey, Charles Powers, Reuben Simpson, Frank Syrell, Herman Trapp, and Robert Walsh.

The service of the Ninth Infantry in Luzon began in April, 1899, and terminated in June, 1900; and the cable message from Washington ordering a regiment to China was dated June 16, 1900. The Special Order No. 65, an Extract read:

In compliance with cable instructions from the Secretary of War, dated June 16, 1900, the Ninth Regiment of Infantry will be concentrated in Manila, with the least possible delay, for transfer to Taku, China, upon arrival, the commanding officer will report to the United States Minister for the protection of the American Legation and the lives and property of American citizens in China.

The regiment left June 26, 1900, for China; the entire regiment served in China from July, 1900, until May 27th, 1901, when it returned to Manila.

Samar had been occupied since January, 1900. Finally (May, 1901) the time came to clean up Samar, that impenetrable island, which had never been subdued by the Spaniards, and counted itself unconquerable. That the Ninth Infantry was looked upon by General Arthur MacArthur as a lusty, available regiment for service in the same place, appeared as early as May 15th ten days before the regiment left China. The order for the movement, issued from Headquarter's Division of the Philippines, July 24, 1901, directed four companies to proceed to Samar to relieve four troops of the Ninth Cavalry. Company C was placed at Balagiga, a point previously unoccupied at the southern end of the island. The movement to Samar began August 7th.

The officers of Company C were Captain Thomas W. Connell and First Lieutenant Edward A. Bumpus; Major Richard S. Griswold, United States Volunteers, was assigned as surgeon to the station. The company was landed at Balagiga without opposition, and the officials of the town professed friendship. The public buildings were appropriated for the use of the company, the upper part of the tribunal being used as barracks, and the lower floor as commissary storehouse, guard and prison room. The kitchen was in a building immediately in rear, large tents between the two buildings were used as mess rooms. Conical tents were erected at the northwest corner of the main building as shelter for native prisoners, sentinel post No. 1 guarding them on one side and another sentinel on the other. Two small houses a short distance were occupied as additional barracks, the main building not being sufficient to accommodate the whole

302

company. The tribunal faced an open square or plaza, and in front of it, on the opposite side of the plaza, was the church and convent. The latter building was taken for the hospital, and the officers occupied one part of it as its quarters. It was separated from the church by a narrow passage which was bridged by a closed hallway from the church on the level of the main floor of the convent, a staircase ascendinng from a door of the church to the level of the hall. A guard and sentinel were posted in the convent at the foot of an interior staircase, near a door looking out toward the plaza. This building which was on the south side of the church was slightly further than the latter, and immediately in its rear was the river—a deep and rapid stream. A few yards below was a dock at which landing was made from barotas. The river flowed into a small open bay a short distance from the dock, and the bay, with a shelving beach, lay on the south side of the town. On the other sides the tangled tropical shrubbery bordered the town, and the shrubbery about the native houses offered places of concealment. Immediately in front of the church was a large wooden cross, the stone base of which was crumpled somewhat, and to the left (north) side was the bell tower, a separate structure, about thirty feet high, holding several bells of different sizes, which were rung at stated hours of the day.

The Uprising

It is not the intent of the writer to give a detailed description of the attack on the morning of September 28th. A few facts are necessary to make the scene clear. The morning came and the usual reveille calls aroused the men, who lazily prepared themselves for breakfast. Already the natives were gathering for the day's work, and many were lounging about the plaza in groups of 15 or 20, their working bolos in their hands. The prisoners, of whom there were 64 in the guard tents the night of the 27th, were within a few feet of fifty or more bolos which they had thrown together in a pile for the night near their tents.

Corporal (Sylvester) Burke, (Oswego, New York), with others, were at breakfast under Barracks G. The Chief of Police came near him and leaned against pillar of building, then walked along post No. 2 towards Barracks No. 3. As the sentinel passed him he seized the sentinel's rifle, gave a loud call, the church bell rang, and a rush was made by the natives simultaneously on the different barracks,

303

officers' quarters, and the men at breakfast table and kitchen. The sentinel on No. 1 and the Sergeant of the guard were killed at once, and the native prisoners and others rushed into main barracks. From the east of the kitchen the natives rushed upon the men at Breakfast.

The details of the plan of attack were evidently thought out with care and were well nigh perfectly arranged. The time was the breakfast hour, when the men were all assembled and absent from their arms, and the officers still sleeping. A certain number of individuals were assigned to assassinate particular persons, such as the sentinels on post, of whom there were four; one or two were to ring the church bells as the general signal for the attack; the Chief of Police was to see that all were ready at their posts, and at the proper moment to call out to men at the bells, and at the same time grab the rifle of the sentinel on Post No. 2. Small groups were told to kill the officers, the Acting First Sergeant, and the few individuals who might be at the two outlying houses used as barracks. A large number were to be in the plaza near the entrance to the barracks, having their bolos in their hands as though ready to begin work of the day, to rush in and up the stairs to the main dormitory to secure the arms and ammunition belts. With these the prisoners, most of whom had been brought in from the surrounding country during the few days immediately preceding, were to arm themselves. They were doubtless, an organized lot of insurgents prepared to do the bidding of their leaders, and the fifty bolos, which they had been using at their work the day before, were never at hand to be seized as they sprang forth from the guard tents. Finally a large number were assembled along the beach and in the grass and shrubbery among the houses, just south of the kitchen, to rush on the men at breakfast.

The slaughter was indescribable. In the few minutes of hurrying, stabbing, cutting, all the officers and more than half of the 71 men were killed, at least half of the remainder received serious wounds, and only 4 escaped without wounds of some nature. The assailants were believed to have numbered 400, and an estimate of the number killed, based on the statements of the survivors, is placed about 100. The others were driven to cover. Much more can be told of individual courage. Briefly, the town was reoccupied by a company of the Eleventh Infantry.

The Ninth Regiment left Manila for the United States on May 27, 1902; a happy day for all. An elaborate welcome was given by the city of Watertown. After a parade by the regiment, a supper was

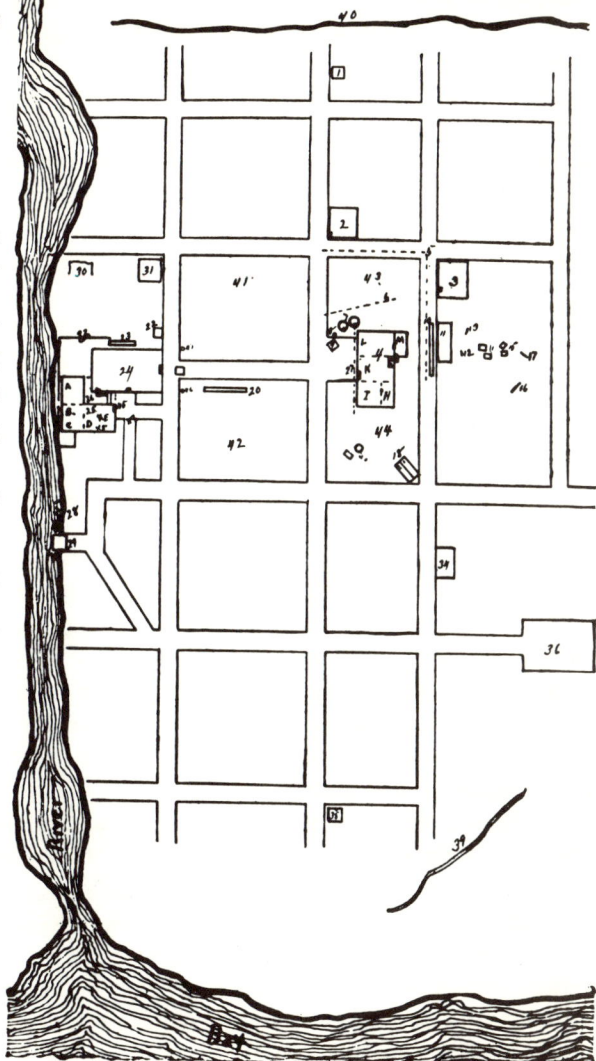

PLAN OF BUILDINGS AND GROUND OCCUPIED BY COMPANY "C" NINTH U. S. INF. AT BALANGIGA, SAMAR. SCALE, 1"50 YARDS. SEPT. 28, 1901. CORP'L C. M. MUMBY, CO. "C" NINTH U. S. INFTY., CALBAYOG, SAMAR

INDEX

1. Residence of chief police.
2-3. Small barracks.
4. Main barracks.
5. Post No. 2.
6. Post No. 4.
7. Conical tents for prisoners.
8. Flagstaff.
9. Well for drinking water.
10. Dining tents.
11. Kitchen.
12. Buzzacot.
13. Woodpile.
14. Bake oven and Bakery tent.
15. Hen-coop and pig-sty.
16. Lavatory.
17. Where Prvt. Wright was buried.
18. Graves of Schechterle and McGilligan.
19. Bath tent and well for wash water.
20. Where 33 Americans' dead were buried.
21. Large cross.
22. Bell tower.
23. Where enemy's dead were buried.
24. Church.
25. Convent.
26. Passageway between church and convent on ground.
27. Post No. 1.
28. Barotes survivors escaped.
29. Docks for small boats.
30-1-2-3. Ruins of old cathedral.
34. Police headquarters.
35. Residence of presidente.
36. Cemetery.
37. Bridle path to Caloogan, 7½ miles.
38. Bridge over small creek.
39-40. Insurgents trenches.
41-2-3-4. Plaza.
45. Stairway and Post No. 3.
46-47. Trees.
A. Kitchen for officers' mess and hospital mess.
B. Hallway.
C. Room used for hospital.
D. Room used for officers' barracks.
E. Where Lt. Bumpus was killed.
F. Where Major Grisswold was killed.
G. Where Capt. Connell was killed.
H. Orderly room on 2nd floor.
I. Sales commissary on 1st floor.
K. Guard room and prison, 1st floor.
L. Store room and prison, 1st floor.
M. Squad room, Srg't. Hickman and four (4) men.

305

enjoyed by the troops at the armory. The regiment was thus once more at its old home at Madison Barracks. Four years of campaigning were closed.

Oswegonians At Belangiga

Sylvester Burke was born in the Town of Scriba, the son of Jeremiah and Hannah Newstead Burke. He spent practically all of his life in Oswego. After service in the Spanish-American War and the Philippine insurrection, Sergeant Burke was connected with the United States Lighthouse service at Oswego and Sandusky, Ohio. Leaving the federal service, he established a hotel at Vernon, Oneida County. After retiring from the hotel business, he operated a tavern in Oswego. His last location was at East Bridge and Eight Streets.

Sylvester Burke enlisted December 12, 1898, at Fort Ontario, Oswego, New York, at the age of 22, (height 5' 5"), in the Ninth Infantry, Company C; and, was discharged August 6, 1901, at Manila.

In 1928 Col. E. G. Payton, U. S. Army, commanding the Ninth Infantry, recommended the awarding of Congressional Medals of Honor to Sgt. Burke and Roland T. Clark of Oswego who as members of Company C of the regiment were among those in the Belangigan massacre who performed "acts of heroism and bravery beyond and above the normal call of duty." At the time of the massacre Mr. Burke was promoted to corporal in the company.

Colonel Peyton letter to the War Department recommending congressional recognition of living as well as the deceased members of the regiment who participated in the massacre follows:

In compliance with authority contained in a letter from the War Department, dated January 26, 1928, to the commanding officer of the Ninth Infantry, I strongly recommend that the following named survivors of the Belangigan massacre be awarded the Congressional Medal of Honor for exceptionally meritorious and self-sacrificing services far beyond the normal call of duty in heroically assiating and saving lives of comrades overwhelmed by hostile natives, then rescuing under fire and later caring for their helplessly wounded comrades.

There were other survivors of this fight, but the records at hand fail to reveal their participation in any of the phases of the fighting described above.

This almost forgotten fight in faraway Philippines really deserves a place in history alongside of Thermopylae, Balclava, the Alamo and Little Big Horn.

A brief history of the insurrection is already related above and the part Sgt. Burke played in it but let Sgt. Burke describe the incident in a letter, dated October 2, 1901, to his mother, Mrs. Hannah Burke, of East Tenth Street:

George Allen, Will and I are alive and well, but because of that fact we have nothing to thank the natives. Will and Dan Donovan were not with us, they having been left in Manila. Its a good thing for both that they were not with us. Will, in particular, for he would have become so excited that he would have jumped right into the thick of the scrimmage and would have been cut down.

[Will and Dan Donovan were brothers, residents of 142 East Seneca Street. In the list of names in the company from this city, one was given to Daniel J. Donovan. Oswego *Daily Palladium*, October 1, 1901.]

I suppose, however, that you heard all about this affair. It occurred on the morning of September 28th at Belangiga. It was half-past 6 in the morning when the 'brown men' came at us. We were eating, or had just concluded breakfast. There were about 500 of the bolomen and before we could get out of the dining room, they were among us chopping and stabbing right and left. I was not feeling well that morning and was sitting under my quarters when the attack was made. The company occupied 3 'shacks' apart from each other. When they charged our 'shack' myself and 4 or 5 others rushed inside and we had a hand-to-hand battle of it. Two of the men were killed, but I managed to get hold of a six-shooter that belonged to the Hospital Corps and I made good use of it. I killed all the natives in the 'shack'. Myself and the few men that were able to fight got to the rifles and commenced firing through the windows. At muster time that morning we had 71 men strong and of that number 46 were killed and 18 wounded, leaving only seven who escaped uninjured. Three officers were among the killed and the company records were carried away. Many of the men were killed at breakfast table while washing their dishes, a number of them started to run when they saw the natives with our guns, but were shot down.

When we began shooting and the bolomen began falling there was a lively scramble to get out of range or hide themselves from view. We captured about 30 of our rifles that they had taken when the charge was made, but we had no one to use them. We were obliged to destroy them. Picking up our wounded we started in canoes a distance of 35 miles to Basey, where Company G was stationed. We atarted at 7:40 A. M. ; it took us till 3:30 A. M. the next day to make the distance.

Several of the wounded died on the trip, including poor Charlie Powers. He was cut in the head and back. The last time I saw him he was alive and being placed in a canoe with others. I was in the first boat assisting in propelling it, with others stretched out behind. Charlie died on the trip and his body was buried in the sea. The passage was a rough one for all of us and one of the boats filled and sunk, but we managed to save 2 of the wounded men that was in it, and took them in our boat. To save ourselves and give the others a like chance, the ropes holding the canoes together were cut and drifted apart. Two of the men in one boat died before we reached our destination and 2 others died here in the hospital. I got a stab over the right eye from a stiletto. I believe the fellow was trying to hit me in the eye, but I ducked and caught the blade over the eye. Joseph Godon was killed instantly. I saw him when he was hit and he was dead when I reached his side. Guy Dennis was killed in the doorway of his quarters. His throat was cut with a bolo knife.

We went back to Belangiga next day and buried our dead marking each grave. We got a few of the company records back and expect to get the others, as the troops are after them. We lost all our clothing and everything we owned excepting the clothing on our backs and rifles we were able to recapture. My time will be cut in two months and if they don't get me inside of that time I will return home. An effort is being made, however, to recruit the company here. With the exception of Custer massacre, in which every member of the Cavalry troop was killed, I believe the affair at Samar was one of the most disastrous engagements that a company of regulars has ever been engaged in.

Sgt. Burke's letter describes the engagement but not a word was said about his bravery. Stephen Bonsal, a correspondent in the

Phillippine Islands for the New York *Herald* wrote a description of the slaughter to the local press. An excerpt follows:

Beaten down on their knees, bleeding from a score of wounds, the little band that followed Betron and Burke were driven inch by inch out of the larger room took refuge in a smaller room adjoining, and here, with their backs to the wall, so that few bolomen could get at them, they were preparing to sell their lives dearly.

The Chief of Police led the band that was pressing them so closely, Burke was growing weaker every minute for the loss of blood, and at last he decided not to fight any more, but to take the Chief of Police, their ruthless pursuer, down to death with him. So he watched his chance and sprang upon him, and before the Chief knew his danger Burke was past the murderous dagger and the crimson bolo. With his hands entwined about the scoundrel's throat with all the strength his courage could summon, he closed in the death grapple. Over and over they rolled.

The Chief was a sinewy fellow and hold his own, but no one of his henchmen dared to aid him, so inextricably intertwined were the bodies. Burke was weakening fast. His blood was flowing from many wounds, his grasp upon the savage's throat relaxed and together they fell on a cot.

Stretching out his hand, as a drowning man does for a saving straw, Burke grasped, to his astonishment, a revolver. It belonged to the hospital man who was killed in the first rush, and no one had known of its presence there. Burke placed the pistol against the Chief's head and blew his brains out, but so tenacious was the man that with his last breath he bit into Burke's arm so firmly and wrapped his arms and legs about him so tightly that when the breath left the body of his antagonist Burke in his weakness found that he could not move.

Sgt. Sylvester Burke died on November 20, 1953, at the age of 78. At that time there were three survivors of the unit; namely, Warren Sheldon, Ernest Mond and Roland T. Clark.

Roland T. Clark was born in Hornell, New York, May 12, 1880. He served during the Spanish-American War, enlisting May 12, 1898, as a private in Co. D, 3rd Regt, N. Y. V., and was mustered out on November 30, 1898. Mr. Clark then enlisted February 22, 1899, at Fort Ontario, Oswego, New York, as a private, Company C,

9th United States Infantry and was honorably discharged March 20, 1902, at Angel Island, California. Among momentos were decorations from the State of New York and the city of Oswego, where in 1936 to 1945 where he was superintendent of the State Armory. He retired to La Jolla, California, where he died December 19, 1969, at the age of 88. He was the last Oswego survivor and probably the last survivor of the massacre of Company C, 9th Infantry Regiment, U. S. Army at Belangiga on Samar.

Other Oswegonians in Company C at Belangiga were: George Allen, wounded; Guy C. Dennis, Killed; William J. Gibbs, wounded; Joseph I. Godon, killed (Spanish-American War, Co. D, 3rd Regt. N. Y. V.); James Pickett, wounded; Charles Powers, wounded, died later. His last words to Pvt. George Allen were, "Tell mother I died fighting like a hero."

On November 20, 1953, the *Palladium-Times* listed the Oswego men who served with Ninth Infantry:

J. Archambeau, George Bell, killed at Tungehow, China; Al Breckinridge and (first not available) Breckinridge; William Burke; Daniel J. and William Donovan; Joseph Dory, wounded at Tientsin, China; Ned Lacey; Charles Lavere, killed At San Fernando, P. I.; Charles Meeker, sent back sick from China; Ernest Mond; James J. O'Neil, killed at Tientsin, China (Spanish-American War, Co. D, 3rd Regt., N. Y. V.); Owen O'Neil; (first name not available) Seymour; Warren Sheldon; Charles and James Southgate; Herman Trapp, sent back sick from China; John Turner; Robert Walsh, killed in Pekin, China, (Spanish-American War, Co. D, 3rd Regt., N. Y. V.); James White.

Hon. William H. Taft, President of the Philippines Commission, reported that nothing could be more unfair than to attribute to the Filipino people at large motives of those who carried out the well laid plot at Belangiga. That was in a remote and always turbulent island, still devastated by war, and was devised by persons with all the war passions who have experienced none of the benefits of either peace or civil government.

Postscript

Article found in Elbert Hubbard's Scrapbook, copyright 1923:

"The perfect historian is he whose work the character and spirit of an age is exhibited in miniature. He relates no facts, he attributes no expression to his characters, which is not authenticated by sufficient testimony. By judicious selection, rejection, and arrangement, he gives to truth those attractions which have been usurped by fiction. In his narrative a due subordination is observed : some transactions are prominent; others retire. But the scale on which he represents them is increased or diminished not according to the dignity of the persons concerned in them, but according to the degree in which they elucidate the condition of society and the nature of man. He shows us also the nation. He considers no anecdote, no peculiarity of manner, no familiar saying, as too insignificant for his notice which is not too insignificant to illustrate the operation of laws, of religion, and of education, and to mark the progress of the human mind. Men will not merely be described, but will be made intimately known to us."

—Macauly

Sources

The French and Indian Wars

1. Stanley Pargellis, ed., *Military Affairs In North America 1748–1765*, Selected Documents From The Cumberland Papers In Windsor Castle, Archon Books, 1967.
2. Diary of Stephen Cross, "Up To Ontario," *Yearbook*, Oswego County Historical Society, 1941.
3. M. Francois Pouchot, *Memoir Upon The Late War In North America Between The French and English, 1755–1760*, Translated and edited By F. B. Hough, Roxbury, Massachusetts, 1866, 2 Volumes.
4. Boston Gazette And Country Journal, August 1, 1757.

Silas Town—An American Spy

1. E. B. O'Callaghan, *Documents Relative To The Colonial History Of The State Of New York*, Weed, Parsons And Company, Albany, 1858, Vol. VIII, p. 718 et. seq.
2. John Albert Scott, *Fort Stanwix And Oriskany*, The Rome Sentinel Company, Rome, New York, 1927.
3. Elizabeth M. Simpson, *Mexico, Mother Of Towns*, J. W. Clement Company, Buffalo, New York, 1949.
4. *History Of Oneida County*, Published by Oneida County, 1977.

Colonel Willett's Expedition Against Oswego

1. Letters Of George Washington And Marinus Willett:
   Willett to Washington, Fort Rensslaer, December 7, 1782.
   Washington to Willett, Newburgh, December 18, 1782.
   Washington to David Brooks, Headquarters, January 18, 1783.
   Washington to Willett, Headquarters, Newburgh, January 20, 1783.
   Willett to Washington, Fort Rensslaer, January 28, 1783.
   Washington to Willet, Newburgh, February 2, 1783.
   Washington to Willett, Headquarters, 2nd February 1783.
   Willett to Washington, Fort Herkimer, 8th February, 1783.
   Washington to the President of Congress, Headquarters, Newburgh, February 26, 1783.

Washington to Willett, Headquarters, March 5, 1783.
2. William M. Willett, *Narrative Of Military Actions Of Colonel Marinus Willet Taken Chiefly From His Own Manuscript Prepared By His Son*, (1831).
3. Howard Thomas, *Marinus Willett*, Prospect Books, Prospect, New York, 1956.
4. Jeptha R. Simms, *Frontiersmen Of New York*, 1883, Vol. II.
5. Wallace F. Workmaster, "The Study of Defenses of Oswego," *Yearbook*, OCHS, 1966–1967.
6. *Fort Plain (N. Y.) Standard*, March 30, 1933.

The New Orleans

1. Letter from A. W. Barnes, Canton, Fulton County, Illinois, to Ephraim Barns, New Haven, Oswego County, New York, April 8, 1843.
2. Dr. James Sullivan, ed.-in-chief, *History Of New York State 1523–1927*, Lewis Historical Publishing Company, Inc., New York, 1927, Vol. III.
3. Charles J. Ingersoll, *Historical Sketch Of The Second War Between The United States Of America And Great Britain*, Lea and Blanchard, Philadelphia, 1845, Vol. I.
4. Crisfield Johnson, *History Of Oswego County*, L. H. Everts & Company, Philadelphia, 1877.
5. Letter from General Haines, Sackets Harbor, May 30, 1814, to Secretary Of War.
6. Letter from Major Appling, May 31, 1814.
7. Mrs. Earl V. De Long, "Battle Of Sandy Creek," *Yearbook*, OCHS, 1949.
8. Richard F. Palmer, "Sackets Harbor and the *New Orleans*."

The Patriot War

1. Albert B. Corey, *The Crisis Of 1830–1842 In Canadian-American Relation*, Russell & Russell, New York, 1941, 1970.
2. Captain James Van Cleve, *Illustrated Manuscript Reminiscences Of Early Vessels Of The Lakes And River St. Lawrence*, 1877, City Clerk's Office, Oswego, New York.
3. Edwin M. Waterbury, "Oswego County In The Patriot War," *Yearbook*, OCHS, 1943.

4. Wallace F. Workmaster, "The Study Of Defenses At Oswego", *Yearbook*, OCHS, 1966–1967.
5. John Michael Sullivan, "Oswego Citizen Soldiers, A History Of The Local National Guard", *Yearbook*, OCHS, 1966–1967.
6. Oswego *Commercial Herald*, 1837–1842.
7. Oswego *Palladium*, 1837–1842.
8. Oswego County *Whig*, 1837–1842.
9. Oswego *Palladium-Times*, November 20, 1945.

The *Vandalia*

1. Captain Van Cleve, *Illustrated Manuscript*, 1877.
2. Herbert Lyons, "The *Vandalia* The First Screw-Propelled Vessel On The Great Lakes," *Yearbook*, OCHS, 1941.
3. Dr. Harold D. Alford, "Shipbuilding Days In Oswego," *Yearbook*, OCHS, 1945.
4. Oswego County *Whig*, 1841–1843.
5. Oswego *Palladium*, 1841–1843.
6. Oswego *Palladium-Times*, November 20, 1945.

Hotels

1. Oswego City Directories.
2. Local Newspapers.
3. Dorothy Rogers, *Oswego: Fountainhead Of Teacher Education*, Appleton-Century-Crofts, Inc., New York, 1961.

Public Schools

1. Oswego *Free Press*, June 1, 1831.
2. Oswego *Palladium & Republican Chronicle*.
3. Oswego *Daily Commercial Times*, July 14, 1849.
4. Oswego County *Whig*, June 16, 1841; July 10, 1844.
5. Oswego *Times*, November 8, 1848; November 27, 1848; December 1, 1848; August 23, 1865; January 31, 1872.
6. *Autobiography Of Edward Austin Sheldon*, edited by Mary Sheldon Barnes, Ives-Butler Company, New York, 1911.
7. Thomas Davidson, *A History Of Education*, Charles Scribner's Sons, New York, 1900.
8. Annual Report Of The Board Of Education, 1854, 1856, 1865.

9. Mayor's Annual Reports, 1861, 1863, 1964, 1895–96, 1900–27.
10. Report Of The Superintendent Of Public Instruction Of The State Of New York.
11. Rogers, *op. cit.*

Ned Lee—City Missionary

1. *Edward Lee, Prison, Camp, Pulpit, (The Life Of A City Missionary In The Slums,)* edited by Charles Dunning Clark, (R. J. Oliphant, Oswego, New York, 1889.
2. City Directories.
3. Writer's knowledge of the history of the city of Oswego.
4. Dr. Lida S. Penfield, "Ned Lee, His Life And Times," *Yearbook,* OCHS, 1943.
5. Oswego Town Clerk's Records.
6. Johnson, *op. cit.*

The Civil War—The Draft

1. Oswego *Commercial Times,* July 21, 1863; August 5, 1863.
2. Charles McCool Snyder, "Oswego County, New York, In The Civil War," *Yearbook,* 1962, of the OCHS And Oswego County Civil War Centennial Committee.
3. Shandy Maguire, *Random Rhymes And Rhapsodies Of The Rail,* The Cleveland Printing Company, Cleveland, Ohio, 1907.

Elmina P. Spencer

1. Fred P. Wright, "Elmina Spencer, Heroine Of The Civil War," *Yearbook,* OCHS, 1954.
2. L. P. Brockett And Mrs. Mary C. Vaugh, *Women's Work In The Civil War, A Record Of Heroism, Partriotism, And Patience,* King & Baird, Philadelphia, 1867, pp. 404–415.
3. Adjutant General's Report.

Dr. Mary E. Walker.

1. Charles McCool Snyder, *Dr. Mary E. Walker, The Little Lady In Pants,* Vantage Press, New York, 1962.
2. Fred P. Wright, "Dr. Mary E. Walker," *Yearbook,* OCHS, 1953.
3. The Oswego County *Messenger,* June 10, 1982. Used with the author's permission.

William Steele.
1. George W. Cullum, *Biographical Register Of The Officers And Graduates Of The United States Military Academy At West Point, New York*, D. Van Nostrand, New York, 1868, p. 613.
2. *The Annual Reunion Of The Association Of Graduates Of The United States Military Academy, West Point, New York*, June 12, 1885, Vol. II, pp. 69–70.
3. Walter Prescott Webb, And H. Bailey Carroll, *The Handbook Of Texas*, Vol. II, p. 665.
4. Walter Prescott Webb, *The Texas Rangers*, Houghton Mifflin Company, New York, 1935.
5. Ezra J. Warner, *Generals In Gray*, Louisiana State University Press, 1959, pp. 289–290.
6. The State Of Texas, Adjutant General's Department, Austin, Texas.
7. San Antonio *Express*, January 15, 1885.
8. Oswego *Times*, November 6, 1848; May 22, 1876.
9. *The War Of The Rebellion Official Records Of Union And Confederate Army*.
10. *Photographic History Of The Civil War*, (1911).
11. Gratitude is expressed to Eugene Hamel, Oswego; Kenneth W. Rapp, Archivist, United States Military Academy; and Colonel Hugh B. Hoeffler, U. S. Army, Ret., (Houston, Tx.); Orlo L. Bundy, Superintendent Riverside Cemetery, Oswego, New York.

John P. Hatch.
1. George W. Cullum, *op. cit.*
2. *The Annual Reunion, etc.*, June 8, 1901, p. 196.
3. Dumas Malone, ed., *Dictionary Of American Biography*, Charles Scribner's Sons, Vol. VIII, pp. 392–93.
4. Snyder, "Oswego County In The Civil War," pp. 20–31.
5. Common Council Proceedings, October 27, 1848.
6. Oswego *Commercial Times*, January, 27, 1863.
7. Oswego *Commercial Advertiser & Times*, January 5, 1863.
8. *New York Times*, April 14, 1901.

George N. Barnard.
1. Donald F. Eddy, "George N. Barnard," Rochester Institute of Technology, March 6, 1963.
2. Photographic Art-Journal, Vol. V, January 1853.

3. James D. Horan, *Matthew Brady*, Bonanza Books, New York, 1960, p. 36.
4. Oswego *Palladium*, March 6, 1847.
5. Oswego *Times*, November 20, 1848.
6. Oswego *Daily Commercial Times*, July 1, 1851.
7. Oswego *Daily Times*, July 12, 1853.
8. Oswego *Times and Journal*, June 24, 1854.
9. Oswego *Commercial Times*, September 23, 1862.
10. Oswego *Palladium-Times*, June 1, 1963.
11. Oswego City Directory, 1852, p. 127.
12. Courtesy of Richard N. Wright, President, Onondaga Historical Association. Mr. Wright gathered the information of Mr. Barnard's activities in Syracuse and elsewhere. He furnished the photos of Barnard on Sherman's march.

Literature
Morgan Robertson
1. *Dictionary Of American Biography*, Vol. XVI, p. 27.
2. Max J. Herzberg, *The Reader's Enclyclopedia Of American Of American Literature*, Thomas Y. Crowell Company, New York, 1962.
3. Dr. Lida S. Penfield, "Morgan Robertson And His Sea Stories," *Yearbook*, OCHS, 1942. Dr. Penfield, former head of the English Department of Oswego State Teachers College had been helped by many old friends of Morgan Robertson. Dr. Penfield's expertise is gratefully acknowledged.
4. Major John W. Vess, Jr., U. S. Army, Ret., "Never Less Than a Dollar," '(The Skipper, The Magazine For Yachtmen, (The Skipper Publishing Company, Annapolis). The Writer gratefully acknowledges Major Vess, Jr's., permission to use his material in his biography of Morgan Robertson.
5. Oswego *Palladium* March 25, 1915.
6. Oswego *Daily Times*, January 25, 1902; January 27, 1902; October 1, 1914.
7. Oswego City Directories, 1861–1897.

Henry C. Bunner.
1. Dictionary Of American Biography, Vol. III, p. 264.
2. Herzberg, op. cit., p. 122.

3. Biographical Directory Of The American Congress 1774–1961.
4. Oswego City Directories, 1852–1870.
5. Dr. Lida S. Penfield, "Henry Cuyler Bunner", *Yearbook*, 1944. Dr. Penfield's expertise is gratefully acknowledged.

Art
Thomas H. Wentworth.

1. Oswego City Directories.
2. Oswego Palladium, March 23, 1823.
3. Oswego Palladium-Times, December 19, 1933; February 7, 1937; February 27, 1937.
4. Riverside Cemetery Of Oswego, Inc.
5. Mrs. Beulah S. Schroeder, Records Of Riverside Cemetery, 1855–1910, Oswego City Library.
6. Johnson, op. cit.
7. *Antiques Magazine*, May 1930; January 1937; June 1937; July 1937.
8. Carolyn Helmetsie, "The Stone Store," Historic Oswego Building Survey No. 1, June 1974.
9. Henry Bronson, *The History Of Waterbury, Connecticut*, Bronson Brothers, Waterbury, Connecticut, 1858.
10. Oswego County Historical Society.
11. Onondaga Historical Association.
12. Yale University Art Gallery.
13. New York Historical Society.
14. Mattatuck Museum.
15. Munson-Williams-Proctor Institute, Utica, New York.
16. Litchfield Historical Society.

Charles H. Grant.

1. Mantle Fielding, *Dictionary Of American Painters, Sculptors, & Crafts*, Green Farms Connecticut, Published 1926, Enlarged and Revised, 1974.
2. Daniel L. Williams, "Oswego County Painters," *Yearbook*, OCHS, 1943.
3. Diary of Claude Fayette Bragdon, (The Watertown Daily Times, Watertown, New York, 1974).

James G. Tyler.

1. Fielding, *op. cit.*, p. 377.
2. Williams, *op. cit.*

John F. Murphy.
1. Fielding, *op. cit.*, p. 252.
2. Williams, *op. cit.*

The Spanish War

1. Sullivan, *History Of New York.*
2. Admiral H. G. Rickover, *How The Battleship Maine Was Destroyed.*
3. J. M. Sullivan, *Yearbook,* 1966–7, *op. cit.*
4. Oswego *Palladium,* April-December 1898.
5. Oswego *Times,* April-December 1898.
6. *New York In The Spanish-American War,* 1900, 3 Vols, New York State Adjutant-General's Office, (James B. Lyon, Albany, 1900), Vol. I, p. 34.
7. Report Book, 48th Separate Company, N. G. N. Y.
8. Descriptive Book, 48th Separate Company, N. G. N. Y.

The Massacre at Samar

1. Captain Fred R. Brown, *History Of The Ninth United States Infantry,* R. R. Donnelly & Sons Company, Chicago, 1909.
2. Oswego *Daily Palladium,* December 1898-March 1899; December 3, 1901, December 7, 1901; December 19, 1901; December 23, 1901.
3. Oswego *Palladium-Times,* November 19, 1953; November 20, 1953.
4. War Department National Archives And Record Service, Register Of Enrollments.
5. State Of New York Division Of Military And Naval Affairs, Albany, New York.
6. The writer was acquainted with several participants. For instance, John Turner, invariably broke out in tears when the subject was mentioned. Roland T. Clark, would on occasions talks to groups, when asked, on the massacre.